WORTH SAVING

WORTH SAVING

The story of
The Staffordshire Regiment's
fight for survival

by BRUCE GEORGE MP
and NICK RYAN

SMITH SETTLE

First published in 1996 by
Smith Settle Ltd
Ilkley Road
Otley
West Yorkshire
LS21 3JP

ISBN 1 85825 070 6

A CIP catalogue for this book is available
from the British Library.

Edited by Christopher Pick,
41 Chestnut Road, London SE27 9EZ

Printed and bound by Smith Settle
Ilkley Road, Otley, West Yorkshire, LS21 3JP

Dedication

This book is dedicated to all who have served in the 38th, 80th, 64th and 98th Regiments of Foot, The South and North Staffordshire Regiments, The Staffordshire Regiment and its Territorials, Militia and Volunteers; to those who currently serve in the 1st and 3rd Battalions of The Staffordshire Regiment; to the campaigners who secured for the Regiment its continued independent existence; and to those who will yet serve in The Staffordshire Regiment.

My empathy with the Regiment and its predecessors is far more eloquently expressed in the words of Rudyard Kipling, in his Prelude to *Barrack-Room Ballads*:

To Thomas Atkins

I have made for you a song,
And it may be right or wrong,
But only you can tell me if it's true;
I have tried for to explain
Both your pleasure and your pain,
And, Thomas, here's my best respects to you!

O there'll surely come a day,
When they'll give you all your pay,
And treat you as a Christian ought to do;
So, until that day comes round,
Heaven keep you safe and sound,
And, Thomas, here's my best respects to you!

Contents

Acknowledgments

A book of this kind could not possibly be written without the very willing participation, and tremendous support, of a huge number of people. But for them this book could not have gone beyond the preliminary stages, and I am enormously grateful. I apologise to the many people whose names are not recorded but who contributed to the Save Our Staffords campaign with great dedication. I would like to extend my gratitude to all the members of the Regimental Association and the Friends of the Regiment, not only for the part they played in the campaign but also for their personal help in recording its activities. The members of the Walsall Branch of the Normandy Veterans Association, particularly Ernest Blincow, were extremely generous with their time and efforts. The Chief Executives, Mayors and many councillors of the local authorities of Staffordshire and the West Midlands helped a great deal as well. It hardly needs to be said that every individual who helped, whether as part of an organisation or as a concerned citizen, deserves a vote of thanks and can rest assured that their part in the campaign is embodied in the continued existence of the Regiment. At least 250 people co-operated in the research for this book, by completing my questionnaire or writing to me or in interviews, and, at the risk of repeating myself too many times, I am most deeply grateful to them all.

I would like to express my especial appreciation to Nick Ryan, MA, my Parliamentary Researcher and joint author, without whose efforts this book would have been very difficult to complete. John Levey and Simon Nayyar, both of whom feature so prominently in this book and whose diligent efforts on behalf of Levey's beloved Staffords are recorded in detail, also had their hands full with research, verifying information, filling gaps and checking the developing manuscripts. These three devoted an enormous amount of time to seeing this project through and receive my heartfelt thanks.

Major General Ian Freer CB CBE has supported this project from its infancy, and I thank him most heartily for his advice, for his forbearance and for his dedication to the Regiment which is recorded herein.

Major Mac McLean, Major Mike Mogridge, Major Ted Green, the staff of RHQ and the Regimental Museum, and the members of the Save Our Staffords Campaign Committee all played a major role in compiling this book. I also talked to many soldiers from the 1st and 3rd Battalions, to all of whom I am most indebted. I hope that the finished book lives up to the Regiment's expectations and reflects the very deep respect in which the Staffords are held by the people of Staffordshire and the West Midlands.

A very special thank you should also go to all the library staff who selflessly tolerated my incessant demands for information. Staff at the House of Commons Library, the National Army Museum, the Ministry of Defence Library (utilised for historical research only), the Royal Military Academy Library at Sandhurst, the Public Records Office and the Walsall Local History Centre all gave generously of their expertise.

The members and staff of the House of Commons Defence Committee put up with my seemingly obsessive interest in the Staffords' survival with selfless good humour, for which I owe them my most sincere gratitude.

Alison Graham helped to trawl through mountains of documents to make this account as complete as possible; and Mark Swerling assisted with the historical research. Both deserve my very great thanks. I would also like to extend my gratitude internationally to Gilbert Riddle, an unexpected American source of information about the 38th Foot during the American War of Independence, and to John Murray, who helped in the final stages.

Christopher Pick undertook editorial work with diligence and enthusiasm, and I would like to thank him as well.

My thanks also go to someone whom I have not met, but whose researches into the Regiment have been immense: Colonel Hugh Cook.

Many authors ritually thank their wives for their tolerance and support. I do so, to my wife Lisa, in all honesty. With this study on top of my normal Parliamentary duties, we only occasionally met. There were times during the writing of this book when she complained that she only ever met me at Staffordshire Regiment functions!

The 'finally, and by far most important' award must of course go to Watchman III (aka Winston), the Regimental mascot Staffordshire Bull Terrier who won over many hearts, campaigned incessantly, and who, with his handler Sergeant Malcolm Bowers, was undoubtedly the most photogenic member of the campaign. It goes without saying that they won this campaign 'single-pawedly'.

Bruce George
House of Commons
June 1996

Chapter 1

The Regiment

On 25 July 1991 Tom King, Secretary of State for Defence, announced the proposed amalgamation of The Cheshire Regiment, raised in 1689 as The Duke of Norfolk's Regiment and later named the 22nd Regiment of Foot, with The Staffordshire Regiment, which dates from the raising of Colonel Luke Lillingston's Regiment of Foot at the King's Head public house in Lichfield on 25 March 1705. A year and a half later, on 3 February 1993, before a packed and tense House of Commons Malcolm Rifkind, King's successor, announced that:

> After considering all the reductions currently under way or planned, it is our [the Government's] unanimous view that the amalgamations of The Cheshire Regiment and The Staffordshire Regiment and of The Royal Scots and The King's Own Scottish Borderers should not now proceed.

This book is a study of the activities of the regional and national campaign that supporters of The Staffordshire Regiment mounted to oppose the amalgamation during those eighteen months. The Ministry of Defence argued, as with other amalgamations of historic and distinguished regiments, that the new regiment would embody the traditions of the two former regiments, that the old titles and emblems could be retained in the new title and badge, and that anyway it was in the interests of the Regiment and the Army not to fight the decision now that it had been made. However, few people in The Staffordshire Regiment, in the county of Staffordshire or in the Regiment's wider recruiting area succumbed to these reassurances.

This first chapter is not intended to be a potted regimental history. (The most recent and complete histories remain Vale's *History of The South Staffordshire Regiment*, Jones's *History of The South Staffordshire Regiment* and Cook's *The North Staffordshire Regiment*.) While it is the first attempt to integrate the four Staffordshire Regiments and Reserve Regiments into one historical analysis, the task of a serious, up-to-date and (of necessity) lengthy history remains to be undertaken.

The purpose here is to demonstrate why so much effort was mounted to retain the Regiment. 'Worth Saving' — one of the slogans of the 'Save Our Staffords' anti-amalgamation campaign — neatly encapsulates this intense feeling. This chapter explains the regimental ethos and the fact that *Options for Change*, the defence cuts first revealed by Tom King on 6 February 1990, was not a unique exercise but one repeated periodically throughout the nation's history, in which the armed forces — in particular the Infantry of the Line — have been cut substantially at the cessation of hostilities. It highlights long periods of neglect and indifference by Government, Parliament and public opinion towards the Army, interspersed with occasional periods of frenetic enthusiasm and commitment of resources; currently, in the last decade of the century, we are experiencing a downward swing in this cycle of interest. It explains, by outlining the Regiment's history, just why there was so much passion in the campaign and why the Regiment's roots run so deeply in the county. In other words, it sets the scene for the story of the campaign which starts with Chapter 2.

Lest we step off on a bad foot, we should emphasise that, although the Staffords have tasted their share of disasters, defeats and disease, these were usually attributable to bad politico-military leadership, climatic conditions, or sometimes just bad luck — but rarely to the incompetence or weakness of the soldiers, who were often sent into impossible situations. The Regiments of Staffordshire have been consistently strong, professional and successful. They have been on the losing side in only one war in three centuries, the probably unwinnable American War of Independence. They have spent most of their time posted 'over the hills and far away' dealing with an enormous range of military tasks as imperial policemen, with occasional long postings at home and in Ireland and later Northern Ireland performing home defence tasks and assisting the civil authorities. They have come under many great military leaders, but they have had the misfortune to experience several incompetents and even downright charlatans.

Periodically the Staffords have also displayed great versatility in different theatres of war. They engaged adversaries of incredible bravery in what have been termed 'small wars' — the Zulu, Sikh and Dervish, for instance — and armies of their own calibre, such as the French in the Napoleonic Wars and the Germans in the two World Wars. As Infantry regiments, the Staffords have fought largely on land and on foot, but they have had to adapt to local conditions, so much so that they seem to outdo the US Marine Corps' motto 'On Land, Sea and Air'. They built their own boats during their interminably long sojourn in the Caribbean in the eighteenth century. They fought on board ship against the French, as well as against pirates, and made amphibious landings. They took to camels and rowing boats in the abortive attempt to rescue the besieged Gordon at Khartoum and to horses in South Africa against the Boers. In the Second World War they provided anti-aircraft detachments for Royal

Navy vessels in the Mediterranean during the evacuation of Greece and the battle for Crete, and later landed on Sicily and at Arnhem and in Burma as glider-borne battalions. Most recently, they changed roles to armoured infantry when they took possession of Warrior Armoured Infantry Fighting Vehicles during their posting to Fallingbostel as part of the 7th Armoured Brigade and that formation's Gulf War deployment in 1991 — a role they undertook with relish and, as described on page 32, with success.

The story of the Staffords is one of endurance and determination, of the creation of a regimental identity over centuries by soldiers whose common bond has been forged by time and tradition within a fighting unit that is second to none and that deeply values its geographical and cultural roots. The disasters that this chapter will recount are as much a part of the regimental tradition as the successes. The ability to withstand disaster, to rebuild with the same pride, and to go on to success have been hallmarks of the Staffordshire Regiments over the years. This is an account of a military body that was — and is — well and truly 'Worth Saving'.

The regimental system

The regimental system is the backbone of the British Army, and will continue to be unless further mergers or massive expenditure cuts are implemented. Though much criticised for its social elitism, it instills a centuries-old culture of loyalty to the regiment, transmitted through regimental history — recounted in barrack-room anecdote, talks, books and regimental journals — celebrating the great victories of the past, the heroes of the regiment, and the minutiae of regimental exploits.

The bonds that develop through the regimental system are strong and complex. Whereas soldiers in other armies, such as the USA's, swear allegiance to their country, regimental soldiers enter into a pact with history. They take on the honours and disappointments of their regiment as their own. This sense of history not only instills group loyalty in the soldier, it also promotes his control. The soldier realises that all he does in battle and in peace will be recalled and passed on to later generations. Bravery and achievement, whether leading to victory or defeat, will be remembered, and this makes the soldier reluctant to let his comrades down.

Each county regiment has its traditions, reinforced through its educational programmes, parades, social functions, freedom marches, receptions and regimental dinners. Even small differences in uniforms attest to individual regimental identities. Thus the Staffords wear the

Holland Patch behind the Stafford Knot on their badge to commemorate the Regiment's service in the West Indies, while the 'Glider' emblem on the upper right sleeve signifies the South Staffords' involvement in the glider-borne landings in Sicily in 1943. When red coats were worn by the soldiers, they were distinguished from other regiments by the colour of the facings and linings of their coats — and this is reflected even today in the yellow field (or background) to the Regimental Colour carried by the Battalions of The Staffordshire Regiment. However, the clearest distinguishing feature is the Stafford Knot, the traditional emblem of the county, which has been worn on the badges of Staffordshire's Infantry regiments since 1782.

Regimental marches are designed not only to entertain, but also to provide inspiration and boost morale. They nearly always reflect some aspect of the regiment's history. Thus, for instance, the Approach March ('Gamel Jeger Marsch') represents the involvement of the 2nd South Staffords in the peaceful liberation of Norway in 1945, and the Assembly — 'Zakhmi Dil', also known as 'The Afghan March' or 'The Wounded Heart' — is believed to have been adopted by the 2nd North Staffords from the Pathans of the North-West Frontier in about 1912. Other marches have simpler origins. For example, the Quick March, 'The Staffordshire Knot', was composed by Bandmaster Duthoit of the South Staffords in 1923.

There is a tradition of animal mascots in the British Army, which in the past have ranged from an understandable drum horse to a less obviously relevant hen and goose! The Staffords have had an animal mascot intermittently since the late 19th century in the form of a Staffordshire Bull Terrier. The first was 'Boxer', who was with the South Staffords when they arrived in Egypt to relieve General Gordon at Khartoum. Unfortunately Boxer jumped from the train taking the men south from Cairo just as it started and was left for dead at the side of the track. Showing true Stafford grit, Boxer rejoined his Battalion a few days later, having recovered and followed them almost 200 miles along the railway track.

At the 1949 Royal Tournament, 6th North Staffords were presented with an English Bull Terrier by War Minister Emmanuel Shinwell with the Band, Drums and an Honour Guard present. Watchman, as he was known, participated in many ceremonial functions before his death in 1959, as did his successor Watchman II, a brindle Staffordshire Bull Terrier who lived until 1974. Both were presented to the Queen: Watchman in Burton in 1957, Watchman II at the presentation of new Colours to the South and North Staffords Reserve Battalions in 1962. Both dogs are commemorated on a plaque at their resting place in the lawns of Burton Town Hall Square.

The mascot tradition was revived when the 3rd (Volunteer) Battalion of The Staffordshire Regiment was formed on 5 April 1988. Burton again showed its generosity, and Watchman III, a Staffordshire Bull Terrier bred by Mr and Mrs Gough of Erdington, was formally presented to the Battalion at a civic parade on 13 May 1989. On parade Watchman III wears a fine embroidered full-dress uniform, the cost of which was met by donations from a number of prominent Burton firms; he is handled by the equally resplendent Sergeant Malcolm Bowers, whose rank Watchman III has recently managed to equal. As we shall see, Watchman III's media appeal was quickly recognised, and he played a pivotal role in the anti-amalgamation campaign.

One of the most important regimental traditions is the possession of The Colours, which consist of the Sovereign's Colour (with the Union Flag) and the Regimental Colour; on both are displayed the Regiment's Battle Honours. The Colours are near-sacred, and were always carried into battle until modern military technology did away with the practice. The last recorded incidence of Colours being carried in action was when the 1st South Staffords brought theirs ashore at Alexandria in 1882. The Colours remain a powerful symbol today and are carried at all ceremonial functions. The laying-up of old Colours and presentation of new Colours continue to be invested with particular regimental significance.

Regimental Days, which are marked by a parade and other festivities designed to commemorate the celebrated historic victories, also serve to link a Regiment's past and present. Like every great regiment, the Staffords found it necessary to reduce the number of Regimental Days to an acceptable number, particularly as the choice had to reflect the victories of four separate regiments. The two main days selected are Ypres Day, 31 July, and Ferozeshah Day, 21 December. Ferozeshah Day, formerly the main South Staffords' day, honours the distinguished part played by the 80th Foot (later the 2nd South Staffords) in the Battle of Ferozeshah in the First Sikh War of 1845. Ypres Day was originally the main North Staffords' day; it marks the anniversary of the successful attack by the 1st North Staffords on the opening day of the Third Battle of Ypres in 1917 and also commemorates the part played by the 1st South Staffords in the First Battle of Ypres in 1914. Anzio Day, 22 January, and Arnhem Day, 17 September, which recall the exploits of the 2nd North Staffords and the airborne 2nd South Staffords, are also marked and celebrated.

The foundation of the Regiment

The present-day Staffordshire Regiment has its origins in four Regiments of Foot dating back to the eighteenth and early nineteenth centuries, although the men of the county had already fought at home and abroad for many hundreds of years. The first of these — Lillingston's Regiment of Foot, which later became the 38th Regiment of Foot — owes its existence to a rare moment of Parliamentary enthusiasm for military spending, when £5 million was authorised for the raising of new Infantry regiments to fight in the War of the Spanish Succession. Thus from the start of their history the Staffords have been subject to the swings of political and public opinion, which for long periods remains indifferent to the spending necessary to maintain a strong Army but is occasionally willing to commit substantial resources to counter a perceived threat.

The regiment was formally raised by Colonel Luke Lillingston at the King's Head public house in Lichfield on 25 March 1705, an historic link utilised for the launch of the 1991 campaign. Lillingston, a professional soldier with over thirty years' experience including a spell in the West Indies, had been ordered to raise his regiment in Cheshire. Why he stopped in Lichfield and decided to raise the Regiment in Staffordshire is unclear.

As we shall see, Lillingston's new regiment did not participate in the glorious campaigns of the Duke of Marlborough on the continent, ending up instead in the pestilential Leeward Islands. One of the few advantages of being isolated in the West Indies was that Lillingston's unit survived the ending of the war in Europe, when regiments that returned home were disbanded in an attempt to reduce military expenditure.

In those days the British Army was little more than a collection of regiments virtually owned by their founders, who often ran them corruptly as private enterprises. They were raised with the sanction of the Monarch, but the Colonel was to all intents and purposes a proprietor who frequently contracted command of the regiment, usually by sale, to a Lieutenant Colonel. While Lillingston cannot be faulted in his choice of location for the raising of his regiment, he does not appear to have taken much part in regimental life. He did not join his fellow-officers when the Regiment sailed for the West Indies in 1707, and the following year he either resigned or was deprived of his Colonelcy — it is not clear which.

Lillingston was a Yorkshireman, but the family's Staffordshire connection remains. The 'Save our Staffords' campaign was proud to have as one of its patrons Commander George Inge-Innes-Lillingston, a direct descendant of Luke Lillingston; he served for many years in the Royal Navy and lives close to the Regimental Headquarters.

In its early years the Regiment survived the worst that fate could throw at it — and emerged strong and fit at the end. After Lillingston, its initial Colonels, James Jones and Francis Alexander, can best be described as rogues; the author believes that Jones has claims to being the worst Colonel in the Regiment's history and also that he could compete for the position of worst Colonel in the British Army. During fifty-seven years of service defending the West Indies against France, the Regiment was grossly neglected by the War Office in London. Weapons were out of date, uniforms were reduced to rags, and officers and men suffered dreadfully from tropical diseases. That said, the Regiment, which became the 38th Foot when the system of numbering regiments was introduced in 1751, did much useful work in the West Indies, defending British possessions and ships alike against both the French and the pirates prevalent in the area.

The Regiment's dress distinction of the Holland Patch, referred to earlier, was awarded by King George V in 1935 to commemorate this unprecedentedly long stay in the West Indies. It recognises that the Regiment was the first to wear a form of tropical uniform when tattered coats had to be replaced by ones made of sacking or holland, used to pack locally grown sugar.

The second Staffordshire Regiment, the 64th, was raised during the Seven Years War, another period of military expansion, thus echoing the 38th's origins. It was not raised in Staffordshire and initially had no link with the county. In 1756 fifteen regiments were ordered to form Second Battalions. The 11th Regiment of Foot, later the Devonshire Regiment, formed a 2nd Battalion; the War Office changed its two-battalion policy in 1758, and the 2nd Battalion of the 11th became a regiment in its own right — the 64th. Its first Colonel was the Honourable John Barrington; he was a distinguished soldier and unlike many Colonels planned to serve with his Regiment when it was posted to the West Indies in 1758. This was not to be, as he soon became second-in-command, and later commander, of the expedition. He returned to England in 1759 with his health broken, like so many others who served out there. He continued to serve, as Colonel of the 40th, but died five years later at the age of forty-four.

The first direct links between regiments and counties were established in 1782. Recruiting had declined because of the unpopularity of the American War of Independence. The War Office hoped to reverse this trend by giving Regiments of the Line a territorial designation. Each Colonel of Regiment was asked to select a county; Sir Robert Pigot, the Colonel of the 38th, already had strong local connections, and so it was no surprise that he selected Staffordshire. (With the benefit of history it is amusing to note that the Colonel of the 22nd Foot, which later became The Cheshire Regiment, also selected Staffordshire but was turned down.) Thus the 38th became the 1st Staffordshire and the 64th, with no obvious county links to call upon, was granted the subsidiary title of 2nd Staffordshire. Both regiments were sent to Staffordshire as soon as possible to reinforce the county connection. However, despite the county designations, the numbers remained the paramount titles for each Regiment up to, and indeed way beyond, the Cardwell reforms of the late nineteenth century (see page 19). To this day many veterans of the Battle of Arnhem refer to the 80th rather than to the 2nd South Staffords.

The third Staffordshire Regiment was raised as 'The 80th Staffordshire Volunteers' in 1793 during the French Revolutionary Wars. Government and Parliament, facing the most serious threat to the country since the Norman invasion of the eleventh century and the attempted Spanish invasion of the sixteenth, were again panicked into raising additional regiments. The 80th was led by the charismatic Lord Henry Paget, who later succeeded his father as Lord Uxbridge and finally became the 1st Marquis of Anglesey. As well as serving as Member of Parliament for Caernarvon, he was one of the country's most distinguished cavalry officers and Wellington's second-in-command at Waterloo.

As the current Marquis of Anglesey relates in his superb book *One Leg*, Paget heard that regiments were to be raised for an expedition to the Continent while at Beaudesert, the family home in Staffordshire. Aged only twenty-five, and with his experience of military affairs limited to serving with his father's militia, he rushed to London, where he met the Prime Minister, William Pitt, and informed him of his desire to raise a regiment of Cavalry. As Cavalry were not required, Pitt told Paget that he could raise a battalion of Infantry and take the rank of Lieutenant Colonel. 'I instantly closed with him', Paget wrote, [and] 'got my father's leave, who generously contributed everything that was necessary to effect the object.'

This was Paget's first commission. Quickly overcoming his youth and inexperience, he proved himself the antithesis of the oafish colonels so prevalent at the time. After the 80th's formation the

Regiment of 700 men, largely drawn from the Staffordshire Militia, was sent to defend Guernsey against a possible French invasion. The young Colonel pulled every possible string to have his new Regiment sent to the Continent, and in 1794 he joined the Duke of York and the 38th in Flanders. The expedition was a disaster; the 80th and the 38th did a lot of fighting, a lot of marching and a lot of dying, in Arctic-like weather, without food, drink, pay or proper medical assistance, marching in rags and virtually shoeless. The 80th returned to England in 1795 with fewer than half its men fit for service. Like the 38th, the 80th survived an early disaster to go from strength to strength. In later life Paget received many honours. He was made Field Marshal in 1846, Lord Lieutenant of Staffordshire in 1849, and his burial in 1854 was attended by various Staffordshire Regiments, including the Militia in which he started his career.

The fourth and final Staffordshire Regiment, the 98th, was raised in Chichester in 1824 by Lieutenant Colonel Mildmay Fane of the Westmoreland family, whose current Earl sits in the House of Lords. The inevitable spending cuts after the end of the Napoleonic Wars soon proved to be too deep, and the reduced Army found itself grossly over-committed, facing unrest at home, in Ireland and abroad. In 1824 the Army was augmented with six new regiments of Infantry, numbered 94th to 99th, and was increased again the following year. Unlike the other forbears of The Staffordshire Regiment, the 98th had a rather leisurely introduction to military life. However, its relatively good fortune was eventually repaid with its experiences in the Far East and India in the 1840s. In nine years there were 1,164 deaths, all from disease, none from enemy action. There was no connection between the 98th and Staffordshire until the Cardwell reforms of the 1870s and early 1880s.

The early years

The popular, if romanticised, picture of raising a regiment portrays recruiting staff in red jackets, drums beating and fifes playing — all combining to convince young men to take the King's Shilling and march off to glory. For Lillingston's troops in 1705, as also for young Paget's eager-to-fight Staffordshire Volunteers nearly ninety years later, reality failed to match up to the ideal. Lillingston's Regiment of Foot was almost immediately designated for 'sea service' (i.e. as a form of marines), spent two relatively uneventful years in Ireland and then nearly six decades in the West Indies, a British Army record.

The 64th, too, went out to the West Indies. Contemporary military planners regarded the West Indies as strategically important, particularly to Britain and France, who fought incessantly for mastery of the region; however, many historians have regarded the area as a sideshow, especially during the Napoleonic Wars. The 38th fought against France between 1710 and 1712. With the 64th it captured Guadeloupe from the French on 1 May 1759 and again during the French Revolutionary Wars. One of the regimental anniversaries is 23 March, commemorating the 38th's seizure of Martinique in 1762; in 1794 the 38th and 64th took Martinique again — victories remembered on the Regimental Colours. The 64th was in St Lucia in 1803 and defeated the Dutch in an expeditionary force to Surinam in 1804. The 64th stayed on in the West Indies for most of the Napoleonic Wars. It returned to Europe too late for Waterloo, but did become part of the occupation force in Paris in 1815.

The West Indies was the graveyard of the British Army. The cost in lives of the campaigns against the French was catastrophic, less from death in the field than from disease — yellow fever (known as 'yellow jack'), typhoid, malaria. Michael Duffy, the distinguished military historian, wrote of the West Indies campaigns that 'the principal executioner was not a visible enemy but pathogenic micro-organisms unseen, unsuspected, and totally devastating.'

The American War of Independence 1775-83

The 38th and the 64th were engaged throughout the entire American War of Independence (even before in the case of the 64th, which arrived in 1772), though fortunately they missed the memorable defeats of Saratoga and Yorktown. The war was never really winnable. It was fought 4,500 miles from home in a largely hostile country, while Washington and his Continental Army became progressively more confident. There was political division at home, and the King was suffering bouts of madness. The uninspiring generals in charge were antagonistic towards each other and could not agree on strategy and objectives. The apparently large British Army was dispersed across a vast territory in small garrisons, and the field armies lacked the strength required to achieve their objectives.

Paradoxically, although Britain lost her American colonies, the 38th and 64th had very good wars. Neither lost a battle, although there were a few draws. In the months before the outbreak of hostilities, the 64th garrisoned Castle William, an island dominating Boston harbour, while the 38th were in Boston. In 1775 Colonel Alexander

Leslie of the 64th was sent to seize munitions stored at Salem, a sortie that ended in a bloodless impasse. Had it not been for Leslie's diplomacy and tact, it is quite possible that the 64th would have been on the receiving end of the first 'shot heard round the world'. Instead that dubious honour fell to the 38th when they fought what is deemed to be the first engagement of the war at Lexington. They then fought courageously and well at Bunker Hill, where they suffered twenty-five dead and one hundred wounded. Wearing their red coats, they marched in line up the hill and made a brave bayonet charge in the face of American sharpshooters.

After Bunker Hill and the subsequent American blockade of Boston the Army withdrew temporarily to Canada (the 38th and 64th were in Halifax, Nova Scotia) and then returned to campaign around New York in 1776, where they were involved in the successful battles at Flatbush, Brooklyn, White Plains, Haarlem Heights, Forts Lee and Washington, and Danbury. Following the capture of New York the 38th spent most of the war garrisoning the city with occasional sorties, mainly to Long Island. The 64th remained on the move; in 1777 they took part in the campaign to capture Pennsylvania, in 1778 they were one of the units in Grey's naval attack on New Bedford and Martha's Vineyard, and in May 1779 they were involved in the capture of Stony Point. The 64th then went south to the campaign in the Carolinas. At Eutaw Springs in September 1781 they bayonet-charged the midst of the enemy — an 'unauthorised plunge upon the American centre', in the words of one historian. The regiment finally left Charleston for the West Indies in 1782. Elements of the 38th and 64th (their former Flank Companies) probably participated in the defeat at Yorktown, after which the British evacuated New York and the war petered out. The 38th returned to Nova Scotia and then to England, where they were based in Stafford for a short time.

The diary of Richard A. Wyvill of the 38th (now in the Library of Congress) gives a fascinating picture of the war in America, which was by no means all privation and fighting. Although Wyvill had attended a military academy in Strasbourg — which gave him a level of training almost unique in the British Army — there is little sign that he did much fighting around New York. He concentrated on enjoying the social life (even though he arrived without any money) and chasing girls (often unsuccessfully). On one occasion he wrote that he passed 'several dreary months [with] no hospitable landlady or fair daughter to solace my melancholy days'. While in New York the 38th helped to found the first black masonic order; one Prince

Hall, a 'free black', was admitted to the Regiment's Lodge #441. After the 38th left America, he went on to establish his own lodge.

Wars against France

For many years the Staffordshire Regiments were involved in conflicts with France, England's traditional enemy, in the Caribbean, in the final stages of the American War of Independence, and on the continent. Once again, in the traditional pattern in times of threat, the Army was permitted to expand; among the new units formed was a second battalion of the 38th, which was raised in Lichfield in 1804.

As we have seen, the 80th, and also the 38th, participated in the Duke of York's expedition to the Low Countries in 1794. The 38th then fought in the Peninsula War with Wellington's army, not always the best dressed or best disciplined but one of the toughest and most professional armies ever put into the field; the Battle Honour 'Peninsular' was well earned. In 1808, under the command of the brilliant but ill-fated Sir John Moore, the 1st/38th took part in the crushing defeat of the French at the Battles of Rolica and Vimiera in Portugal and thence marched into Spain. They had almost reached Madrid when they unexpectedly encountered Napoleon with overwhelmingly superior forces. In his retreat to Corunna Moore lost some 6,000 men (20 per cent of the entire army); following a second battle outside Corunna, in which Moore was killed, what was left of the bedraggled 1st/38th sailed back to England in a storm.

After a few weeks, the 1st/38th was patched up and despatched on an even more disastrous expedition to the Low Countries. The 1809 Walcheren Expedition, commanded by the Earl of Chatham, was intended to divert Napoleon's attention from Austria and capture Antwerp. A fleet of thirty-five ships landed at Walcheren Island and Flushing, but the expedition became bogged down, allowing Antwerp to be reinforced. Chatham withdrew, leaving a garrison of 15,000 at Walcheren. Here disease quickly took hold, as an anonymous diarist of the 38th attests:

> We had not been many days upon the island before our men began to fall bad of the Ague and Fever and so fatal did that disorder prove that in less than one month we buried more than 600 men, so that out of 1000 that we took out with us we did not bring 400 back with us.

Both battalions of the 38th were now involved in major engagements in the Peninsula again, including Busaco (1810), following which

Wellington remarked 'I have never witnessed a more gallant attack than that made by the 38th.' Both also played a major part in the 5th Division rearguard during Wellington's strategic withdrawal to the Torres-Vedras Line and in the successful delaying action at Villa Muriel. The 2nd/38th played a key part in the desperate fight to take Badajoz in April 1812 and fought with 1st/38th at Salamanca the following July. The 2nd/38th returned to England for disbandment in December 1812, although many men remained with the 1st/38th in Spain, taking part in Wellington's decisive victory at Vittoria and the subsequent pursuit of the French across the Pyrenees. The siege of Bayonne was the 38th's final engagement of the campaign.

The Army of Empire

When relative peace descended in Europe in 1815, the British Army, grossly overstretched as always, found itself largely engaged in the small wars of colonial conquest that created Britain's imperial might. The Staffords saw more than their fair share of action in building up and policing the far-flung Empire.

India and Burma

In all, the four Staffordshire regiments spent nearly 170 years (thirty-seven, fifty-five, forty-four and thirty-one respectively) on the Indian sub-continent, including Ceylon and Burma. Life in India was far preferable to other postings, particularly for officers, for there were plenty of sporting and social distractions. Yet disease could cause havoc; between 1857 and 1871 the 38th lost seventeen officers and 409 other ranks and nearly 650 men were invalided home.

From 1824 to 1826 the 38th formed part of Sir Willoughby Cotton's Bengal Division, which was sent to Burma as a reprisal against a Burmese invasion of British-controlled India. In 1852 and 1853 it was the 80th's turn to fight in Burma. While only nine men were killed in action, over 350 died from disease either in Burma or on their return home. A memorial in Lichfield Cathedral to the dead of this period records the names of the Colonel of the Regiment (Daubeny), fourteen officers (including a father and son named Hunt), nineteen Sergeants, seventeen Corporals, two Drummers and 316 Privates. One of the officers named is Matthew Kirkland who was commissioned in the field for capturing a black Sikh flag, a centre for enemy resistance, at the battle of Ferozeshah in 1845. Several officers died trying to take the flag, which now hangs in Lichfield Cathedral; each year on Ferozeshah Day the officers still hand over the Colours for one day to the Warrant Officers and Sergeants as a sign of trust and in memory of Kirkland's bravery.

The 64th made history in 1856 when they took part in the expeditionary force to pacify Persia. Colonel Hugh Cook, the historian of the North Staffords, states that a form of khaki, which is Persian for 'dust-coloured', was first worn at this time. The names of Reshire, Bushire, and Koosh-ab were added to the Regiment's list of Battle Honours.

India brought the Staffords their first Victoria Cross out of a total of thirteen gained by the future Staffordshire Regiments. Drummer Thomas Flynn of the 64th was just fifteen years and three months old — and thus probably the youngest-ever to receive the award — when he took part in a counter-attack on Indian Mutineers at Cawnpore in 1857. The citation remarks on his 'gallantry in engaging 2 rebel artillerymen, although himself wounded'. Flynn served for a further twelve years, during which he spent no less than 586 days in detention or prison due to drink, the traditional scourge of the nineteenth-century army. He died in 1892, aged fifty, in the workhouse of his home town, Athlone, County Westmeath — such was the way the Victorians sometimes treated their heroes.

Australia and New Zealand

From the start of the occupation of Australia the British Army was used, with precious little enthusiasm on the part of the officers and men, in policing operations and in guarding convicts *en route* from England and during their incarceration. In all the task consumed just over eight years, from 1836 to 1844, during which time the 80th contributed in their own way to the expansion of the Empire. Many of the soldiers due for discharge settled in Australia on farms granted to them. More importantly, in 1840 a detachment commanded by Major Thomas Bunbury annexed much of the South Island of New Zealand for the Crown, thus preventing the Americans and French from doing so.

Bunbury was a professional soldier who had been seconded to the Portuguese Army in the Napoleonic Wars and later commanded the 80th at Ferozeshah. It was he who took charge in 1844 as the 80th were moving to India; their ships, the *Briton* and *Runnymede* (containing soldiers and families from another regiment), were wrecked on the Andaman Islands, where the travellers had to defend themselves against a barbarous tribe of cannibals. Bunbury would have made a welcome addition to the Save Our Staffords campaign

150 years later, as his *Reminiscences of a Veteran* are full of cases when he took on authority over poor treatment of himself or his soldiers. Even the Duke of Wellington felt his wrath after the Andaman Islands shipwreck.

The Chinese Wars

The 98th were the first British regiment to garrison Hong Kong and, in a pleasing example of historical balance, the Staffords will be among the last in 1997. The 98th were in China from 1841 to 1845 under the command of the brilliant Colin Campbell, later Lord Clyde, who had built the Regiment up into a formidable infantry force. Accompanied by 116 women and children, 810 officers and men sailed for Hong Kong on the battleship *Belleisle*. Already decimated by disease on the journey, the Regiment then joined the expedition that set out in 1842 under Sir Hugh Gough to the Yangtse Kiang, Shanghai and Nanking, where the Chinese army capitulated. After an early small battle the ravages of sunstroke and disease — cholera, dysentery, 'fever' — took hold. Things got worse on the return to Hong Kong, from where Campbell wrote to his sister:

> The regiment has lost by death up to this date 283, and there are still 231 sick, of whom some 50 or 60 will die. ... This is the history of the 98th Regiment, which sailed from Plymouth in so effective a state in all respects ... and all this destruction without having lost a man by the fire of the enemy.

Campbell was always greatly concerned for the welfare of his men and later, in India, put great pressure on his young Regimental Surgeon, one John Collis Browne, to find a remedy to combat cholera. His preparation, Chlorodyne, has long been out of date for this purpose but has proved ideal for tummy upsets. Sadly Collis Browne failed to take out a patent, and so never made his fortune from his celebrated 'Compound'.

The Crimean War

The Crimean War of 1854-56 was a major test for the British Army. It was the first major conflict in Europe for forty years, and the first also to be waged against opponents of roughly similar military experience and resources, in contrast with the relatively small skirmishes of the Empire. Many defects in administration and training soon became apparent to the detriment, as always, of the soldiers in the field, who fought in appalling weather and conditions of great hardship. The 38th did not see a great deal of major action throughout their time in the Crimea. They were present at the Battle of the Alma, shortly after their arrival in September 1854, but were held with the rest of their Division in support. Subsequently action fell to trench warfare and was concentrated around attempts to seize the great Russian fortress and port of Sevastopol, and the Army suffered tremendous privation during the bitter winter that followed. Because of the efforts of Lieutenant Colonel J J Louth, their experienced and humane commanding officer, the men of the 38th suffered less than their comrades in other Regiments. In addition to 'Alma', the 38th were awarded the Battle Honours 'Inkerman' and 'Sevastopol'. In June 1855, in a disastrous attack on the Redan, one of the great redoubts protecting Sevastopol, Colonel Louth was severely wounded and was invalided home, only to die within an hour of reaching England.

Africa

The 80th played a prominent role in the Zulu Wars of 1878-79. At the disastrous engagement at Intombi Drift in March 1879, when sixty-one officers and men of H Company, the 80th, were killed in an attack by 800 Zulus, the Staffords produced a hero in Colour Sergeant Anthony Booth, who organised a hurried defence when his company, which had taken inadequate defensive positions, was suddenly attacked. He gained a VC and is buried in St Michael's churchyard, Brierley Hill.

The same engagement also produced an anti-hero, a Lieutenant Harward, whose hasty departure from the field on the only horse available, ostensibly to get reinforcements, was not considered to be the behaviour of an officer. Harward was court-martialled but to general amazement was acquitted. This was not the end of the matter, for General Sir Garnet Wolseley, the Commander-in-Chief, refused to confirm the court's finding. Wolseley, a very correct officer with a keen sense of duty, may have been affected by the fact that his first active service had been as an Ensign in the 80th in Burma in 1852. (Wolseley is one of three officers with Staffords links who became Field Marshals; the others were Lord Henry Paget and Colin Campbell.)

Another junior officer who faced court-martial was Lieutenant Carey of the 98th. He was seconded to a detachment escorting the young Prince Imperial, Louis Napoleon, son of Napoleon III of France, who was killed in a Zulu attack. Following the Prince's death, accusations of cowardice were levelled at Carey, who demanded a board of enquiry. Instead he was court-martialled, found guilty of desertion and sentenced to be cashiered. For a variety of reasons the sentence was not confirmed, but many people, including Queen Victoria, continued to believe in Carey's guilt, not least because of an incriminating letter he wrote to his wife. Opinion continues to be divided, with some historians believing that Carey was made a scapegoat for Louis Napoleon's recklessness and unwillingness to heed advice while others take the view that he could have made greater efforts to rescue the Prince. Eventually Carey was allowed to return to the 98th, but he failed to restore his good name and died four years later.

The Zulu Wars also produced a VC for Private Wassal, seconded from the 80th to the Mounted Infantry, for his gallantry while escaping from the military disaster at Isandhlwana. At great risk to himself he rescued a drowning comrade from the Buffalo River while under a shower of bullets and assegais. The 80th took part in Chelmsford's revenge on the Zulus for Isandhlwana and were in the fore at the rout of the Zulus at their capital, Ulundi.

Egypt and the Nile

In 1882 the 38th, by now 1st South Staffords (see page 19), helped to defeat Arabi Pasha and a troop of mounted infantry prior to the battle of Tel-el-Kebir (to which they returned some seventy years later). The large key to one of the gates of Cairo removed after the battle is on display in the Regimental Museum. In 1884 the 38th participated in an extraordinary expedition led by Sir Garnet Wolseley to rescue the beleaguered General Gordon at Khartoum. Most of the Staffords were in the River Column, which sailed up the Nile in specially commissioned oarboats, called 'whalers', commanded by Major General Earle. The second arm of the rescue force, the Desert Column under Sir Herbert Stewart, which contained thirty-one South Staffords as part of A Company The Mounted Infantry Camel Regiment, had a dangerous journey in the face of the Mahdi's Dervish forces. The River Column, led by the Staffords, advanced 550 miles upstream — rowing, sailing, carrying the whalers, fighting — only to learn that Khartoum had fallen. They turned back, but not before a final engagement at Kirbekan in 1885, where the Staffords helped to secure a notable victory, even though Colonel Eyre, who in thirty-two years had risen from Private to Commanding Officer, was killed, together with General Earle.

The North Staffords, under Lord Kitchener, participated in the Dongola Expedition of 1896 which culminated in the defeat of the Dervishes at Hafir. Kipling wrote that of all the British Army's opponents 'the Fuzzy was the finest o' the lot', saluting in an unfortunate turn of phrase the Mahdi's Dervish forces for their bravery and tenacity in breaking British Infantry squares at Abu Klea and Tamai in 1884.

The Boer War 1899-1902

Yet another military debacle into which the Staffords and their auxiliaries were pitched was the Boer War. The 2nd Battalion of the North Staffords was one of the first units to reach South Africa, in February 1900; 1st South Staffords joined them shortly afterwards. Neither Staffords Battalion saw much in the way of hard fighting, nor did they share in any of the major inglorious episodes of this mishandled affair. Both Battalions were reinforced from Staffordshire, with strong detachments of the Militia and Volunteers joining them for periods of six months to a year. The involvement of what was to become the Territorial Force did much to cement the feeling between the county and its Regiments at a time of heightened patriotism.

Home postings

It would be a mistake to think that a home posting was to be looked forward to after years of action in hostile lands thousands of miles from home. For much of the 19th century, soldiers led a miserable life in the British Isles. Until the middle of the century Parliament was unwilling to vote funds to build barracks, and so soldiers were poorly fed and inadequately housed, often in alehouses (with poor consequences for military efficiency and good relations with the local people). Because there was no police force until the mid-19th century, soldiers became the sword in the hand of the state, and were hated for breaking up riots and demonstrations and for coming to the aid of employers in dispute with their workforce. Until the Cardwell reforms regiments were rarely posted to the counties with which they were linked. Perhaps this was deliberate so that they were not often called to deal with incidents in their 'home area'.

The country experienced many food riots and industrial disputes and agrarian unrest and violence were also common. In 1865 seventy men of the 64th, then posted in Manchester, were despatched to Market Drayton on the border of Staffordshire and Shropshire to deal with riots, ostensibly over poor sanitation! Nineteen inhabitants were tried for riot and damage to buildings, most receiving prison sentences of three weeks to nine months.

The Staffords were also involved in what was, after the Peterloo Massacre, probably the most notorious incident of military/civilian confrontation in British history, at Ackton Hall Colliery, Featherstone,

Yorkshire in September 1893. The local constabulary was otherwise engaged at the St Leger races at Doncaster and the nearest available troops, the 38th, were at Bradford. Twenty-eight men and Captain Digby Barker engaged the rioting coal miners, and two bystanders were killed. The subsequent inquiry, which had far-reaching consequences for the future deployment of soldiers in industrial disputes, exonerated Barker and his detachment.

Another incident that revealed the Army's appalling position in industrial disputes was related by a soldier of the South Staffords. Patrolling the Scotland Road, Newcastle-upon-Tyne, during the 1912 dock strike, he found himself under attack. Asking his company commander what to do, he was told: 'Shoot him, man, shoot him' — an order he obeyed. A remark from a civilian after this incident so aggrieved the company commander that he ordered five rounds, which 'had a startling effect on clearing the road'. Men joining the Army intensely disliked getting involved in industrial disputes for exactly these reasons.

The Cardwell reforms

One consequence of the Crimean War was a series of military reforms. Probably the most important of these were instituted by Edward Cardwell, Gladstone's Secretary for War from 1868 to 1874. Among many other changes, Cardwell extended to the whole Army the system of double-battalion regiments, with one battalion generally serving abroad, the other at home. Regimental depots also acquired a more important role as centres for training recruits for the home battalion and for Militia and Volunteer Battalions, and also for fostering local interest in the county regiment.

These proposals took some time to come into effect, and it was not until July 1881 that the new South and North Staffordshire Regiments were formed. The 38th and 80th became the 1st and 2nd Battalions of The South Staffordshire Regiment, while the 64th and 98th became the 1st and 2nd Battalions of The Prince of Wales's (North Staffordshire) Regiment. (In the original plans formulated in 1873 the 38th and 80th were to have been translated into The North Staffordshire Regiment and the 64th and 98th into The South Staffordshire Regiment.) The depots for both Regiments were located at Whittington Barracks in Lichfield, where the first buildings came into use in 1881. In 1920 the North Staffords' title was reversed to The North Staffordshire Regiment (The Prince of Wales's), since they had been known as the North Staffords throughout the First World War.

The North Staffords' designation as Prince of Wales's came via the 98th. The title The Prince of Wales's, which had once belonged to a completely different 98th Regiment (the Prince of Wales's Tipperary Regiment), was resurrected in 1876 when the Prince of Wales presented new Colours to the 98th in Malta. The Commanding Officer asked the Prince whether the old title could be restored, and six months later Queen Victoria granted the request.

The First World War

The post-Crimea reforms produced a force of half a million men that had great difficulty in subjugating the Dutch Boers. The real reforms, however, came after the South African Wars and were associated largely with the names of Richard Burdon Haldane (the Liberal Minister of War after 1906) and Lord Esher (who sat on the Royal Commission on the South African War and was subsequently appointed by Balfour in 1903 to head a committee to report on reform of the War Office). These reforms produced, in just over a decade, the British Expeditionary Force (BEF), a small, professional army that was capable of challenging Europe's best. In essence there were four British Armies in the First World War, and the Staffords were in all four: the BEF, made up of professional soldiers from Regular Regiments (a force largely destroyed by the end of 1914); the county-based Territorial Force (for which Kitchener, wrongly, did not have a high regard); Kitchener's New Armies; and those who were conscripted under the various Military Service Acts after 1916, when the flow of volunteers for the first three armies began to dry up.

In August 1914 each Staffordshire Regiment consisted of two regular battalions (1st and 2nd), two special reserve battalions (3rd and 4th) and two territorial force battalions (5th and 6th). By the end of the war, the South Staffords had had a total of seventeen battalions, of which eleven had served overseas, and the North Staffords had had eighteen, of which twelve served overseas. The two Regiments made enormous sacrifices, losing over 10,000 men, as recorded on the numerous memorials in the towns and villages of the county. The South Staffords gained fifty-six Battle Honours, the North fifty-two. The majority of Battalions served on the Western Front, and remarkably every one of these fought in the Ypres Salient. 46th (North Midland) Division, including three Staffordshire TA battalions, was the first Territorial Army Division to see action in

France, and contained the most highly decorated other rank of the War, Lance Corporal Coltman VC, DCM and Bar, MM and Bar of the 1st/6th North Staffords. Coltman, who carried out his feats of bravery as a stretcher-bearer and conscientious-objector, remains Britain's most decorated soldier. Between them the two Regiments were awarded seven VCs. An eighth was won by Lieutenant Alan Jerrard of the South Staffords as a pilot in the Royal Flying Corps in Italy in March 1918.

The contribution of one family (all North Staffords) to the county's war efforts is documented in a privately produced monograph by Andrew Thornton entitled *The Thompson Brothers in the Great War* (1994), which details the exploits of Company Sergeant Major William Thompson, Lance Corporal John Thompson (killed in action in 1917), Private Walter Thompson, Gunner Joseph Thompson and Lance Corporal C E Smith (related by marriage). Smith was a stretcher bearer who, according to the *London Gazette*, 'displayed the utmost indifference to personal danger, and set a magnificent example by his coolness and courage under heavy fire'.

The efforts made to fight for King and Country by young (and not so young) were quite breathtaking — the young men of whole streets joined up, and many were slaughtered within weeks or months of arriving on the continent. Although they were both under-age, two lads from Bilston, William Turner and his younger brother Rubin Vernon Turner, joined up at the outbreak of war — recruiting officers sometimes turned a blind eye to enthusiastic young men. William saw his younger brother at the Front (in a Scottish regiment) and wrote to the War Office informing them of Rubin's age. As a result both were discharged. The moment he reached the requisite age William walked to Whittington Barracks to join the South Staffords.

From 1914 until November 1917 1st South Staffords were in France, but were then transferred to Italy with the 9th Battalion to fight against the armies of the Austro-Hungarian Empire, remaining there until 1919. 2nd South Staffords were present at the Battle of Mons, the first of the war, and served on the forlorn Western Front throughout, participating in most of the major battles. 1st North Staffords also served in France continuously, fighting in many major battles including the Somme and Ypres. 2nd North Staffords, in contrast, spent the whole war on the Indian sub-continent, fighting on the North West Frontier in 1915 and later in the Third Afghan War. In June 1915 the 7th South and the 7th North deployed to Gallipoli in the 78,000-strong army under the command of Sir Ian

Hamilton. Having survived that debacle, 7th North Staffords continued to fight against the Turks across the Middle East to Baghdad and Baku, where they also had to defend themselves against attack by Bolshevik forces in the Russian Civil War.

Of the many battles fought by the South and North Staffords, one stands out as epitomising the Regiments' strength of character, resolve and bravery. The breaching of the Hindenburg Line and the crossing of the Saint Quentin Canal on 29 September 1918 was an outstanding Allied victory, and incidentally one of the few occasions when South and North Staffords fought side by side. The 46th (North Midland) Division, which consisted of Territorials of the Lincolns, Leicesters, Sherwood Foresters and South and North Staffords, captured over 5,000 prisoners and seventy guns. John Terraine, a leading historian of the war, wrote: '[The 46th] made possible the deepest penetration on the whole Army front — some 6,000 yards. And the price of this scarcely believable triumph was less than 800 casualties.' Terraine chose the famous picture (reproduced in this book) of the Staffords gathered at the side of the Canal, some still wearing the lifebelts they used to cross it, for the cover of his book.

The attack began at 05.50 in a series of waves. The 137th (Staffordshire) Brigade (1st/5th South Staffords, 1st/6th South Staffords and 1st/6th North Staffords) took the leading role on a three-battalion front, with 1st/6th North on the left, 1st/5th South in the centre and 1st/6th South on the right. Advancing almost a mile to the forward German trenches, the Staffords tore through, crossed the Canal and completed the assault on the Hindenburg Line defences on the far side of the Canal between 08.30 and 10.00, by which time the next waves of attackers were exploiting the breach. In only about three or four hours the 137th Brigade had advanced well over a mile, stormed three lines of defence and taken 2,000 prisoners. Although it caused considerable confusion in the rear, fog greatly assisted the surprise of the attack. Many Staffords were saved by the instruction to shout through the fog 'Are you Staffords?' With hindsight, this seems a little unsporting, as the chances of a terrified German infantryman being able to comprehend the Black Country and Stoke dialects seem improbable! The cry also has a greater long-term significance, auguring the gradual merger process that led to the present Staffordshire Regiment. Not long after this staggering victory, German resistance collapsed and the bloody Great War came to an end. Terraine described this action, won by a Division not regarded as one of the finest on the Western Front, as a 'wonderful feat of arms'.

Between the wars

As after the defeat of Napoleon, the destruction of the Triple Alliance (Austro-Hungary, Germany and the Ottoman Empire) led to substantial reductions in the British armed forces and a lack of preparedness for war that almost brought about the liquidation of the British Empire in the early years of the Second World War. Churchill called this period the 'locust years'. The substantial growth of pacifism, underfunding combined with overstretch, lack of adaptability (the Army was the slowest of the three Services to adapt to changing battlefield technology) and, above all, weak and indecisive military leadership debilitated the British Army.

Immediately after the Armistice the Army was engaged in settling the many disputes and wars arising from the collapse of four major empires, the Ottoman, Austro-Hungarian, German and Russian. 1st North Staffords were deployed to Turkey and Thrace in 1922 and 1923, while 2nd North Staffords fought in the Third Afghan War and then came home via Egypt in 1920. Thereafter the Army, much diminished in size, returned to imperial policing duties. One battalion each of the South and North Staffords were based in the UK and played a role in home defence, Ireland and internal security tasks, as well as spending much time preparing for overseas tours of duty. In 1929 the 2nd South Staffords travelled to Palestine aboard an aircraft carrier, the first unit to use this form of transport.

At home there was much political unrest. During the 1926 General Strike, which many people believed was a precursor to a Bolshevik-style revolution, the 2nd South Staffords sailed from Plymouth to the Clyde, where they were stationed around Glasgow. The Battalion, which was less than 350 strong, spent most of the time not bayonet-charging revolutionaries but playing military music to them and football against them. According to one contemporary account:

> As regards the football, suffice it to say that once the ice had been broken, the numbers of offers of games became positively embarrassing. No fewer than nine challenges were received on one day, mostly from strikers' teams. Both regimental and company sides had their full whack of football.

There was also some sightseeing, including a bus excursion to Loch Lomond.

Ireland

For many centuries the British found it necessary to subjugate Ireland, and control of the country was only maintained through a permanent presence of substantial British forces. In all there have been some forty-four Irish deployments totalling some 110 years by the various component regiments of the present-day Staffords. Ireland has also provided a major source of recruits — indeed sometimes one could more easily encounter men from Limerick than Lichfield, Strabane than Stoke. For much of the 19th century, the 64th was nearly three-quarters Irish. Ireland also provided some of the finest officers in the British Army (such as Wellington) as well as in the Staffords. One example is General Sir Robert Pigot, Commanding Officer of the 38th during the American War of Independence and Colonel of the Regiment for twenty years afterwards.

The Staffords performed a variety of military and policing tasks in Ireland, often being used to quell civil disturbances. In 1801 the 38th dealt with rioting in Dublin; in 1809 the 64th helped to quell a French-aided rebellion; and in 1871 the 98th put down and 'disembodied' the Tipperary Light Infantry Militia, which had attacked a police station. In 1916 the 176th (Staffordshire) Brigade, containing 2nd/5th and 2nd/6th South Staffords and 2nd/5th and 2nd/6th North Staffords, was hastily sent to Ireland to assist in resisting the Easter Uprising. In the 'Troubles' of the early 1920s three of the Staffordshire Regiments, barely out of the carnage of the Great War, formed part of a British force deployed to defend British interests; this consisted of Regulars, 'auxiliaries', the Royal Irish Constabulary and the infamous 'Black and Tans'. Lieutenant Colonel James, the Commanding Officer of 2nd South Staffords, was threatened with assassination by the IRA after presiding over the court martial of the Mayor of Cork, who died as a result of a hunger strike. In March 1922 the 2nd South Staffords took part in a brigade attack with supporting artillery on Pettigoe, Fermanagh, which was still, officially, British soil.

The Second World War

Both the South and the North Staffords played an important part in the long years of conflict with Germany. They tasted victory on distant battlefields such as Sidi Barrani, Sicily and Anzio, in the Chindit Campaign and in Normandy. They also experienced failure at the retreat to Dunkirk and the Battle of Arnhem.

The South Staffords

Early in the war the 1st/6th Battalion, composed of Territorials, joined the Expeditionary Force to carry out pioneer work. They then fought gallantly in the retreat to Dunkirk under dangerous fire from enemy dive-bombers and artillery and left France in the famous flotilla; some stretcher-bearers were among the last to be evacuated.

At the outbreak of war, 1st South Staffords were in Palestine, and the 2nd Battalion were in India. The 1st Battalion eventually moved to Egypt, fighting the Italians at Sidi Barrani, and spent the early part of the war in the eastern Mediterranean and North Africa, later moving with 70th Division to India and Burma.

In Burma the 1st South Staffords formed part of the 'Chindits'. The endeavours of the Chindits under Orde Wingate, their brilliant but controversial leader, are often dismissed as insignificant. Yet the South Staffords have frequently extolled the virtues of their commander. The late Colonel Eric Butler (who posthumously played a vital role in the Staffords' battle against amalgamation) received the MC in this campaign and later campaigned strenuously to perpetuate Wingate's memory. A statue honouring the Chindits stands outside the Ministry of Defence in London; beneath Chinthe, the hideous beast of Burmese mythology, are the names of The South Staffordshire Regiment and of Cairns, VC. Lieutenant George Cairns was one of the heroes of the campaign. Slain at Henu in what has been characterised as 'medieval' hand to hand combat, with 'rifle and bayonet against two-handed feudal sword', Cairns is said to have continued fighting even after losing his arm, swinging a Japanese ceremonial sword and then a rifle until he fell, mortally wounded. For his courage he was posthumously awarded the VC.

The Staffords were in Calvert's 77th Brigade. Calvert later described them as

> an amazingly compact and solid battalion. One thinks of them as a team rather than as a series of individuals ... the perfect example of the difference between a group of men and a firm, trained, efficient unit, fighting as one man, while their marching and spirit were terrific right through the worst possible conditions. ... The South Staffords were the solid bulwark of the brigade.

Perhaps the most memorable part of this eulogy was Calvert's comparison of the South Staffords with the redoubtable Gurkhas — they were not as fast across country but had 'greater go and dash'.

Before its arrival in North Africa in May 1943 the 2nd Battalion, which was led by Lieutenant Colonel W D H McCardie, who had been injured in 1940 with 1st/6th South Staffords, was moved from India to the UK and designated an airborne battalion. Following extensive glider training they were put in the lead, together with The Border Regiment, in the invasion of Sicily. As part of Operation Husky they were towed from their base in northern Africa, but met disaster when the Horsa gliders encountered rough air and anti-aircraft fire. Some of the pilots of the Dakota tugs panicked and released the gliders prematurely. Sixty-nine of the 144 gliders came down in the sea, and only twelve managed to make the drop zone; in all over 600 casualties were sustained and 326 men drowned. The remaining troops were scattered around Syracuse (the Staffords unfortunately missed their intended drop zones of 'Walsall', 'Bilston' and 'Dudley'); to their credit they managed to improvise and adapt their battle plans in order to press on. The mission was eventually successful despite its tragic beginning.

The next airborne landing, at Arnhem in the Netherlands, was a true disaster. The intention was to send three airborne divisions (the British 1st and American 101st and 82nd) to capture the bridge over the Rhine at Arnhem and other bridges in the Netherlands, while Dempsey's 2nd Army raced north some 65 miles to link with the glider-borne British, Polish and American forces. By flanking the German Siegfried Line, Montgomery intended to hasten the end of the war and wrong-foot the Americans in the process — but, as everyone now knows, this was 'a bridge too far'.

2nd South Staffords, which formed part of the British 1st Airborne Division, set off in Horsa gliders in two lifts on 17 and 18 September 1944. The first lift was commanded by Lieutenant Colonel McCardie, the second by Major J C Commings, whose father was Colonel of the Regiment. McCardie's landing met little resistance, but Commings was less fortunate. Fighting in and around Arnhem was fierce. Instead of weak resistance, the troops encountered Panzer divisions with inevitable and disastrous consequences. Losses were heavy, many men were captured, while the rest managed to escape across the Rhine to Nijmegen.

The Battalion received two VCs, the only one to do so in a single battle during the entire conflict. Major R H Cain — whose unit was cut off from the Battalion for six days but fought successfully to rejoin it — confronted a German Tiger tank, waiting until it was only 20 yards away before firing with a Piat. Cain won this unequal duel, as he did another the next day against three tanks. Lance Sergeant J D Baskeyfield, a young man from Stoke, was awarded a posthumous VC for his action in manning an anti-tank gun single-handedly and wounded, knocking out two tanks and two self-propelled guns before being killed. Of the 765 Staffords officers and men who set off to Arnhem, only 139 returned to base; McCardie was wounded and captured. Major Commings served on to become a Brigadier and, like his father, Colonel of the Regiment.

The North Staffords

Immediately after the outbreak of war the 2nd North Staffords moved to their allotted position near the Belgian border, coincidentally near the village of Nomain where the 1st North had ended the First World War over twenty years before. The 'phoney war' meant that they did not see action for eight months, but then they had more than their fair share in the seventeen-day fighting withdrawal to Dunkirk. Although all heavy equipment was lost, every man had his personal weapon when the battalion embarked on 1 June. The cost was 140 men killed and wounded as well as many posted missing. In his book *Tribute*, A W Turner wrote that 'it was a source of some pride that the enemy had never managed to break through the Battalion at any stage.' After reinforcement and retraining the Battalion fought in the 1943 North Africa campaign in the 1st Army. They then fought in Italy for a year, landing south of Rome in December 1943 and again at Anzio on 22 January 1944 in order to circumvent the Germans. German resistance was heavy and victory came at a high cost. On one occasion they took twenty-six casualties when German shells caught the Battalion mustered for roll-call; another time an attack across a dry river bed caused fourteen fatalities and over fifty wounded. In all twelve officers and 134 NCOs and men were killed in the campaign.

The 1st North Staffords spent the whole war in India and Burma. The Battalion was originally sent to Calcutta to quell civil unrest, but when the Japanese began to advance through Burma they switched from a peacekeeping role to a fighting one. One company was despatched to defend the Andaman Islands where the 80th had been shipwrecked in 1844. In 1943 the Battalion moved into Burma as part of 26th Indian Division, spiritedly attempting to stem the Japanese advance in appalling climatic conditions with inevitable loss of life from disease. They were far from fully-trained for this jungle role and lacked equipment. However, the campaign provided some of the expertise later used by commanders to plan jungle warfare. After five months the Battalion withdrew to India in September 1943 to re-group and the 64th saw no further action in Burma.

The Territorial battalions of South and North also fought bravely in Normandy in 1944, and this is described in more detail on pages 34-50.

Post-war operations

At the end of the Second World War, and after the formation of the rival NATO and Warsaw Pact military alliances, Central Europe became the focal-point of Western security capability and strategy. The region was the most heavily militarised in the world, with two million troops confronting each other across the Iron Curtain. One major role of the Army was to supply, in the form of the British Army of the Rhine (BAOR), Britain's contribution to the Western presence. Another was, at first, to continue imperial policing operations and then to participate in the dissolution of Empire and the passing over of virtually every former colony to local rule. Throughout the entire post-war period the Army was also subjected to a series of defence reviews designed to rationalise organisation and to reduce expenditure.

The Staffords had surprisingly few postings to BAOR. The South Staffords were in Minden from 1952 to 1954 and in Lüneburg for two years from 1957. The North Staffords were in Minden at the same time — the two Regiments were to be amalgamated there in 1959. The amalgamated Staffordshire Regiment was posted to Osnabrück from 1973 to 1977 and to Fallingbostel from 1986 to 1991, where they heard that they were to be deployed to the Gulf. The Staffords also spent two years in Berlin from 1968 to 1970, when Major John Levey, whose name appears frequently in this book, was Second in Command. Duties included guarding Rudolf Hess, Hitler's deputy and the sole occupant of Spandau Prison. The brigade headquarters were in the Olympic stadium, where the controversial 1936 Games were held. Berlin was a popular posting with good shopping and good sport; John Levey recalls the importance of providing extensive sporting facilities — it was unwise to give soldiers too much free time in Berlin since they invariably got into trouble.

Further afield, in the late 1940s the South Staffords were in Hong Kong as part of 40th Infantry Division, reinforcing the colony to prevent it becoming involved in the civil war in China. Though neither the South nor the North Staffords fought in the Korean War, which started in 1950, the South Staffords sent over seventy men as reinforcements to the Middlesex Regiment and the Argylls. It was at about this time that Mac McLean (another prominent figure in this book) volunteered to join the North Staffords, who were going to Korea as one of the British Army units in the UN peacekeeping forces; however they arrived in November 1953 just after the war had ended. McLean remembers Korea not for the horrors and heroics of war but for bad weather, digging 'miles and miles of trenches' and laying barbed wire fences.

In 1954-55 the South Staffords endured a rather boring posting in Egypt, at Tel-el Kebir on the edge of the desert. Having left Egypt shortly before the Suez crisis, they were propelled into the Cyprus conflict. They fought EOKA (the Cyprus independence movement) in the towns and the hills, patrolled the streets, searched for bombs, and engaged in riot control, dawn ambush parties and internal security operations, including the arrest (or abduction, as some might prefer to describe it) of Archbishop Makarios, the Greek Cypriot leader, codenamed Black Mak. In Kenya from 1962 to 1964, the now amalgamated Staffords helped to put down military rebellions in Tanzania, Uganda and Zanzibar. They were the last battalion to leave Kenya in 1964, and in 1971 again watched the British flag descend in Bahrain and Sharjah. As Spearhead Battalion in 1977, 1st Staffords deployed to Belize, which was threatened by neighbouring Guatemala. The lead company was commanded by Major Ian Freer, who features later in this book as Colonel of the Regiment. Within days of returning to the UK he remembers deploying for a firemen's strike.

When Argentina invaded the Falkland Islands in 1982, the 1st Staffords, now under the command of Freer, were in their ninth posting to Gibraltar. They were very disappointed not to be part of the invasion force, especially since they were the closest Infantry regiment to the South Atlantic. Corporal Rob Hyde, from Bentley, Walsall, recalled that the mood was 'a real downer' when the Regiment heard that it was not to participate. He regarded fighting a war as the culmination of a soldier's training and experience, and as a chance to put it to good effect on behalf of oneself, one's Regiment and one's country.

Home defence

Between 1945 and amalgamation in 1959, both 1st South Staffords and 1st North Staffords spent only one year in Lichfield. The amalgamated single-battalion Regiment then spent thirteen years in home defence postings (excluding Northern Ireland) at Colchester, Dover and Lichfield with a brief touchdown at Chester in 1991 before going off again to Northern Ireland. These home postings included training for NATO roles and for Northern Ireland, Spearhead Battalion and military aid to the civil authorities (MACA).

Amalgamations

In 1948 the two Regiments experienced the first of two major post-war amalgamations, when each was reduced to a single Battalion. The justification for these cuts was Indian independence and the consequent fall in the number of troops required. The two Battalions then in India, the 38th and the 64th, were put into 'suspended animation' — ironically these were the two oldest of the four Battalions. The 80th and the 98th were renumbered the 1st Battalions of the South and North Staffords respectively. The 64th/98th held an amalgamation parade in 1948 in Fayid, Egypt, to mark the 'amalgamation' of the two Battalions.

The 1957 Defence Review put forward a major rethink of strategy, commitments and manpower in an attempt to relieve military overstretch and to reduce the financial strain of national military commitments. Many Infantry regiments disappeared or were amalgamated into single-battalion regiments. So it was that on 31 January 1959 The South Staffordshire Regiment and The North Staffordshire Regiment (The Prince of Wales's), which shared a Depot at Whittington Barracks, became The Staffordshire Regiment (The Prince of Wales's). Although the two Regiments came from the same county, the Staffords' merger was nevertheless painful and a great deal of effort was expended in achieving a smooth transition.

On 21 December 1958, at Lüneburg, West Germany, the South Staffords held their last ceremonial parade to celebrate Ferozeshah Day. Major General A W Lee, Colonel of the Regiment, told the assembled soldiers and guests of a telegram sent to the Queen pledging the loyalty of the new Regiment. This read:

> With sincere sorrow, after 250 years of service, we say goodbye to Your Majesty, but we pledge the new Regiment (The Prince of Wales's) to maintain that high tradition which we have endeavoured to follow.

At the first post-amalgamation parade in Minden, Lee, who was also appointed Colonel of the new amalgamated Regiment, gave a rousing exhortation:

> I may have been a South Stafford for a long time, but that is past — and I am now a Stafford, and proud to be so. I promise you

> that, as long as I continue as your Colonel, I will guard the interests of the Regiment as zealously as I ever guarded those of my former Regiment.

The amalgamation prompted an epic poem, written very much in the style of William McGonagall by Colour Sergeant Sceales, *The 38th/80th on Amalgamation*, which conveyed the feelings of ordinary soldiers and tried to foster a common identity. One verse runs:

> If you're from the industrial South
> Or the Northern County parts
> Come and swell the ranks of glory
> Come and serve with our proud hearts.

The various regimental nicknames proved difficult to merge. From the South Staffords came 'The Staffordshire Volunteers', after the 80th's original title, along with 'The Staffordshire Knots' and the intriguing 'Pump and Tortoise' ('on account of its sobriety and the slow, methodical manner of the men while doing their work when once stationed at Malta', according to *Nicknames and Traditions in the Army*). The North Staffords brought just one nickname, 'The Black Knots'. Numerous religious services and other ceremonies marked the amalgamation. On 23 August 1959 the Colours of The North Staffordshire Regiment were temporarily laid up at the Garrison Church. As the Colour party moved down the chancel to the Regimental March, the Chaplain spoke these words:

> We are gathered together in this chapel to lay up and lodge the Colours of The North Staffordshire Regiment. No more fitting place could be found wherein to deposit these emblems of Duty and Service than the house of God. ...

The Gulf War

The Staffords were in the thick of the Gulf War; we shall not discuss the action in detail as it is admirably covered in Nicholas Benson's *Rats' Tales*. In late summer 1991 they had just returned from Exercise Medicine Man in Alberta, Canada, and were starting intensive training for a six-month emergency tour of Northern Ireland. On 14 September, six weeks after Saddam Hussein's invasion of Kuwait and only seven after Tom King's amalgamation statement in the House of Commons, it was formally announced that 1st Staffords would be deployed to the Gulf as the armoured infantry component of 7th Armoured Brigade, commanded by Brigadier Patrick Cordingley. The

Quartermaster's Advance Party arrived in Saudi Arabia on 11 October and the rest of the Battalion between 20 and 24 October, reinforced with soldiers and units of nine other formations. After a period of training, which included some of the most intense live-firing exercises ever conducted by British Infantry, the Battalion was declared operationally effective on 16 November. Initially it came under the command of 1st (US) Marine Expeditionary Force. At the end of 1990 4th Armoured Brigade was sent to supplement 7th Armoured Brigade, which together came under the command of 1st Armoured Division. On 11 January 1991 1st Armoured Division was reassigned to VII (US) Corps.

On 17 January, the day the air war started, 1st Armoured Division began to move forward to the concentration area, codenamed Keyes. On 30 January practice began for the operation to breach the Iraqi border defences, and on 14 February 1st Armoured Division, along with its US counterparts, was in place for the assault. After several days of withering Allied artillery fire, the assault began at 04.00 hours on 24 February 1991, with 7th Armoured Brigade leading the British forces out at 10.00 hours on 25 February. The first of the Staffords' two casualties was suffered just an hour and a half before this, when sadly Private Shaun Taylor was accidentally shot by another soldier checking his weapon. The second casualty was Private Carl Moult, who died at Objective Platinum II when an RPG7 anti-tank missile was fired at Callsign 32 (a Warrior) from behind an Iraqi white flag.

The Staffords' final objective on 28 February, the day of the provisional ceasefire, was Cobalt, a position across the Kuwait-Basra road, which had to be reached to prevent any movement of Iraqi forces along the road after the ceasefire came into effect. Reaching that objective meant a headlong dash and the Staffords Battle Group covered 290 kilometres in less than 100 hours, an impressive rate for an armoured battle group. The Staffords were involved in as much, if not more, fighting than any other British Infantry battalion in the Gulf; this mainly involved clearing trenches and bunkers and taking on armour and vehicles with MILAN anti-tank missiles.

As Robert Fox, the *Daily Telegraph*'s Defence Correspondent, attested, the Staffords had good reason to be proud:

> One of the less glamorous and under-rated of the county Regiments ... they were one of the most successful formations in the British offensive, and one that was to see the most action.

The author met a dozen men of the 1st Battalion at Al Jubayl shortly before their departure from theatre. It was impossible not to feel immensely proud of these men, who had shown only brave, steely resolve. On 19 October 1993 Malcolm Rifkind, the Secretary of State for Defence, announced to the House of Commons that Her Majesty the Queen had approved the award of the Theatre Honour 'Gulf 1991' and the Battle Honour 'Wadi Al Batin' to The Staffordshire Regiment (The Prince of Wales's).

The Volunteers

Britain has depended on the voluntary principle (sometimes supplemented by ale!) in Army recruitment for hundreds of years, with the exception of two periods of conscription during the twentieth century: from 1916 to 1918, and again from 1939 until the early 1960s. Throughout the 18th and 19th centuries the voluntary principle governed the raising of regular regiments even during times of crisis. The voluntary principle has also been maintained through various 'reserve' structures, notably the Volunteers, Militia, Fencibles and the variously designated Territorials.

Staffordshire contributed with enthusiasm to the raising of voluntary auxiliary battalions. The 1st Staffordshire Militia — which so impressed King George III that he bestowed upon them the title of The King's Own Staffordshire Militia — had no less than four incarnations between 1776 and 1857. In 1797 two additional regiments of militia were raised and re-raised, of which the 2nd Staffordshire Militia continued until 1805. These two regiments served in a home defence capacity against the threat of invasion from Revolutionary and Napoleonic France, but principally provided the Line Regiments with officers and men. After the Napoleonic Wars both the full-time Army and Militia were swiftly and comprehensively reduced in size and effectiveness as the French threat receded; until the middle of the century the 1st King's Own Staffordshire Militia had only two, geriatric, officers. Old habits die hard, however, and despite allying with France during the Crimean War the country continued to fear a French invasion for the next fifty years.

Between 1794 and 1802 twelve Volunteer units were also raised in Staffordshire but lapsed with the temporary peace with France. Twenty-eight Staffordshire towns raised Volunteer units in 1803, but these were again disbanded in 1813. In 1859 the Volunteer movement surfaced again, as a 'middle class militia', and proved much more robust than its counterpart sixty years before. A meeting at the Shire Hall, Stafford, convened by Lord Hatherton, the Lord Lieutenant, established the six-battalion 40th Volunteer Corps, which was then set up between 1859 and 1860. There was little Government assistance and uniforms and rifles were largely paid for locally.

In 1883, as a result of the Cardwell reforms, the Militia was made the 3rd and 4th Battalions of the two Regiments, thus creating a more formal link with the Regular Regiments. Each Regiment also had attached Volunteer Battalions descended from the Staffordshire Rifle Volunteers, raised in 1859. The South Staffords had three Volunteer Battalions based at Handsworth, Walsall and Wolverhampton, while the North Staffords had two Volunteer Battalions, at Stoke-on-Trent and at Burton-upon-Trent. Staffordshire also contributed Army Reserve, Pensioner, Yeomanry Cavalry and Artillery Volunteer Corps units. As mentioned earlier, several of these, together with the Regular 1st South Staffords and 2nd North Staffords, saw service in South Africa during the Boer War.

The Territorial Army as we know it today was formed in 1908 and played a major role in the First World War, serving on the Home Front as well as in nearly every theatre of war. Three Staffordshire battalions formed part of 46th (North Midland) Division, which, as we have seen (page 22), secured one of the most decisive breakthroughs of the war.

As part of a reorganisation of the TA reflecting new requirements for anti-aircraft, armoured and anti-armour units, 46th Division was disbanded in 1936. This produced a dearth of TA Infantry, and when war came in 1939 each TA division was ordered to 'duplicate' itself. As a result, 59th (Staffordshire) Motor Division was created. With the addition of units from the disbanded 66th Division, this became 59th Infantry Division (The Staffordshire Division). The Division contained two Staffordshire brigades (which included 7th Royal Norfolk Regiment) and one Lancashire brigade; the inclusion of the Royal Norfolks and the Lancashire brigade resulted from geographical rearrangements of other divisions. The Staffords TA battalions were 5th, 1st/6th and 2nd/6th and 7th South Staffords and 6th North Staffords; initially 7th North Staffords were included, but were replaced in October 1942 by the Royal Norfolks.

After spending the first five years of the war in a home defence role (except for 1st/6th South Staffords which went to France, see page 25), the Division landed on the Normandy beaches on 26 June 1944 (D Day plus 20). Initially the Division was concentrated between Bayeux and Cruelly; on 3 July it entered the battle around Caen. A series of hard-fought engagements (59th Division suffered 239 deaths with 1,029 injured or missing in two days outside Caen) saw the Division advance from Caen, past Noyers, across the River Orne and past Thury-Harcourt. The disbandment of 59th Infantry Division was announced on 20 August 1944, even as 5th South Staffords were chasing and engaging the retreating enemy 20 miles south of Thury-Harcourt. In the words of Major Len Roberts, a TA Company Commander: 'Thury-Harcourt was the Division's last cohesive battle. It can be said that the Division went out in a blaze of glory!'

The Division was broken up only because it was the most junior in Normandy, and its troops were dispersed by unit to maintain the morale and *esprit de corps* of seasoned fighting units. The transferred troops were well received and many divisional commanders had a high opinion of them. Nevertheless the disbanding caused much unhappiness. Peter Knight, a former 59th Division officer, wrote in his book *The 59th Division: its War Story*: 'It was all very difficult for the ordinary soldier to grasp ... and yet, had we not shown in five weeks that we were capable of great deeds?'

In 1994, during the 50th anniversary commemoration of the D-Day invasion, the author had the opportunity to meet many members of the Division and their families and the people of Epron and Thury-Harcourt. A few months after this visit, the author again had the honour of meeting present residents of Epron and Thury-Harcourt, this time at the Palace of Westminster. One said that 'we wish to pay our respects, honour the dead, and say thank you once again to the men of the Staffordshire Division.' The importance of the Staffords has not been lost on the people whom they so courageously liberated.

In 1967, 5th South Staffords and 5th/6th North Staffords amalgamated to form the 5th/6th Battalion, The Staffordshire Regiment (The Prince of Wales's) (TA), and subsequently became the Mercian Volunteers. In 1988 the Mercian Volunteers (headquartered at Wolverhampton with Companies in Burton-upon-Trent, Stoke-on-Trent, Tamworth and Walsall) were disbanded and 3rd Staffords (V) were established in their place. However 3rd Staffords retained the Colours of the Mercian Volunteers until 1991 when The Duke of York presented them with new Colours. The present-day Staffordshire Regiment therefore now includes 3rd Staffords (V) as its Territorial Army Battalion. The use of the Regiment's mascot, Watchman III, helps to unite the Territorial and Regular Battalions.

This has been a short account of the four regiments that have gradually coalesced into the present-day Staffordshire Regiment and nearly became half of The Cheshire and Staffordshire Regiment. It highlights the achievements, the disappointments, the traditions, the vicissitudes of public and political support and the exploits of the soldiers themselves. Their uninterrupted service over the centuries — contributing enormously to the British national interest serving in home defence, the expansion and the twilight of empire, the maintenance of the Cold War's delicate standoff, and on UN duties — came within an ace of being fractured. Many men had laid down their lives — in great battles and through plague and pestilence. The Regiment had close links with the county, and was held in extremely high esteem, yet all this was to become a piece of history.

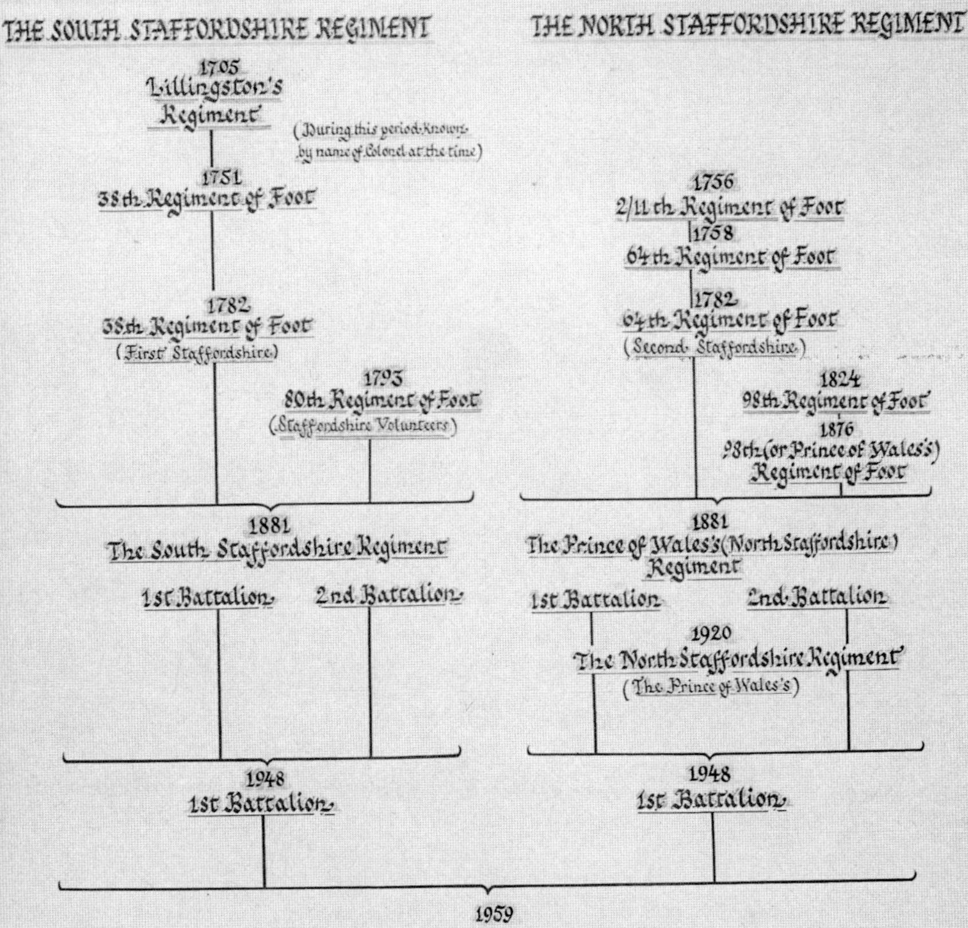
THE REGIMENTAL TREE
THE SOUTH STAFFORDSHIRE REGIMENT
THE NORTH STAFFORDSHIRE REGIMENT
1705
Lillingston's Regiment
(During this period known by name of Colonel at the time)
1751
38th Regiment of Foot
1756
2/11th Regiment of Foot
1758
64th Regiment of Foot
1782
38th Regiment of Foot
(First Staffordshire)
1782
64th Regiment of Foot
(Second Staffordshire)
1793
80th Regiment of Foot
(Staffordshire Volunteers)
1824
98th Regiment of Foot
1876
98th (or Prince of Wales's) Regiment of Foot
1881
The South Staffordshire Regiment
1881
The Prince of Wales's (North Staffordshire) Regiment
1st Battalion
2nd Battalion
1st Battalion
2nd Battalion
1920
The North Staffordshire Regiment
(The Prince of Wales's)
1948
1st Battalion
1948
1st Battalion
1959
The Staffordshire Regiment
(The Prince of Wales's)

THE MILITIA

The origins of the Militia in the County go back to the 17th. Century and there are records of their being embodied on a number of occasions, including the years 1776 – 1783, 1793 – 1801, 1803 – 1814 and 1815 – 1816. It was in 1805 that King George III conferred on the 1st Staffordshire Regiment of Militia the title 'Kings Own Staffordshire Militia'. From 1816 the Militia was in abeyance until:

1852

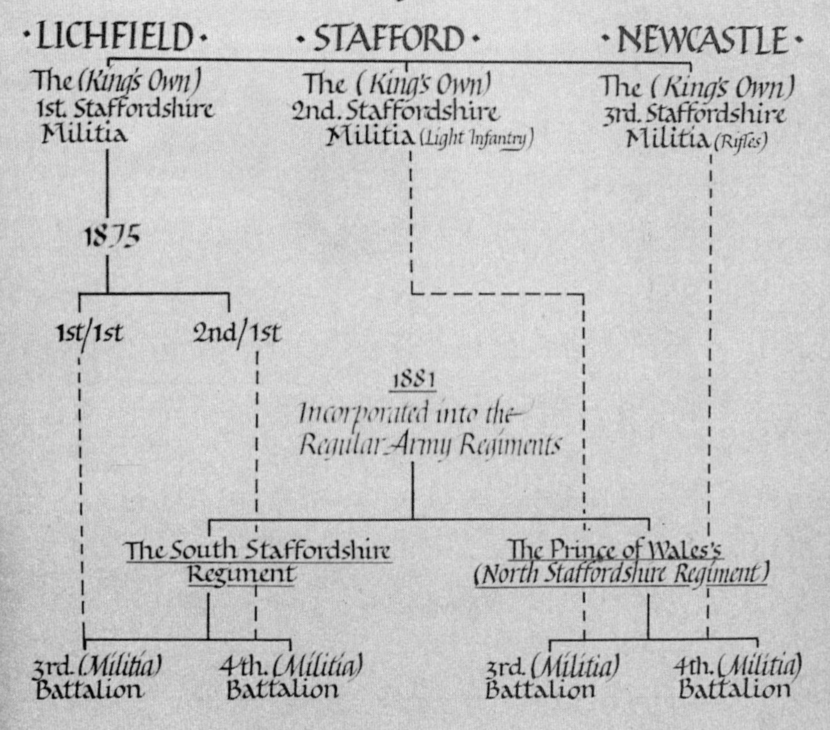

1918 – 1919

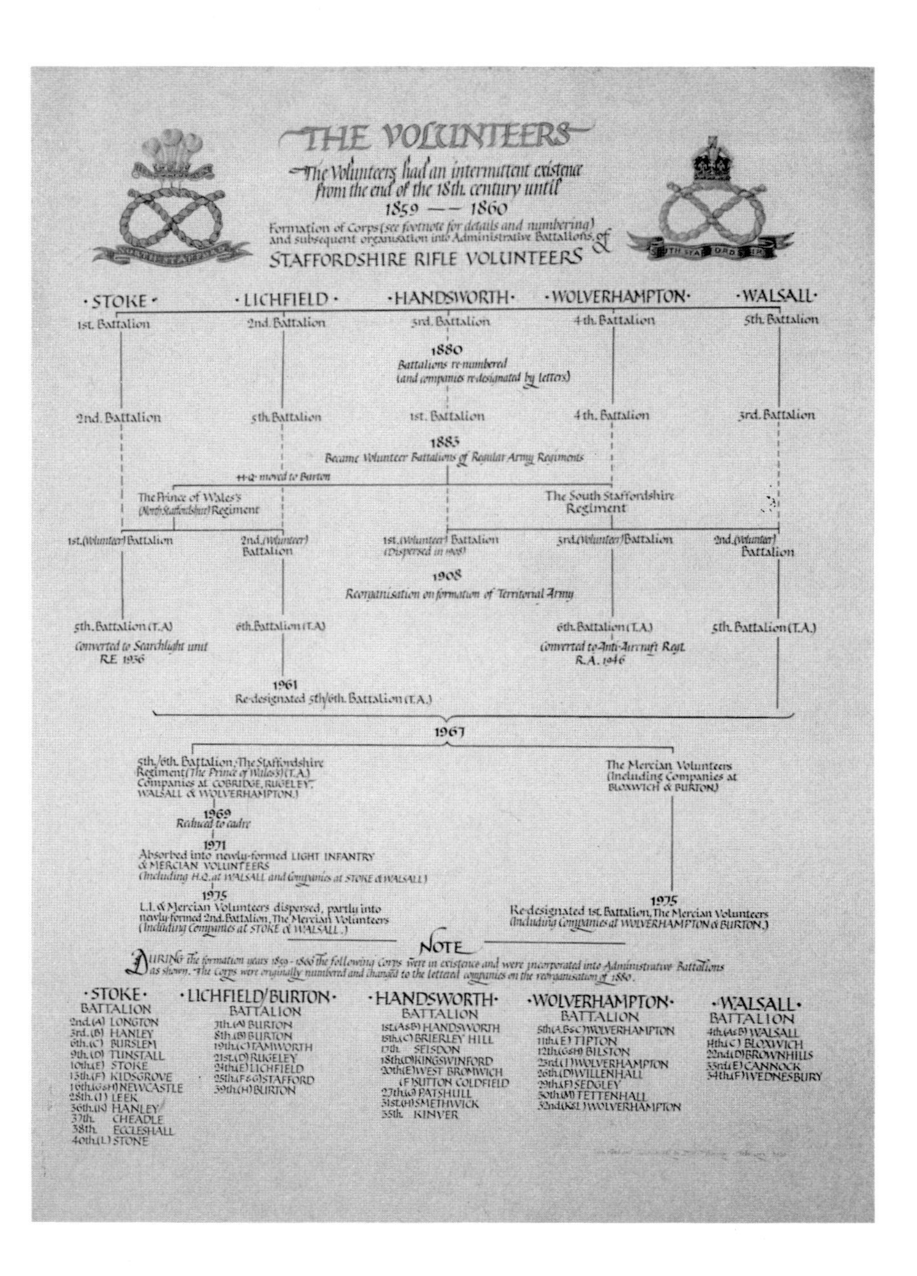

As a result of a reorganisation of the territorial battalions in the Midlands, on 5 April 1988 the Mercian Volunteers was disbanded and a new 3rd (Volunteer) Battalion of The Staffordshire Regiment was formed.

Regimental Museum

Officer of Lillingston's Regiments c. 1705.

Antigua 1715.

Mark Chapman – Walsall

Regimental Museum

Capture of Monte Video 1807 during the Napoleonic War.
(38th of Foot)

Regimental Museum

The capture of Reshire during the Persian War by the 64th of Foot in 1856.

Imperial War Museum

137 Staffordshire Brigade at the Riquerval Bridge being addressed by the Brigade Commander Brigadier General J V Campbell on 29 September 1918.

Lance-Corporal Coltman, VC, DCM and Bar, MM and Bar, 1st/6th North Staffords, 1914-18 War.

Regimental Museum

Lance Sergeant Baskeyfield 2nd South Staffords manning his 6 inch anti-tank gun at Arnhem in 1944; in this action he was awarded a posthumous VC.

Regimental Museum

Soldiers of 1st Staffords in final training for the Gulf War 1991.

Regimental Museum

The Prime Minister John Major visits 1st Staffords 1991 after the Gulf War.

Chapter 2

The Strategic and Political Background

Pressure for a peace dividend

The pattern of United Kingdom defence policy over the centuries has had a consistent theme: a contraction in resources at the conclusion of major hostilities followed by a rush to reconstitute forces at the outbreak of a major new conflict. Throughout the post-war period governments have had to balance changing defence commitments and resources within the constraints of the overarching strategic environment. At the same time as old colonial commitments were shed, equally demanding new roles were being established. These included membership of NATO, which entailed maintaining forces in the Federal Republic of Germany and within the naval theatre; the development of an independent nuclear deterrent; and, from the 1970s onwards, the commitment of substantial resources to Northern Ireland.

A series of defence reviews (in 1957, 1966-68, 1974-75, 1981 and 1990) has led to a steady reduction in both the size of the UK armed forces and national expenditure on defence. Since 1971 the United Kingdom has experienced NATO's second largest reduction in military personnel. Defence expenditure fell from its 1951-53 high of 10 per cent of gross domestic product to 4.2 per cent in 1991-92 and is projected to fall still further to 2.8 per cent in 1997-98.

Following the end of the Cold War the Government set about reducing the strength of the armed forces. In his invaluable and revealing *Diaries*, Alan Clark, who served as Minister of State for Defence Procurement until the April 1992 general election, states that a number of competing 'reduction exercises' were being conducted simultaneously. He himself wrote one paper, which he used to pre-empt proposals in the form of a Departmental Paper drawn up by Sir Michael Quinlan, the MoD's Permanent Secretary. Then Clark's own proposals were sidelined by the interloper known as *Options for Change*, whose origins are unclear. Clark's description of its impact is illuminating:

> The whole Department is in a state of frustration. What is happening to the Review?
>
> 'Options for Change' — I ask you! Spastic title. There shouldn't be any f***ing 'options'. It should be — 'It's like this. Now get

on with it.' As it is, we're just haemorrhaging away on needless expenditure, and morale is plummeting with the uncertainty.

Options for Change was so called after Tom King, Secretary of State for Defence, used the phrase in an answer to a Parliamentary Question in February 1990. The particular significance of the term for the Army was that a series of organisational options was considered and developed. Each of these was described alphabetically, and it is interesting to note that it was 'Option Whisky' that was eventually implemented. *Options for Change* continued the broad trend of earlier reviews, proposing a further contraction in resources, force levels and defence expenditure. Yet so much changed between February 1990 and July 1991 (when specific details of the Infantry reductions were announced, including the merger between the Staffords and the Cheshires) that the suspicion arises that the Government's acknowledgement of these changes was designed to provide a retrospective justification for its strategic rationale and that this in turn was designed to obscure Treasury pressure to reduce public spending.

Throughout the Cold War defence planning was based on a relatively stable strategic rationale. Central to this was NATO's assumption that conflict with the Soviet Union and its eastern European allies would take the form of high-intensity armoured warfare. This scenario largely dictated equipment standards, force structures and training requirements. Equally important, by requiring forces to plan for only a limited range of responses, it failed to set a high premium on preparing for a diversity of scenarios and responses, and on adaptability to different forms of warfare.

The democratisation of the eastern European states and the collapse of the Soviet Union led to a radical shift in strategic thinking. The new NATO catchwords were mobility, flexibility and multinationality. The New Strategic Concept, unveiled at the Rome Summit in November 1991, stressed that, following the removal of a single unified threat, the major risks to European security until well into the next century would be likely to arise from sources such as ethno-nationalist conflict arising inside or outside NATO's geographical area. The earliest and most striking example of this was the conflict in former Yugoslavia. The uncertainties associated with such conflicts would demand flexibility and mobility and a new willingness to operate outside NATO's area.

To some extent, *Options for Change* did anticipate the future needs of United Kingdom and European defence. The knowledge that the

UK was to play a major role in future NATO multinational mobile formations was reflected in the decision to maintain 1 (UK) Armoured Division in Germany. Yet the decision to reduce the number of Infantry battalions from fifty-five to thirty-six amazed most observers. In view of the development of the UN's peace-keeping potential and of NATO's capability to support the UN through new mobile and flexible force structures, the decision represented a severe reduction in the very troops who would be needed most. The scale of Infantry reductions would make the UK increasingly dependent on 'double-hatting' and even 'triple-hatting' Infantry units (giving units two or three alternative roles) in order to cover the range of commitments that an uncertain environment might demand.

Most critics argued that the force reductions had been worked out well before any concrete strategic rationale had been developed to justify them. Who could know how many peace-keeping operations might have to be undertaken as conflicts arose across the new Europe? Could major threats to Western interests be foreseen? Could, for instance, the Government have anticipated the Gulf War when it first announced *Options for Change*? In 1991 and 1992 the Government seemed to be formulating UK defence policy through a series of *ad hoc* decisions. These were governed by the dictates of a growing budget deficit and justified, in the Government's eyes, by public expectation of a 'peace dividend' following the end of the Cold War; they were not based on a well-founded understanding of the nation's strategic needs into the next century. Opponents of *Options for Change*, and of the regimental amalgamations in particular, were quick to seize not only on the lack of clarity of the general policy but also on the inconsistency and lack of transparency surrounding specific decisions within the overall policy and within the *Options* decision-making process.

Opening salvoes

Tom King presented the broad outlines of the *Options* strategic review to Parliament on 25 July 1990, just before the summer recess. The significance and seriousness of the review was immediately obvious, as was the extent of the changes proposed, which were of a magnitude comparable with previous defence reviews and went far beyond tinkering at the margins of defence spending. The main elements of the Ministry of Defence's plans for 'smaller but better' armed forces were an approximate halving of the Army commitment to Germany, together with a reduction in RAF bases there from four to two; the reduction of the Royal Navy's frigate/destroyer fleet from 'around fifty' ships to 'around forty' and a cut in the conventional submarine fleet from twenty-seven hulls to 'about sixteen'; personnel reductions in the Royal Navy and the RAF to 60,000 and 75,000 respectively; and, of greatest importance to The Staffordshire Regiment, a future Army of 'about 120,000' troops.

In a perceptive question following the announcement, Sir Hector Monro, the Conservative MP for Dumfries and soon to become a loyal supporter of the Scottish anti-amalgamation campaign, asked for an assurance that 'the regimental system will be maintained and that the old regimental area and county names and Scottish regimental names will be retained'. Perhaps not hearing the second half of the question, King replied that he could 'give him that confirmation' — yet four Scottish Infantry regiments were selected for amalgamation and county names proved far from safe. Perhaps not quite realising how prescient his words were, King also said, in reply to Sir Geoffrey Johnson Smith, the Conservative MP for Wealden: 'I do not conceal from the House the fact that we will have to face some very difficult decisions and problems.' How right he was.

When Parliament reassembled in the autumn, events had conspired to prevent sensible debate. Saddam Hussein's annexation of Kuwait only eight days after King's announcement put a temporary hold on King's proposals. The US-led operation that pushed Saddam out of Kuwait served to underline the fragility of the new post Cold War strategic environment and pointed to the need for a comprehensive strategic reassessment of the global situation. And in the Gulf War the Staffords themselves played a decisive and distinguished role.

The amalgamation announcement

Tom King returned to the despatch box on Tuesday 23 July 1991, only a few months after the ceasefire in Iraq. It immediately became clear that the Gulf War had not led the Government to undertake a strategic reappraisal. Indeed the Ministry of Defence was sticking rigidly to its original plans. The Army as a whole was to be reduced to 116,000 personnel (the reality of the 'about 120,000' figure), and the Staffords were stunned by a single seemingly unremarkable sentence:

> Within The Prince of Wales's Division, recruiting from Wales, the Midlands and the West Country, The Cheshire Regiment will amalgamate with The Staffordshire Regiment and The Gloucestershire Regiment with The Duke of Edinburgh's Royal Regiment.

Staffordshire and West Midlands MPs greeted this with incredulity. There was no obvious strategic justification for the Government's decision to reduce the number of Infantry battalions from fifty-five to thirty-eight; within that reduction the abolition of the Staffords' separate identity beggared belief. Throughout the entire consultation process within the Infantry about how to achieve the Government's reductions there had been no indication that the Staffords would be recommended for amalgamation with any regiment.

In their immediate reactions to King's statement, MPs seized on the two themes that were to become the bedrock of the case against amalgamation. Nicholas Budgen, Conservative MP for Wolverhampton South West, who as a young man had served as an officer in The North Staffordshire Regiment, fired the first salvo. Asking King to reconsider the proposed amalgamation, he noted the Staffords' excellent recruitment record:

> I remind [the Secretary of State] that The Staffordshire Regiment is already an amalgamation of The North and South Staffordshire Regiments in 1959, that it has shown splendid service in Northern Ireland and, more recently, in the Gulf, and that its recruiting figures are very good.

King's reply was the first portent of the Government's approaching and protracted intransigence. Acknowledging Budgen's concerns for the Regiment, King nevertheless went on: 'This is the decision reached by the Army Board and — tough as it is — it cannot be changed.'

Jerry Wiggin, another Conservative MP and a former junior Defence Minister, voiced what later became the second main theme of the Staffords' campaign: the lack of a rationale for the reductions.

> Does my right hon Friend accept that, in mounting the recent expeditionary force to the Gulf with only one division, all the ancillary services in the Army were stretched to the limit? Does he recognise, therefore, that some of us do not believe in the basic calculations on which he propounded his statement?

Again, King's reply anticipated the months of debate that lay ahead. He defended the 'restructuring' by asserting that better equipment and better manned units would counter overstretch, a refrain that flowed from the basic premise of the 'smaller but better' Army.

The Save Our Staffords campaign subsequently went to great lengths to point out that the initial responses of local MPs to the Government's plans for the Infantry and the Staffords were not a parochial knee-jerk reaction. The Campaign Committee — and a large body of supporters, including most MPs with constituencies within the Staffords' recruiting area — was convinced that there were very good reasons to challenge the strategic and organisational rationale upon which the decision was based.

The debate with the Government also focused on the issue of accountability. What most irritated the Regiment and its supporters was the secrecy shrouding the decision, the inconsistency of the 'strategic rationale', the seeming failure of the Government to abide by its own criteria for amalgamation, and uncertainty about where the crucial breakdown within the decision-making process had taken place.

The political decision-making process

The main purposes of this book are to explain how the Staffords campaigned against amalgamation and to highlight the various arguments put forward during their campaign. But before we embark on that story, it is important to try to elucidate how the decision was reached to amalgamate the Staffords and the Cheshires and to identify the institutions and individuals involved.

Cabinet level

In 1964, a single unified Ministry of Defence (MoD)was created, replacing the previous three Service ministries, each of which had its own secretary of state. Bringing the three Services together in one ministry was designed to make defence policy planning more cohesive and to provide a single defence-oriented voice within Cabinet. The parallel creation of the post of Chief of Defence Staff (CDS) was also designed to reduce the traditional inter-Service rivalry that resulted from the inclusion of three separate Service chiefs in the Cabinet.

The strength of the Secretary of State for Defence within a Cabinet of approximately twenty-two members depends on a variety of factors. As the departmental minister concerned, the Defence Secretary clearly has a prominent voice on defence matters. Yet dominant Prime Ministers (such as Margaret Thatcher and Harold Wilson) regard themselves as major decision-makers and seek to steer the Cabinet on significant decisions. Furthermore, the Defence Secretary is generally ranked only about eighth in the Cabinet hierarchy. Much also depends on the experience and weight of the individual minister; since Margaret Thatcher came to power in 1979 there have been no fewer than seven Defence Secretaries.

Much of the work of Cabinet ministers is carried out in numerous committees. The world of Cabinet committees is a secret one about which little is known with certainty. Some committees consist of ministers alone, some of civil servants alone, while others are mixed. The most important committee relating to defence is the Overseas and Defence Policy Committee, which is chaired by the Prime Minister. Other members include the Foreign Secretary, the Chancellor of the Exchequer, the President of the Board of Trade, the Defence Secretary and the Attorney-General; the Chief of Defence Staff and the Chiefs of Staff of the three Services attend when necessary. Many other committees and sub-committees can also play an important role. For instance, in 1991-92 the Northern Ireland Committee was influential in the calculations of troop numbers in Northern Ireland, a factor that in turn had a considerable bearing on the reversal of two Infantry amalgamations. Other ministries involved are the Foreign Office — for defence is, of course, closely linked with foreign policy — the Home Office, and the Transport, Environment and National Heritage departments. The Treasury, which controls the purse-strings, always has an enormous influence on expenditure and, in consequence, on policy as well.

Parliament

As far as policy-making is concerned, especially in the field of defence, the House of Commons is one of the weakest democratic legislatures in the world. (The author can speak with some confidence on this, having conducted a survey of forty defence committees throughout the world and presented a paper to an international conference on the subject.) MPs, it is true, have many opportunities to raise issues of concern, and, as we shall see, Staffords supporters made use of all of these. They also exploited every possibility for behind-the-scenes pressure, which can be particularly effective when undertaken by backbenchers of the governing party, especially when the Government has a small majority. Yet these opportunities are essentially reactive and do not permit MPs to become closely involved in the development of policy. Decision-making remains highly centralised, and most key decisions are taken by a small group of ministers (assisted by their political advisors), civil servants and, the case of defence issues, the Services' chiefs of staff. This is more true of policy formation in defence than in other areas, since defence was for centuries the exclusive preserve of the Monarch, whose powers were later transferred not to Parliament but to the Cabinet.

The House of Commons Defence Committee

The system of select committees, as it has developed since 1979, has had some effect in countering the excessive and exclusive power of the executive in policy-making. The House of Commons works in an adversarial way, as do the standing committees of MPs appointed to scrutinise legislation. Select committees, however, which are composed of backbench MPs from all parties, generally function in a more consensual manner, scrutinising departmental policy and practice and making often very detailed recommendations for changes. Most ministries are monitored by a select committee, which develops significant expertise in the policy area concerned. Committee chairmen in particular become known as experts whose opinion carries considerable weight in Parliament and in the media.

The Defence Select Committee (of which the author is Senior Opposition member, and as such *de facto* Vice-Chairman) carved out for itself a unique role in the debate about *Options for Change* and in particular about the regimental amalgamations. As we shall see, debates in both the House of Commons and the House of Lords served a valuable purpose, but it was in the Select Committee that MoD policy and practice was subjected to intense and prolonged interrogation. While the Committee lacks the power of Senate and House of Representatives committees in the USA, its inquiries and subsequent reports have some impact on policy.

Since new select committees are appointed after each general election, the Save Our Staffords campaign worked with two Defence Committees. The 1987-92 Committee was chaired by Michael Mates, who retired as a Lieutenant Colonel in The Queen's Dragoon Guards to fight, and win, his first election in October 1974. He was not given ministerial office by Margaret Thatcher and spent many years on the backbenches, during which he courageously opposed aspects of Government policy (notably the ill-fated Community Charge) and acted as Michael Heseltine's Chief of Staff during the contest for the leadership of the Conservative Party in 1990. After the 1992 general election he served as Minister of State for Northern Ireland with responsibility for security before resigning in 1993 over the Asil Nadir affair; this concerned donations to the Conservative Party by a major public company which later collapsed.

The new Committee, appointed after the 1992 general election, consisted of six Conservative MPs, four Labour and one Liberal Democrat, in line with party strengths in the House. After considerable politicking, notably by the Opposition members, Sir Nicholas Bonsor was elected as Chairman to replace Michael Mates. He was considered (in particular by the author and his Labour colleague John Home Robertson) to be the best choice from the standpoint of the regiments fighting to retain their identity as well as the most likely to maintain the consensual tradition. Bonsor, a baronet, wealthy landowner and MP for the Upminster constituency in the Essex suburbs of London, was an independent-minded politician who had frequently voted against the Government in backbench rebellions, including one on the Defence Estimates. (After sixteen years on the backbenches, Bonsor was made a full Minister of State at the Foreign Office in July 1995; he was replaced as Chairman by his fellow-Conservative Michael Colvin.)

The Defence Select Committee has acquired a reputation for independence of mind. Tory members in particular, who might be expected to toe the Party line, have often behaved in what the MoD perceives as an unnecessarily inquisitive and truculent manner. The Committee has been remarkably successful in warding off party-political pressure and keeping above the usual inter-party warfare, even during the 1980s when the consensual approach to defence politics was much less in evidence than it was in the mid-1990s.

The Defence Select Committee's most important contribution to the campaign against the regimental amalgamations was its doggedness and persistence in probing the MoD. In a highly public fashion it exposed the process — and deficiencies — of policy-making through press coverage, in televised sessions, and through its damning and cogently argued reports. Ministers and civil servants knew that every time they appeared before the Defence Committee, whether or not the session was directly related to the Army, there would be no escape from the core question of the Infantry. There was little love lost between ministers and Committee members. If ministers hoped that their Conservative colleagues on the Committee would soften the impact of the repeated and sometimes heated questioning, they did so in vain.

Perhaps one reason why ministers and civil servants became so defensive and irritable was because they could be sure that, at some point, a Committee member would start to probe into the darkest recesses of the MoD, where information tends to be treated with extreme possessiveness. The Select Committee forced information out of the system through sheer persistence, damaging the MoD's case as the Ministry's own claims became ever harder to support with its own information. Allied to this persistent questioning were important links with the regiments themselves and with other supporting organisations. These gave the Committee invaluable insights into the 'real' situation and the 'real' pressures on fighting men; these could never have been gained solely from the information provided by official sources, which were often 'economical with the truth'.

Chapter 3

Implementing Options for Change

As the previous chapter has explained, it is clear that the initial proposals to reduce defence expenditure originated in the Treasury and were approved by the Cabinet. How the Ministry of Defence then determined what proportion of the cuts would fall on the respective Services is a mystery. For all the regiments threatened with amalgamation, but especially for the Staffords and Cheshires, the important issue was the decision-making process within the Army, as senior officers sought to find ways of implementing the cuts required by *Options for Change*.

The consultation process

Options proposed that the number of Infantry battalions should be reduced to thirty-six. To achieve this the Director of Infantry, Major General Bob Hodges, was required to seek the views of the Colonels Commandant of the nine administrative Divisions of Infantry and then put his considered recommendations to the Executive Committee of the Army Board (ECAB). To guide him in this process the Chief of General Staff (CGS), General Sir John Chapple, laid down five determinants by which individual regiments should be judged for amalgamation. These became known as CGS' Criteria and addressed: recruitability; previous amalgamations (unamalgamated regiments were to be more vulnerable); demography; the cultural and geographic compatibility of regiments (i.e. 'like with like'); and the seniority and precedence of regiments.

This consultation process should have ensured that every regiment had ample opportunity to debate and comment on any amalgamation proposals affecting them. Certainly the Director of Infantry's package of recommendations to ECAB should have held no surprises. For most regiments this was the case, but not so for The Staffordshire and Cheshire Regiments. They were not consulted on a possible amalgamation with each other, and the announcement by Tom King that they were to amalgamate therefore came as a stunning shock. To add insult to injury their requests for an explanation of the decision were firmly rejected and, not surprisingly, they felt deeply hurt and badly treated. This lack of consultation and rationale was a regrettable indictment of all concerned and it prompted the Staffords' decision to campaign against amalgamation.

Major General Hodges' consultation process with the Divisions of Infantry had been completed by early July 1991. The full Army Board received a paper from the Executive Committee on 22 July and submitted recommendations for Cabinet approval. The amalgamation decisions announced in Parliament the following day, 23 July, differed slightly from the original *Options* proposals in that there were to be thirty-eight battalions, two more than originally planned.

The divisive debate that followed the parliamentary announcement focused on the consultation process and on the rationales for the decision to amalgamate Infantry regiments. Although the official criteria were undoubtedly taken into account, at some point crucial additional considerations came into play. This point was later admitted by both Archie Hamilton, the Armed Forces Minister (in a letter on 10 March 1992 to John Levey, who masterminded the Staffords' campaign), and by Sir John Chapple (in a letter to Ian Freer, Colonel of the Staffordshire Regiment, on 13 September 1991).

The critical point is that the rationales for amalgamating the Cheshires and Staffords, or any of the other regiments nominated, were never revealed. Although subsequently the Staffords presented a strong case against amalgamation on the basis of the CGS' Criteria, before the announcement, since they did not know that they were being considered for amalgamation, they were never in a position to do so.

Furthermore, the Divisional Plans — which presumably contained the Infantry's own amalgamation proposals — had supposedly been agreed in discussion with the Colonels of Regiments. Yet both Brigadier Ian Freer of the Staffords and Brigadier Keith Prosser of the Cheshires have made it clear that they had neither recommended amalgamation with each other nor even been consulted about the possibility. The Director of Infantry took the view that the Divisional Plans contained the recommendations of the Colonels of Regiments; yet in a letter to Brigadier Prosser of 6 August he contradicted himself, asserting that 'it was a pity that you did not express in your submission a clear preference for an amalgamation should the Army Board have decided that was what you had to do.'

Amalgamation options

On the basis of the CGS' Criteria, there was not a strong case to recommend an amalgamation between the Cheshires and the Staffords. Both regiments are in the Prince of Wales's Division, whose Colonel Commandant at the time was General Sir John Waters, then

Commander in Chief, UK Land Forces. In terms of geography, the Cheshires had more in common with both the neighbouring Royal Welch Fusiliers (RWF) and The King's Regiment. In addition the RWF, like the Cheshires, had not previously been amalgamated; and although The King's Regiment was the product of an amalgamation in 1958, it was geographically closer for recruitment purposes. The facts that the Staffords had already been amalgamated and had a strong local recruiting base did not give Brigadier Freer any justification for conceding his own Regiment's amalgamation.

Although it has never been made public, the Director of Infantry's submission to the Army Board almost certainly contained three options for the Cheshires; two of these had already been agreed at Divisional level, while the third seemed to come out of the blue. The Divisional preferred option for the Cheshires was amalgamation with the Royal Welch Fusiliers: neither of the regiments had been amalgamated before, they recruited close to each other's areas (and sometimes within them), and their Regimental Headquarters, at Wrexham and Chester, were only 20 miles apart. It was recognised, of course, that straddling the Welsh-English border would prove contentious, but against this it could be argued that the geographic proximity of the recruiting areas was undeniable, and the RWF have traditionally had to import recruits from South Wales to keep their numbers up.

The second, fallback, Divisional option for the Cheshires was amalgamation with The King's Regiment, also close neighbours. Again, this proposal cut across boundaries — in this case the boundary between the King's and the Prince of Wales's Divisions — but there were already precedents for this which the MoD had accepted. Indeed, another Prince of Wales's Division regiment, the Royal Hampshire Regiment, had reluctantly agreed to amalgamate into The Princess of Wales's Royal Regiment, who are in the Queen's Division. In many respects the Cheshire/King's amalgamation was preferable for the Cheshires, since the King's headquarters was in Liverpool and the cultural identity of the Cheshires was closer to that of the north-western regiments than to that of either the Welsh or the West Midlands regiments.

These, then, were the two options discussed and agreed by Colonels of Regiment at Divisional level. In a note accompanying the Divisional Plan Brigadier Prosser made it clear that both were acceptable to him but that he was not enthusiastic about either. Amalgamation with the Staffords — the proposal that later seemed to come out of the blue — was not at the time in the frame, so much so that Ian

Freer was not invited to comment on the Divisional Plan in detail. Interestingly he was invited to put forward a general case against amalgamation for the Staffords, which he did, but for reasons that are not clear the Division did not forward it to the Director of Infantry. Not surprisingly Ian Freer became increasingly confident that the Staffords would not be amalgamated: they had been amalgamated before, they came from a strong recruiting area and other regiments appeared to be more vulnerable. His view was reinforced when he stayed overnight with General Waters in early July and was given no hint that storm clouds were gathering over his Regiment.

However events were conspiring to disturb the situation. Even before the Director of Infantry had received the Divisional Plan, the RWF broke the informal agreement on confidentiality and went public with its plight, assembling a formidable campaign in a very short time. A Welsh public relations consultancy was hired to raise media awareness and undertake political lobbying; the RWF Old Comrades Association collected 85,000 signatures on a petition, which Barry Jones, the Shadow Welsh Secretary, presented to Parliament on 8 July; local authorities were involved; a group of sympathetic MPs of all parties was assembled to fight the proposal in Parliament; and campaigners and MPs alike lobbied key political decision-makers such as David Hunt, then Secretary of State for Wales.

The campaign achieved a great deal in a very short time, with the added benefit (in comparison with the Staffords' later campaign) of having the Welsh national card to play. And play it the RWF certainly did. The campaigners' case relied almost exclusively on national arguments. There was no need to assemble facts and figures to counter the MoD's case, since no announcement had yet been made to Parliament. This also meant that there was no embarrassment to Ministers in making a last-minute alteration to the amalgamation short-list. Even when the RWF campaign did put forward a number of arguments (concerning recruitment and retention, the overall regional military contribution, and the economics of amalgamation) the comparisons were still largely made on Welsh national grounds.

The strong national character of the opposition to the amalgamation of the Cheshires and the RWF would undoubtedly have caused severe headaches in Whitehall had it gone ahead. There is overwhelming evidence that this amalgamation was rejected on grounds of regional diversity and identity. The campaign did its job effectively. The pressure on David Hunt to use his position for the benefit of Wales appears to have been decisive, and it seems that Hunt responded by making sure that the Executive Committee of the Army Board rejected the proposed amalgamation. Indeed any future threat that can be portrayed as discriminating unreasonably against Scottish or Welsh regiments is likely to face similar staunch resistance. Highly placed insiders have also suggested that it is not unlikely that the Royal Household put in a word for the RWF; the Queen herself is the Regiment's Colonel in Chief, although any suggestion that she played a role is pure speculation.

The second option — amalgamation with The King's Regiment — aroused no such campaign. Why it was rejected is not known. As Director of Infantry, Bob Hodges might not have favoured this amalgamation on the grounds that it was cross-boundary. However, the logic for such a stance is difficult to see as he had already accepted the Hampshire proposal. What precisely he thought and recommended is a mystery, and appears likely to remain so. What is known is that in the final phase of the MoD's deliberations the Cheshires/Staffords amalgamation emerged without either Colonel of the Regiment being consulted. Furthermore, the amalgamation, widely anticipated throughout the Infantry, between The King's Own Royal Border Regiment (of which Bob Hodges was Colonel) and The Queen's Lancashire Regiment did not take place, even though both form part of The King's Division. Inevitably the situation caused great consternation and hurt to both Regiments and beyond.

In discussion with many different people at different levels in the Staffords' campaign, the author has often heard suggestions of 'gerrymandering' by the Army Board. Perhaps, the theory runs, the decisions about amalgamation were only partly based on the published criteria but were also biased by the regimental allegiances of the senior officers on the Army Board, and by those of Ministers as well. No one has overtly suggested a conspiracy, but it is certainly not inconceivable that the officers and politicians involved unconsciously favoured their own regiments when choices concerning their very survival were being made. Why should senior officers not be as influenced by regimental loyalties as an ordinary infantryman?

By way of example, accusations were levied that the Staffords were one of the more poorly recruited regiments who would in future struggle to maintain their numbers. This mystified them until they discovered what had happened. The Director of Infantry's calculations for them had been based purely on Staffordshire and had not credited the Regiment with recruits drawn from the northern part of the West Midlands, which used to form part of Staffordshire; this includes four of the Regiment's Freedom Towns and is very much part of their recruiting area. Fortunately the mistake was spotted by the Regiment and the figures were later revised, but for a while a false impression was created. Time has told its own story, and in 1996 the Staffords are the second strongest regiment in the Prince of Wales's Division and are confident of maintaining their strength.

The Cheshires also have an intriguing story to tell with regard to recruiting areas. Traditionally they have always recruited from the Wirral on the south side of the river Mersey. Surprised by a reducing number of recruits over recent years, they investigated possible causes with the MoD's recruiting staff only to discover that at the time of *Options for Change* the Infantry recruiting area map had been revised by the Director of Infantry's staff and the Wirral incorporated into The King's Regiment recruiting area. It was a simple error but, like the omission of part of the West Midlands for the Staffords, it affected recruiting numbers — the life blood of the Regiment. The recruiting map has now been corrected, and the Wirral is once again allocated to the Cheshires.

The author has no hard evidence to support a conspiracy theory. It seems more likely that the officers and one Civil Service member of ECAB listened to the Director of Infantry's recommendations and went along with them. In the end, we cannot say definitely whose allegiances, or indeed if any at all, swung the balance.

The ECAB decision-making process that led up to the announcement on 23 July that the Staffords and the Cheshires were to be amalgamated remains unclear. In addition to the published criteria, which were well known to the regiments, other considerations clearly lay behind the decision. What these were remains a mystery. But there are definitely gaps between the Director of Infantry's original proposal to the Divisions, the recommendations by the Colonels of Regiments for their own regiments, and the proposals presented to and finalised by the Army Board. This incompleteness and incoherence account for the Staffords' dismay when they heard the amalgamation announcement and explains why a formidable campaign against the merger quickly developed.

Chapter 4

Forming up for Battle

July 1991 to September 1991

In July 1991 Brigadier Ian Freer, Colonel of the Staffordshire Regiment, was Chief of the British Commanders-in-Chief Mission to the Soviet Western Group of Forces (inexplicably allocated the acronym BRIXMIS). On the afternoon of Tuesday 23 July, the day Tom King broke the news to Parliament of the Staffords' fate, he was sitting at his desk in Berlin. General staff officers at the Ministry of Defence (MoD) were unable to contact him to break the news that the Staffords and the Cheshires were to be amalgamated; eventually they reached a startled Major Mike Tarbuck at Regimental Headquarters (RHQ) who managed to relay the message to an equally shocked Freer some twenty minutes before the Statement in Parliament.

Freer, stunned, tried to digest what he had just heard. There had been no indication that this amalgamation was being mooted in Whitehall, nor had the possibility been discussed at either of the meetings held to finalise a Divisional Plan. Many thoughts crossed Freer's mind, including intense anger at the way he and the Regiment had been treated; but he had to set these thoughts aside and warn the Regiment urgently, particularly the 1st Battalion, of what lay in store. The 1st Battalion's problems were compounded because half of them were on block leave from their base in Fallingbostel, Germany. Their Commanding Officer, Lieutenant Colonel Charles Rogers, had received a similar last-minute warning and was in the process of mustering and briefing as many of his Battalion as were in barracks at the time. Freer quickly telephoned RHQ and several senior Staffords officers. He could offer no explanation for what had happened or say anything to allay the deep sense of shock and dismay felt by all ranks. Many of the tears shed by the Regiment that night sprang as much from the hurtful surprise of the decision as from sadness at the Regiment's fate. To each and every Stafford, it was a real blow.

Over the next few days, Freer took stock of the situation, trying to establish what had happened. He spoke to General Sir John Chapple, Chief of General Staff (CGS). Sir John was sympathetic about the lack of warning but requested that the Regiment accept the order stoically, in the broader interests of the Army; he spoke of the difficulties of the decision-making process and of the Army Board's keen desire to move forward and implement the changes required of it. At that time Freer hardly felt like being quiet, but it was proving difficult to establish what had taken place at the various Army Board meetings prior to the announcement because of the principle of confidentiality — what others might call excessive secrecy — which covers such meetings. No one was prepared to offer a rationale for the amalgamation or to explain when the Staffords had been selected. The decision was presented as a *fait accompli.*

The announcement on 23 July rocked not only the Staffords but also everyone associated with them and the county. It also revealed a rich seam of loyalty to the Regiment which would be tapped with dramatic effect. If the Government believed that the ties binding regiments and people were loose enough to justify complacency about which regiments to select for amalgamation, it would soon learn that it had chosen a particularly stubborn knot to untie. Almost as soon as the announcement was made in Parliament and the orders went out to the regiments affected, it became obvious that the Staffords would not accept the decision without an explanation. After his discussions on 23 and 24 July, Freer decided to appeal formally to the Army Board; he also felt that the Regiment had strong grounds to mount a public campaign to have the decision reversed.

Freer summarised his views in a Special Order of the Day to the 1st Battalion in Fallingbostel on Thursday 25 July 1991. For the first, but not the last, time he stated that there must be two aspects to the Regiment's reaction. On the one hand, they clearly had grounds for appeal, and he gave every indication to his troops that he would not take the decision lying down. On the other hand, the serving officers and soldiers should show positive leadership and carry out the preparations involved with amalgamation unquestioningly (albeit reluctantly) in the knowledge that the amalgamation might, in the end, go ahead. Over the next eighteen months, this dual approach was adhered to with great professionalism, and only occasionally led to conflicting tensions.

While the serving officers and soldiers were constrained by the need to follow orders (and by the regulation forbidding them to comment publicly on Government policy), the old soldiers, and the families and friends of soldiers and the Regiment, were not so restricted. In many cases, they were as shocked as the Regiment was, and began to ask the same questions as Freer: why had the Staffords been chosen when until then they had met all the criteria for exemption from amalgamation? And why had the decision been revealed to Brigadier Freer only twenty minutes before being announced to Parliament?

The determination to answer such questions would fuel a local, regional and national campaign of considerable duration, of high intensity and with huge appeal. To be understood, the campaign must be seen in the context of the British regimental system, which creates intense *esprit de corps* and equally intense local, often county, loyalty.

A cursory comparison with other amalgamations is instructive. Many previous amalgamations had gone ahead unopposed, and the majority of the post-1990 *Options for Change* amalgamations proceeded with very little protest. The two amalgamations ultimately cancelled by Malcolm Rifkind in February 1993 involved regiments with very strong regional identities which also ran vocal, professional and effective campaigns opposing their loss of separate identity. The Staffords could demonstrate their sustainability by pointing to the demographic strength of their recruiting area, which returns twenty-six Members of Parliament. The threatened Scottish battalions — The King's Own Scottish Borderers, The Royal Scots, The Queen's Own Highlanders and The Gordon Highlanders — could also point to a strong national identity. The Royal Welch Fusiliers, for whom the Staffords had been substituted, had secured their own reprieve on the basis of national considerations, for it was considered politically unacceptable to amalgamate Welsh and English regiments. The analogy between the Staffords, the Scottish regiments and the RWF is by no means exact, but of all the English regiments under the shadow of amalgamation few could claim such intense county loyalty as the Staffords or argue quite so vociferously for their regional homogeneity.

If this strong regional loyalty accounts, to a large degree, for the support that the Staffords' campaign received within the recruiting area, important questions of the role and strength of the Infantry and of British national interests also handed the campaign natural allies in Parliament, so that it could boast significant support at a variety of levels. There was also a fair element of luck: the general election called in the middle of the campaign provided guaranteed media opportunities; a central location in Lichfield provided by a Kuwaiti property company was used as a command centre during the election; and a bequest gave the campaign adequate funding to undertake a protracted fight. It was lucky, also, that as a Staffords supporter the author — Vice Chairman and Senior Opposition member of the House of Commons Defence Committee — helped to keep the Staffords' cause before that Committee, which in turn harried the MoD more or less constantly.

Although these conditions would be of enormous help in making the campaign as effective as it was, it almost certainly would have folded quietly and without success had a strategy not been developed to direct and focus it and had there not been an effective campaigning organisation to carry the fight at a variety of levels and in different arenas.

Formation of a campaign committee

After the initial shock of the amalgamation announcement, Brigadier Freer decided that two things had to be done. First, a stay of execution would have to be obtained to give sufficient time in which to develop and mount a case for the Regiment. Second, a campaign organisation would have to be created to co-ordinate the fightback.

Tom King's original timetable had planned for the Staffords and Cheshires to amalgamate in autumn 1992. However, under a previous order, the two battalions were also programmed to switch locations between Fallingbostel (where the 1st Battalion were stationed in July 1991) and Dale Barracks, Chester (home to the Cheshires) in summer 1992. Freer could see the force of the MoD's arguments for cancelling the switch and leaving the Staffords in place until their amalgamation date. However, this would have been regarded as a second penalty, particularly if the new regiment had continued the Staffords' posting in Fallingbostel. He decided to forestall this possibility by pressing for the unit switch to go ahead and for the amalgamation date to be delayed to create sufficient time to justify the moving expenses.

It was also in the Regiment's interest to delay the amalgamation for as long as possible in order to improve the chances of it not taking place at all. Freer reflected these thoughts in his Special Order of the Day:

> For the immediate future, I am endeavouring to ensure that your arms-plot changeover with the Cheshires goes ahead as originally planned. After all you have been through, you deserve a proper break in the UK and Dale Camp would be a convenient base. I am also trying to ensure that we are allocated a late amalgamation date, i.e. sometime during 1995-97. If we can achieve that then we will have just a glimmer of hope that circumstances will change over the next five years and we might win a reprieve.

Freer then embarked on a campaign of letter-writing, both within the Regiment and outside. He started by expressing the Regiment's dismay and shock to Major General Bob Hodges, Director of Infantry, on 2 August:

> Since I was given no subsequent indication that [amalgamation] was being considered, I was unable to warn the Commanding Officer of the unwelcome likelihood. The battalion was therefore shocked by the Secretary of State's announcement. Their morale has been devastated. Considering the assurances given beforehand that there would be full prior consultation, our treatment has been a painful breach of faith and we feel distinctly let down by all concerned.

Freer told Major General Hodges that he had decided to appeal to the Chief of General Staff, and went on to explain his case in detail and request the Director of Infantry's support. He also urged most strongly that the Staffords be given at least a two-year tour in the UK after Fallingbostel.

On 6 August Freer submitted a formal letter of appeal to CGS. It expressed the Staffords' dismay at the lack of consultation and the importance which they placed on the Ministry of Defence's original determinants (the CGS' Criteria), which should have driven the selection process. In a separate letter on the same day to a senior staff officer in the MoD, he enlarged on the Regiment's strong recruiting potential, reminding his correspondent that in early July 1991 (before the Army Board had made its decision) the Director of Infantry had underestimated the Staffords' recruitment levels in the West Midlands parts of its recruiting area. (Local government reorganisation in 1974 had moved several Staffordshire towns out of the county into the newly created West Midlands metropolitan county.) Those areas, Freer pointed out, included four of the Staffords' Freedom Towns and provided 30 per cent of the Regiment's recruits. If the Director of Infantry had conducted the selection procedure under the misapprehension that the Staffords recruited at only two-thirds of their actual figure, there was every reason to argue the injustice of the decision. As one campaigner went on to observe about this exchange: 'The Regiment was almost ditched over an administrative oversight.'

As Chapter 3 makes clear, we do not know what was argued by whom in the discussions leading up to the final crucial meeting in June 1991 between the Director of Infantry and ECAB, at which the final recommendations for amalgamations were decided for presentation to the full Army Board for approval; nor do we know the criteria the Director of Infantry used to formulate his proposals. Nevertheless it would seem logical to assume that a summary of the Staffords' recruiting potential that ignored one-third of that potential would colour the Director of Infantry's judgment of the viability of the Staffords as an independent regiment in the context of what was, to all intents and purposes, a competition for survival. This was therefore a potentially crucial error. An enormous amount of effort could have been averted if this document, a possible cornerstone of the Director of Infantry's decision, had been accurate. We cannot stress this too much; neither can we discover what role it played until a future Government releases the position papers and the records of the meetings.

According to Freer, one of the most surprising aspects of the process before Tom King's statement was the failure of General Waters, the Colonel Commandant of the Prince of Wales's Division, to indicate — or to even to hint — that amalgamation was being considered. On 9 August Freer wrote him a strong letter pointing out that he could have been advised when it was decided to offer the Staffords-Cheshires amalgamation option to the Army Board. At that time, Freer says, neither the Colonel Commandant nor the Director of Infantry was bound by any rules of confidentiality. Freer argued that it would have been in the Army Board's interest to know his views on the option; instead his exclusion put his Regiment at a disadvantage compared with others.

Following this flurry of correspondence — which did indeed secure a year's respite for the Regiment — Freer approached several influential ex-members of the Regiment to form a Campaign Committee. The decision to mount a public campaign, like that of the Scottish Infantry regiments, had been taken by Freer and promulgated to all senior Staffords officers in a letter of 27 July 1991. Brigadier Sir Louis Hargroves, Colonel Jimmy Baines, Colonel Walter James, Colonel Tony Griffiths, Major Doug Bridges and Major Mac McLean, the Regimental Secretary and ironically also a member of the Amalgamation Committee set up to oversee the amalgamation of the Staffords and Cheshires, were all well known in the county; all agreed to take part, and many devoted much time and energy to the cause.

On his way to the first meeting of the embryonic Campaign Committee Ian Freer stayed overnight with Brigadier John Levey; also staying at Levey's house was Lieutenant Colonel Nigel Alderman, Levey's son-in-law who was soon to become Commanding Officer of the 1st Battalion. Freer remembers that he had been mulling over the matter of a Committee Chairman, and after dinner, over a second scotch, he asked Levey if he would be willing to assume the role. Levey was reluctant, having taken no part in regimental affairs since he retired in 1983, but Freer and Alderman persuaded him that he was the man for the job; his last appointment had been Divisional Brigadier of the Prince of Wales's Division based at Lichfield, and consequently he had just the right sort of experience and background to take on the project. The next morning Levey was on his way to Lichfield with Freer to meet the Committee as its Chairman.

Freer had also spent some time thinking about the position of Secretary to the Committee. Captain Will Stamper was in the process of leaving the Army and was able to take on the job. His role was initially very demanding and he became one of the unsung heroes of the first part of the campaign, taking on an enormous amount of behind-the-scenes planning and work.

Although Freer chaired the first 'Extraordinary Meeting on Amalgamation', reflecting his role in establishing the Campaign Committee, it is incumbent upon serving officers, men and civil servants to refrain from commenting publicly on Government policy without clearance from the MoD. For that reason, Freer had to relinquish his role on the Committee, although he remained closely involved throughout the campaign; after that first meeting, while he was occasionally present, he was not minuted as having attended, nor were his words recorded. Knowing the depth of emotion provoked by the announcement of the Staffords' amalgamation, senior Army officers felt it necessary to remind Freer of the need to exercise control over his Regiment's public utterances. This reminder was, it should be added, extremely sympathetic to the Regiment's plight, and the injunction needed to be invoked in the interests of the soldiers rather than to protect Government policy. This consideration explains not only Freer's 'absence' from the campaign but also the non-serving status of the Committee members.

The Campaign Committee agreed to meet every six to eight weeks at Regimental Headquarters at Whittington Barracks, Lichfield. The first meeting was held on 12 August 1991. The committee discussed the goals, strategy and structure of the campaign, which at this early stage took a fairly imprecise form. Each Committee member stated what he would do in a personal capacity. Brigadier Sir Louis Hargroves, for instance, undertook to explore the possibility of hiring a public affairs consultancy, and it was agreed that John Levey would act as Campaign Co-ordinator. The Committee also decided to call the campaign 'Save Our Staffords' — 'SOS' for short.

To obtain maximum publicity, the Committee decided to stage an official launch. None of the venues discussed seemed suitable. Chatting after the meeting, Levey and Stamper decided that they had to find a location of historical significance with ample space and ease of access. Stamper hit upon the idea of the King's Head, the Lichfield pub where the Regiment was first formed. It proved to be an inspired choice, evoking one of the cases for the Regiment's retention, namely its 300-year association with the local community. It only remained for Stamper to fix it.

The following morning Mac McLean issued a press release announcing a decision taken by the Regimental Association, friends, retired officers and former soldiers of the Regiment to mount a campaign, 'with the support of the Colonel of the Regiment', to fight the amalgamation of The Staffordshire and The Cheshire Regiments. The statement added: 'This decision has not been taken lightly but it is strongly felt that amalgamation is not in the best interests of the Regiment, county or Infantry.'

While the general aims of the campaign had been identified (to be given more substance over the coming weeks), they would have been unattainable without considerable financial support. Most campaigns have to begin with fund-raising. Save Our Staffords was extremely fortunate that on his death in 1985 Colonel Eric Butler OBE (of whom more will be said later) left a significant bequest 'to be applied for charitable purposes for the benefit of the Regiment in such a manner as the Colonel of the Regiment shall at his sole discretion see fit'. The Eric Butler bequest relieved the Committee of much of the burden of fund-raising and meant that it could afford good public relations advice and advocacy, which turned out to be of inestimable value.

The Regimental Council, which advises the Colonel of the Regiment, includes the Trustees who control the allocation of regimental funds. The importance of the Council to the campaign is obvious, and the members were always sympathetic and supportive. A further important factor was that John Levey, although not at that time a Council member, understood and played Regimental politics very well.

The formation of a Campaign Committee did not of itself guarantee that the concerns of the Regiment would be represented effectively to all the varying audiences — local, regional, national — that mattered. Competent as the Committee was, its experience was military rather than political. Dealing with Whitehall and Westminster demanded a different sort of expertise. The Committee understood its own limitations all too well, and, as we have seen, wisely decided to delegate the task of scouting for a public affairs consultancy to Sir Louis Hargroves.

Selecting a consultancy

An initial approach was made to Citigate Birmingham, the West Midlands subsidiary of Citigate Communications Group, a City of London-based financial and corporate PR consultancy with a network of offices across Britain, Europe and the USA. Any relationship between Citigate and the Staffords was bound to appear incongruous at first sight — the Staffords' objectives were very different from those of the average City or blue chip client, and never before had PR experts been called on to save a regiment that Whitehall mandarins had announced was for the chop. However, the Campaign Committee was looking for a company with a good reputation which would be interested in taking on such an unusual client. The question, then, was not 'Why Citigate?' but 'Why not Citigate?'

Keep Our Scottish Battalions (the campaign organisation formed to fight the amalgamations of the four Scottish Infantry regiments) had recently hired Citigate Scotland, another part of the Citigate group; it was in this way that the SOS Campaign Committee, which had established common cause with the Scots, came to hear of Citigate. At a very early stage, it had been recognised that there was a degree of commonality in the arguments against amalgamation that the Staffords and Cheshires and the Scottish regiments might deploy, so it seemed sensible to use a single agency to run these parallel operations. Citigate in turn recognised that, in the Staffordshire region and in Westminster, the Staffords would be addressing very different audiences. So it was that Citigate referred the national component of the campaign to Westminster Communications Group, a leading public affairs consultancy which, at the time, had an informal partnership arrangement with Citigate. Meanwhile, Citigate Birmingham would handle the local elements of the campaign in Staffordshire and the West Midlands.

Westminster Communications Group is a public affairs consultancy — or political lobbying company — operating out of an imposing Georgian townhouse in Little College Street, a stone's throw from the Palace of Westminster. It was created in April 1989 as a merger of two consultancies — Westminster Communications (founded by Richard Faulkner, a former Labour Prospective Parliamentary Candidate and advisor to Neil Kinnock) and Murray Evans Associates — and, at the outset of the campaign, was based at 7 Buckingham Gate, next to Buckingham Palace.

The second meeting of the Campaign Committee, on 15 August

1991, included representatives of Citigate Birmingham and Simon Nayyar from Westminster Communications. Following a 'credentials pitch' and a formal proposal document from the two consultancies, Citigate and Westminster Communications were engaged by the Staffords until 31 October, at which time the situation was to be reviewed. Citigate's proposed strategy was accepted 'in principle', although several minor amendments were found necessary in respect of the aims of the campaign. The amendments were agreed at the third meeting, on 27 August 1991, as was the rationale of the campaign — that the Midlands had been disadvantaged 'both militarily and culturally' due to excessive Infantry reductions. The meeting also agreed to launch the campaign at the King's Head in Lichfield, and proposed to approach several local dignitaries to become Patrons of the campaign. (This group of distinguished persons, all of whom accepted the Colonel of the Regiment's invitation, consisted of Sir Arthur Bryan, Lord Lieutenant of Staffordshire; Colonel Walter James, Vice Lord Lieutenant; Commander George Inge-Innes-Lillingston, a Deputy Lieutenant of the County and descendant of Luke Lillingston; the Rt Hon the Earl of Shrewsbury and Waterford; Sir Anthony Bamford, Chairman and Managing Director of J C Bamford Excavators (JCB); and Sir Eric Pountain, Chairman of Tarmac.)

The SOS Campaign Committee and Westminster Communications had little time to think things through. Simon Nayyar, one of the youngest and newest account executives at Westminster Communications, who was given the Staffords portfolio, had something of a case to prove and took up the assignment with gusto. Levey remembers him as 'utterly, utterly dedicated to us winning'. Enthusiasm notwithstanding, Nayyar had a fair amount to learn, as would anyone with a civilian background fighting the cause of a county regiment against the MoD. Nayyar acknowledges that he was on 'an extremely steep learning curve' from the word go.

A barrage of educational assistance from John Levey (which later included a visit to the 1st Battalion at their temporary home in Chester) and intensive tutorials on regimental history, Army structure and defence policy gave Nayyar enough knowledge of defence matters to make effective judgments for the campaign's political strategy. Nayyar identified the key political objectives, and Levey ensured that he understood the primary concerns of the campaigners. Chief among these was a fear of antagonising the Ministry of Defence and thereby jeopardising the case the campaign had constructed. The arguments needed to be forceful, coherent and convincing, without offending those whose views would be crucial to reversing the amalgamation decisions.

The process of learning and formulating strategy was compressed into a very short period of time. From conception to launch was a matter of weeks.

Chapter 5

Launching the Campaign

September 1991

The official launch of the 'Save Our Staffords' campaign took place at 11 am on 9 September 1991 at the King's Head. The day dawned bright, which at least gave the members of the Campaign Committee a psychological lift on their way to Lichfield. Together with Will Stamper, Major Jim Ellison and his team from the Lichfield branch of the Regimental Association had worked hard preparing a room in the King's Head for the launch. The 'Save Our Staffords' campaign logo was in place, bright yellow pamphlets explaining the campaign's intentions were on the seats, and coffee was made.

The Committee members milled around, watched by Simon Nayyar of Westminster Communications and Ian Hunter of Citigate, who quietly wondered how this *ad hoc* Committee would perform on its first public outing. The Committee members knew few of the guests, and had to rely on prompts to differentiate between MPs, Prospective Parliamentary Candidates (PPCs — candidates planning to challenge sitting MPs at the next election), the press and local dignitaries. One important exception was Jim Guthrie of the *Birmingham Evening Mail*, who had covered the Staffords' activities for many years. John Levey had first met Guthrie while second-in-command of the battalion, stationed in Berlin in 1969, and had invited him to dinner at his home. Such contacts, as the campaigners were soon to realise, can become extremely precious in later years.

Everybody knew that the success of this launch would be crucial to the rest of the campaign. If the media failed to show up, if not enough heavyweights arrived whose support would be critical, if the Committee's arguments lacked sufficient clarity and force to generate publicity and support, then potentially all could be lost in a single throw of the die. It was quite possible that the Regiment might be born and die in the same pub.

Nayyar had earlier sent letters to MPs, PPCs — a general election was, after all, approaching — and local government representatives, inviting them to attend the launch or, if they were unable to do so, to send a message of support to the Regiment and its campaigners. A number of MPs representing constituencies within the Staffords' recruiting area showed their support by attending. The Conservatives were represented by Gerald Howarth, MP for Cannock and Burntwood; Labour supporters were the author (Walsall South), Llin

Golding (Newcastle-under-Lyme) and Sylvia Heal (Mid Staffordshire). Michael Fabricant, the Conservative PPC challenging Sylvia Heal, was also present, as was Brian Jenkins, then Mayor of Tamworth and later to be Labour MP for Staffordshire South East.

The speed with which the campaign was established and the absence of many MPs during the summer recess limited attendance at the launch, but messages of support were received from many MPs, including Peter Archer (Labour, Warley West), whose father had been a South Stafford; Peter Snape (Labour, West Bromwich East), who sent his unconditional support as an ex-national serviceman; Dr John Gilbert (Labour, Dudley East), a former Defence Minister, and Bill Cash, Conservative MP for Stafford. Gilbert wrote that:

> Many families from my constituency have sent their men to serve in the Staffordshire Regiment over the years, and I am sure they are most distressed at the suggestion that the Regiment might lose its identity. The campaign has my full support.

In all, letters endorsing the campaign were received from thirteen MPs, three Members of the European Parliament, seven PPCs and nine local authorities.

Appropriately, John Levey kicked off the campaign, reminding those present of the link between the launch event and the Regiment's long and illustrious history. He asked, rhetorically:

> Why are we here on the 9th of September some 286 years after Colonel Luke Lillingston raised the Regiment in this Public House in 1705? Because, Ladies and Gentlemen, we are here to fight for the survival of The Staffordshire Regiment and to launch our Campaign to 'Save Our Staffords'.

The campaign, he went on to explain, would be two-pronged, operating at both local and national levels. While the national campaign would focus on the complex issues raised by *Options for Change*, the local campaign would concentrate on the apparent underhandedness of the Staffords' last-minute substitution for another regiment, especially as it had met the Army Board's criteria for exemption from amalgamation, and on the MoD's persistent refusal to explain the selection of the Staffords for merger. It would not be a blindly emotional campaign:

> These are facts and not sentiment coming from an old soldier. There is, of course, sentiment. There are many who have given

> their lives to the Regiment. There are those all over the county who have served in the Regiment. There is the Regiment's fine military reputation, tested in the Gulf.

The local campaign would centre on the injustice to the Regiment, and the heavy presence of local media at the launch ensured wide transmission of the campaign's arguments to the regional community. Nationally the campaign would join other groups — particularly the Cheshires and the Keep Our Scottish Battalions campaign — to expose the depth and severity of the cuts, and subsequently the overstretch, within the Infantry. From a national perspective, it was intended that the Staffords would avoid accusations of narrow regimental interest. After this outline of the campaign's broad strategy, Levey ended with a stirring call to arms: 'Ladies and Gentlemen, it is time to make our presence felt.'

A series of speeches by supporters followed. The first was by George Inge-Innes-Lillingston. It was appropriate that he was present at the launch, in the same place where his forebear had raised Lillingston's (38th) Regiment of Foot, not just because of his lineage, but also because he was an ex-sailor: the Lillingston/38th Foot spent countless months on ships between Britain and the colonies. He perceptively pointed out the advantages of the loyalty created by the Army's regimental system over the Royal Navy — presumably a hard admission for an old salt.

The Earl of Shrewsbury, another patron and the Campaign's most prominent supporter in the House of Lords, underlined Brigadier Levey's arguments and exhortations. Speeches were made by MPs George, Heal and Howarth; George McEwan, Chairman of Lichfield Council; Councillor Wills, Mayor of Lichfield; Councillor Heenan, Mayor of Stafford; and Councillor Doug Bridges of East Staffordshire Borough Council. Colonel Walter James, Vice Lord Lieutenant of Staffordshire, closed the meeting, reiterating how unfair it was that the Regiment, already amalgamated in 1959, should be earmarked again when other regiments, unamalgamated since the Second World War, had not been selected.

To those present at the launch meeting it was obvious that this would be a dynamic campaign with the breadth of support necessary to endure. Their optimism seemed to be vindicated when, the following morning, there was a report and photograph of the campaign launch in *The Times* in addition to reports in a number of regional papers and good regional television coverage.

Local ceremonial

The campaign launch was followed, later the same morning, by a Freedom March by 170 soldiers of C Company, 1st Battalion, and the bands of the 1st and 3rd Battalions, in full dress uniform through Lichfield in celebration of the Regiment's part in the Gulf War victory. The Mayor of Lichfield took the salute. Intended to express thanks to the people of Lichfield for their support, the march that day — the first for six years and the first in Lichfield since November 1983 — and others that followed throughout Staffordshire and the West Midlands underlined the sense of bitterness felt by many young soldiers. Those taking part, and many of the thousands watching, knew that the march might be the last by The Staffordshire Regiment.

The Staffords enjoy the Freedom of ten towns and cities in the region — Burton-upon-Trent, Dudley, Lichfield, Newcastle-under-Lyme, Sandwell, Stafford, Stoke-on-Trent, Tamworth, Walsall and Wolverhampton — and, traditionally, may march through any one of these with bayonets fixed, drums beating and flags flying. A Freedom March is a spectacle of sight and sound, a celebration as well as a means of thanking Freedom Towns for their support; conversely, conferring the Freedom of the Town, Borough or City is the greatest honour a civic authority can bestow. For serving soldiers, not permitted to comment on Government policy, a Freedom March was one of the few practical things they could do to promote the Regiment during the campaign. These occasions focused public attention on the plight of the Regiment and on its military capability and viability. They strengthened and renewed bonds between Regiment and community. They were also excellent public relations opportunities.

Just over a week later, on 20 September, Lichfield Cathedral hosted a service of thanksgiving for the Staffords, attended by about 200 men and their families and over 1,500 invited guests. HRH The Duke of York, The Colonel-in-Chief of The Staffordshire Regiment, was present at the service and the same afternoon, on a glorious autumnal day, presented new Colours to the 3rd (Volunteer) Battalion in a ceremony at Whittington Barracks. This was a unique event in the life of the Regiment: it was the first occasion on which the 1st and 3rd Battalions had paraded together.

As MPs had been invited, it was thought that it might be an opportune moment for them to comment, should they wish, on the proposed amalgamation. Unfortunately, some of the Conservative MPs felt that they were being pressurised to comment negatively on Government policy and made clear their unhappiness, much to the amusement of the Labour MPs present. Because of the limited success of this first public encounter of the Committee with MPs, Simon Nayyar, unimpressed with the way the afternoon had unfolded and after consultation with Levey, resolved to work on the campaign's communications skills.

It was also on the occasion of the presentation of new Colours to the 3rd Battalion that Simon Nayyar first glimpsed the Volunteers' mascot at close quarters. A stocky, black Staffordshire Bull Terrier, Watchman III stood to attention during the parade as if following the orders of a drill-sergeant with a voice beyond the threshold of human hearing. In his livery coat and collar, and with his handler, Sergeant Malcolm Bowers, also in parade dress, Watchman was resplendent. The media potential of this highly photogenic Staffordshire symbol — who also possesses a distinct personality of his own — was immediately obvious to Nayyar.

No sooner had the parade ended than Nayyar and Levey agreed that Watchman should join the campaigners' armoury. Nayyar says that Watchman's role was pivotal in securing a reprieve for the Regiment. Watchman, he maintains, provided a highly seductive photo-opportunity for the local and national newspapers and media organisations, and this regularly provided the hook on which to hang the story of the wider injustice of the proposed amalgamation.

The campaign hierarchy

In keeping with the efficiency and enthusiasm of the Campaign Committee and Nayyar's energetic optimism, the challenges facing the campaign in its formative weeks — and throughout the subsequent year and a half — never became insurmountable obstacles. Things just got done. In Nayyar's view, the fact that the Campaign Committee was formed mainly from retired army officers was of considerable importance:

> They were all so used to military discipline, if a senior retired officer said 'jump!' they'd all jump; so if I mentioned to John Levey that something needed doing, it would be as good as done. You could almost hear a chain of commands issuing from John Levey's command cell and growing fainter as they passed down the line. It was really quite remarkable to receive such a level of co-operation, very reassuring and crucial to ensuring that the campaign moved forward credibly and coherently.

It is difficult to overstate the significance of this military discipline, just as it is difficult to avoid the image of a clutch of uniformed ex-officers moving toy tanks and artillery pieces across a map of the field of battle. Caricature though that image is, it is nevertheless not inappropriate. The planning of strategy, the command, control, communications and intelligence, and the deployment of forces which are critical to the outcome of a military campaign were all key elements of this campaign of persuasion, and were utilised with military precision. The abundance of strong and consistent leadership, clear decision-making, protracted planning, understanding of resources and unity of purpose distinguish this campaign from so many goal-oriented exercises over the decades.

The military discipline of the campaign may help to explain its organisational capabilities, but the personal dimension was also of great importance. Two or three personalities stand out in particular. Simon Nayyar is adamant that John Levey was the 'star of the piece', and a host of campaign participants have supported this view in comments to the author. He was the unifying force of the enterprise, prolific in his handling of information as the person at the centre of the campaign. The campaign was dealing with The Staffordshire Regiment, the Regimental Association, the Friends of The Staffordshire Regiment, the local and national media, Parliament, individual MPs, MEPs and Peers, the Government and its advisers, the Ministry of Defence, local authorities, the Cheshires, the Scottish regiments' campaign, the consultancies, and the public. It was a huge brief for anyone unfamiliar with campaigning, and one that he pulled off with aplomb. He was also crucial as an insider: a former Commanding officer of the Regiment, he had considerable knowledge of, and contacts within, the Army and the Ministry of Defence.

Levey had been commissioned into The North Staffordshire Regiment in 1953, prior to the amalgamation with the South Staffords. He served variously as intelligence officer, machine gun platoon commander and officer cadet instructor before reaching Staff Officer level and returning to the amalgamated Staffordshire Regiment, eventually commanding the 1st Battalion between 1971 and 1974. He did not serve directly with the Regiment again, but after jobs in Lichfield, Northern Ireland and the Ministry of Defence he became Brigadier of the Prince of Wales's Division in 1980, from which he retired in 1983.

Ian Freer also deserves mention as a central player in the campaign, although strictly speaking his was mainly an initiating role and his activities were far from the public eye. He was instrumental in setting up the campaign; as he was at pains to point out, without wishing to compromise his loyalties both to his Regiment and to the Army Board, he felt that the merger undermined his position in several ways. For instance, having been given only twenty minutes' prior notice of the amalgamation, he had been taken completely by surprise; yet the process as described by the Ministry of Defence should have included his own opinions, and those of Brigadier Keith Prosser, Colonel of The Cheshire Regiment, in the Divisional Plan submitted to the Army Board, so that at the very least he should have been aware that the merger was likely. Yet because the ostensible criteria by which regiments were to be selected for amalgamation were not adhered to, Freer had no way of knowing what was to come. Hence he felt that the Regiment had been duped — which, after the Staffords' performance in Operation Granby (the Gulf War), was a gross injustice — and that his position of authority had been undermined.

Commissioned into The Staffordshire Regiment in 1961, Freer stayed with the Regiment for most of his early career, interspersed with staff appointments, until commanding the 1st Battalion from 1982 to 1984. He received the OBE after a tour of duty in Northern Ireland, and was honoured with a CBE after commanding 39th Infantry Brigade, again in Northern Ireland. At the time of the announcement of the Staffords' amalgamation, he was Brigadier, Colonel of the Regiment and Chief BRIXMIS in Berlin; shortly thereafter, on 15 November 1991, he was promoted to Major General and became Commander Land Forces, Northern Ireland.

Freer lobbied relentlessly, out of the glare of publicity, within the MoD and the Army and acted as a behind-the-scenes joint strategist with John Levey. His activities were not always appreciated by his superiors who, while respecting his loyalty to his Regiment, must have been irritated beyond words at his refusal to accept the MoD diktat. The Campaign Committee, on the other hand, was more than happy to have Freer on board. His position was made all the more difficult by his coincidental work as Commander Land Forces, Northern Ireland to raise troop levels in Northern Ireland. The reinforcement of the Province by two extra battalions undoubtedly helped to expose the dangers of Infantry overstretch, but it laid him open to accusations of scheming. Freer also felt it better to work behind the scenes to avoid a clash of interests with his role as Co-Chairman of the Amalgamation Committee. John Levey and Freer routinely discussed his role, and Levey regularly reported back to the Committee on the constraints on Freer's actions; the Committee was more than happy to support Freer's 'covert' role. Freer was able to communicate easily, through regular letters, through the regimental network and through *The Stafford Knot*, the regimental journal.

Occasionally Freer's anger spilled over into the public domain, but he made every attempt to balance his campaigning zeal with a grudging acknowledgment of the seeming inevitability of the amalgamation. For instance, shortly after Tom King unleashed the amalgamation on the unsuspecting Regiment he wrote in The Staffordshire Regiment newsletter: 'We have always been a regiment which squares up to reality with maturity and professionalism. If ultimately we are required to amalgamate, then so be it.' As Colonel of the Regiment Freer knew that, were the amalgamation ultimately to proceed, he would be responsible for carrying it through.

Several other key players deserve mention. Bill Cash, Conservative MP for Stafford, and Patrick Cormack, Conservative MP for South Staffordshire, brought interesting, albeit often differing, perspectives and ideas about how best to progress the campaign; each played a central part in bringing the campaign to Parliament's attention, maintaining the media's interest, and hounding the Government. (Patrick Cormack received a well-deserved knighthood in the 1995 New Year's Honours.) The author, as Senior Opposition Member of the Defence Select Committee, also helped to belie any Government hopes that the progress of regimental mergers would be assisted or rubber-stamped by that Committee.

While not present to participate in the campaign, the late Colonel Eric Butler OBE also deserves mention here. Eric Butler was a man of great energy and passion for his county and its Regiment, to which he dedicated much of his life; had he been alive in 1991 he would undoubtedly have been closely involved in the struggle to save the Staffords. His substantial and generous bequest to the Regiment on his death in 1985 provided crucial funding for the campaign and ensured that it would be vigorously fought.

Butler was commissioned into The South Staffordshire Regiment in 1940, joining the 1st Battalion in 1941. He was twice wounded in Burma, the second time during the Second Chindit Campaign, and was awarded the Military Cross. In 1946 he returned to the family brewing firm as a director and became an executive director when Bass Charrington acquired the company, a position he held until he retired in 1977; he was greatly respected and admired in the brewing business. When the Territorial Army was re-formed after the Second World War, Eric Butler joined the 5th South Staffords and served as

Commanding Officer from 1953 to 1956. He became Colonel on the Staff, and in 1957 was awarded the OBE and was made a Deputy Lieutenant; he was appointed Chairman of the Staffordshire Territorial and Auxiliary Forces Association in 1965; and he was a member of the Executive Committee of the South Staffordshire Old Comrades Association and its progeny, the amalgamated Staffordshire Regimental Association, serving as President of the Hednesford branch from 1959 and first President of the Willenhall (1960) and Wolverhampton (1970) branches. He also served on the national committee that established the Chindits Old Comrades Association in 1947, and formed the Wolverhampton branch, of which he was Chairman and later President; from 1971 until his death he was an active Life Vice President of the National Association. In 1969, he and Lord Mountbatten struck up a conversation about a national memorial to the Chindits; Butler kept the idea alive until the National Committee decided to commission a memorial in October 1985, ironically only a month before his death.

When the South and North Staffords were amalgamated, Colonel Butler helped to establish a new Regimental Trust and served as a Trustee for over twenty years; he was also a Regimental Museum Trustee from 1975 until his death. As well as these regimental activities, he devoted a great deal of time to conservation and heritage organisations. Butler died on 28 November 1985; his memorial service filled Lichfield Cathedral.

No account of this campaign would be complete if it omitted the huge part played by Simon Nayyar. Aged twenty-four when the campaign started, Nayyar was a junior member of the public affairs team at Westminster Communications. He had studied history at York University, and (of indisputable importance to public affairs consultancy in the early 1990s and, of course, to the campaign) already had significant campaigning experience within the Conservative Party. When the SOS campaign moved into high gear during the general election campaign, Nayyar was working at Conservative Central Office, in Smith Square, as a media relations adviser to Ministers: an ironical position since many Conservatives in Staffordshire were threatening to withdraw their support for the Government over the Staffords and over the wider implications of *Options for Change*.

A list of everyone who participated in the campaign would end up reading like a telephone directory; it is impossible to acknowledge the roles of all who participated, and the author hopes that this account of the campaign's success will attest to each individual's particular contribution — it was indisputably the sum of many individual efforts. It was also amazing just how many people threw themselves into the campaign — former members of the Regiment and its predecessors (including one centenarian whose memories of the Regiment and its forebears are like gold dust); families of soldiers and their webs of kin radiating from Staffordshire; local government officers and workers; businessmen; politicians; football clubs; in fact, people from virtually every walk of civic and public life in the region. Surely one of the campaign's greatest strengths was this enormous grass roots sympathy and support which translated into action and participation for as long as two years.

For ceremonial purposes, the campaign had its colourful and traditional presentation pack: the 3rd (Volunteer) Battalion's mascot, Watchman III ('known to his friends as Winston'), who was promoted after the campaign's victory for his tireless efforts; and his handler, Sergeant Malcolm Bowers, whose 'dogged' devotion to the campaign cannot be overstated. As a bonus, when the Save Our Staffords and the Keep Our Scottish Battalions campaigns shared platforms a clutch of Scots pipers added to the ceremonial pomp; and there was also the tartan glory of Sir Nicholas Fairbairn, Conservative MP and champion of The Gordon Highlanders, who sadly died in 1995.

Ready for action

By the middle of September 1991, less than two months after Tom King's announcement of the regimental mergers and only weeks after Ian Freer had approached John Levey to form a Campaign Committee, the main structures and strategy of the campaign were in place and activity was well underway. The Campaign Committee had allocated its members distinct tasks; a strategy had been agreed, which separated the campaign into distinct local and national components with corresponding sets of goals and messages; two consultancies had been engaged to manage the implementation of these two levels of campaigning; a cross-party group of Staffordshire and West Midlands MPs had been assembled (with a few temporary exceptions) which would ensure the campaign's access to Parliament and Ministers; and the media were harnessed to the campaign's caravan of support. It was not long before this army of campaigners was called up for active service.

Chapter 6

The Road to Westminster

October 1991

The initial structure of the campaign was envisaged as a two-stage operation, running in parallel with that of the Cheshires and the Scots: first, to bring home to the county the implications of the imminent loss of the Regiment; and, second, to take that concern to Westminster. The vehicle chosen was a petition to Parliament, which the campaigners had initiated at the launch of the campaign in the King's Head. This device was being used with great effect by the Scots, who, having been forewarned of their likely amalgamations, had already begun to gather public support; the Royal Welch Fusiliers had also used a petition in their short but effective campaign. Nayyar suggested to the Campaign Committee that the petition would carry considerable weight if it was presented to the Speaker of the House of Commons on the first day of the annual Defence Estimates debate, 14 October.

This generated a flurry of activity. Captain Will Stamper, the temporary Campaign Committee Secretary, found himself tasked with building support throughout the county and beyond. He achieved this admirably: copies of the petition were spread to all corners of Staffordshire and the West Midlands, largely thanks to the far-reaching network of fifteen Regimental Association branches, Friends of the Regiment, the Gulf Support Groups, and Territorial Army members acting in a private, civilian capacity, plus hundreds of retired soldiers and families of those still serving with the Staffords. No stone was left unturned in the search for support. For instance, the Campaign Committee invited twenty Midlands Army Cadet units, whose Colonel Commandant was on the committee, to compete against each other to collect as many signatures for the petition as possible; silver trophies would be awarded to the three units gaining the best results. The Cadets took up the challenge with gusto. This was typical of the enthusiasm growing for the campaign in the region, as was the signing of the petition by a number of Wolverhampton Wanderers players.

The Blackpool meeting

One of the earliest detailed presentations of the Infantry's case was given at a fringe meeting at the Conservative Party Conference at

Blackpool on 9 October 1991. By then, however, the issue was already in the public eye. As well as flurries of correspondence between private individuals and Ministers, prominent supporters of the Infantry regiments were mounting a campaign of letter-writing to the press. One notable example was a letter published in *The Times* on 26 September, in which five former Colonels of The Staffordshire Regiment — Derek Boorman, John Commings, Louis Hargroves, Jeremy Swynnerton and Gerald Thubron — deplored the unaccountability of the Army Board:

> Those regiments affected are being obliged either to accept amalgamation without justification or to argue against it publicly. They should have been spared such as decision. Good leadership requires contentious orders to be explained. Had the Ministry of Defence consulted fully during its decision-making process, it would have had to contend with fierce debate but would not now be facing heavy criticism. ...
>
> We, as former Colonels of The Staffordshire Regiment, understand that the Army Board has reviewed its decisions but does not intend to change or explain them. If that is true, it is regrettable. Our serious disquiet and desire for explanation remain.

The fringe meeting represented the start of a more focused national campaign, in which the foundations of a well planned and executed strategy were evident. Lieutenant General Sir John MacMillan, the chairman of the Scottish campaign, and Simon Nayyar, who also worked as an advisor to the Scots, had agreed that the Scots should have a presence at the Conservative Party Conference in order to press their case to Conservative MPs and constituency representatives. Both the SOS and Keep Our Scottish Battalions Campaign Committees believed that the more Infantry regiments represented at the fringe meeting, the greater the benefit to their individual and collective cause. So it became a joint meeting of the two campaigns, representing six regiments, the logistics having been discussed at Westminster Communications' offices on 27 September by Nayyar, Levey, MacMillan and Generals Sir Napier Crookenden and Peter Martin of the Cheshires. It was the earliest manifestation of the philosophy that, at a national level, the campaigns should represent opposition to the effects of manpower reductions across the Infantry, rather than the 'parochial' concerns of individual regiments.

Any Conservative Party Conference fringe meeting must be chaired by a Conservative MP. The hunt was on to find an MP willing to perform this role. Nayyar approached a succession of likely candidates, all of whom declined politely, saying that while they would have liked to help they did not want to embarrass the Government on this difficult issue. In early September Bill Cash was invited to chair the meeting, and accepted in a telephone conversation with Simon Nayyar from the USA, where he was on a lecturing engagement.

It was natural that the campaign should focus on the Conservative Party Conference, since the Conservatives were the party in Government, and any seeds of dissent sown on its backbenches would give the Government cause for alarm. At the Labour Party Conference, Nayyar and other colleagues from Westminster Communications had discreetly canvassed individual Labour MPs about their views on defence cuts and amalgamations, but the campaign itself was not present. This was not because the campaign felt that the Labour Party was hostile to defence — indeed some of its most ardent supporters were Labour MPs. The reality was that dissent within the Conservative Party in Parliament, especially if media attention could be focused on it, would have a greater impact on crucial votes on defence, particularly the impending Defence Estimates debate.

The campaigns had chosen a highly suitable occasion to launch their attack on Infantry overstretch. Of the 1,411 motions submitted by Conservative constituency associations to the Conference, the highest number (168) covered defence and international affairs. Of these 168, more than eighty referred to *Options for Change*, many urging a more cautious approach than that taken by Tom King. The motion submitted by the Burton-upon-Trent Association was typical, urging the Government not to 'demoralise the Services and put our defence in jeopardy by over-large cuts'. The motion chosen for debate was 'suitably uncontroversial', according to one observer, 'welcoming' the force levels announced in July; eight speakers were called, all of whom made equally bland speeches, and the 'debate' (one Tory MP described Conservative Conferences to the author as consisting of 'anodyne motions and sycophantic speakers') was wound up — to tumultuous applause — by Tom King, stroking his old Somerset and Cornwall Light Infantry tie.

The Campaign Committees had not anticipated just how much their fringe meeting would expose growing fears within the Conservative Party about the Government's defence policy. Conservative Conferences lack the policy-making role of their Labour counterparts, and historically they have caused less 'bother' to the leadership. Yet on some issues the Conference — and, increasingly importantly, the fringe meetings — has considerable influence. As Simon Nayyar observed in the *Daily Telegraph's* 'Peterborough' column: 'We anticipate a great deal of support.... A lot of Tories feel very strongly about the proposed cuts.'

The meeting — in the Savoy Hotel on Blackpool's seafront — was packed; it was the only fringe meeting to be sealed off and checked with sniffer dogs. A chord had been struck, and whether the Conservative rank and file supported the arguments put forward by the regimental campaigns, or whether they just wanted to hear what the arguments were, they turned up at the meeting in droves, thus providing guaranteed media interest; there were camera crews from as far afield as the United States and Canada. With Bill Cash on the rostrum were Scottish Conservative MP Sir Hector Monro; Sir John MacMillan for the Scots; Generals Crookenden and Martin for the Cheshires; and John Levey for the Staffords. In addition, to provide third-party backing, Colonel Andrew Duncan, Assistant Director for Information at the International Institute for Strategic Studies, spoke in support of the regiments.

Before the day there was considerable discussion about the line to be taken by the representatives of the two campaigns. It was decided that they would concentrate on their substantive concerns about retention, recruitment, demography and the threat of job losses, while making links with the wider issue of the Infantry. The underlying approach was aptly summarised by Simon Nayyar, writing to Will Stamper.

> They [Keep Our Scottish Battalions] feel, as we feel, that this is not the occasion to show public disunity with each regiment attempting, individually, to establish its own *raisons d'être*. Our principal aim, in front of rank and file representatives of the Conservative Party, at their conference, is to show unanimity in our collective view of the implications of the cuts. This is our last public opportunity before the Defence Estimates debate to inform the debate on the cuts, to a constituency that, traditionally, does not like to see itself perceived as anything less than forthrightly supportive of Her Majesty's Armed Forces.

The prominence which the fringe meeting achieved, and its success at raising the issues of Infantry overstretch, delighted the Campaign Committee. Clearly, the campaign was on a roll, and four days later the Defence Estimates debate would carry the fight to Westminster itself, where the Government would be forced to listen and respond under public scrutiny.

By mid-October, meanwhile, almost 100,000 petition signatures had been collected and returned to Regimental Headquarters. The presentation of the petition, it was decided, should be co-ordinated with that of the other regimental campaigns. The Metropolitan Police granted permission for one coach-load of supporters per campaign to congregate in Victoria Tower Gardens and Abingdon Green at the south end of the Palace of Westminster. On 14 October the campaigns, full of energy to kick off the national media campaign, converged on Westminster bearing petitions with a total of some 750,000 signatures. The Staffords took Watchman, the Cheshires took a large effigy of a Cheshire cat, and the Scots took most of the publicity with their pipers — it is always, Levey remarked, difficult if not impossible for English Line Regiments to upstage the Scots. The presentation of the petitions to Parliament was the lead item in every single news bulletin of BBC Radio Four's agenda-setting Today programme (to which politicians of all political persuasions listen religiously), and throughout the remainder of the day the campaigners swept up large amounts of TV news airtime.

There followed a press launch in the House of Commons, and then receptions in the Terrace Dining Rooms. That evening the Staffords' petition was presented to the Speaker of the House, Bernard Weatherill, by three local MPs: Bill Cash, Patrick Cormack and the author, with Llin Golding and Sylvia Heal, two other MPs active in the campaign, in close attendance. The petitions themselves, in large bundles, were brought into the chamber by uniformed custodians, who were all ex-armed forces NCOs; after one of the sponsoring MPs had presented them to the Speaker, one sheaf was placed in the petition bag and the remainder whisked off to their mysterious destination. At the same time, Ann Winterton (Conservative MP for Congleton, Cheshire, and with her husband, also a Cheshire Conservative MP, an active campaigner for the Cheshires) presented a parallel petition for the Cheshires with Gwyneth Dunwoody (Labour MP for Crewe and Nantwich) in support; and a group of six Scottish MPs (from the Conservative, Labour, Liberal Democrat and Scottish National Parties) presented petitions on behalf of the Keep Our Scottish Battalions Campaign. Archy Kirkwood, Liberal Democrat MP for Roxburgh and Berwickshire, reminded the House of Rudyard Kipling's celebrated lines that underscore public ambivalence towards the Army:

> It's Tommy this, an' Tommy that, an' 'Chuck him out, the brute!'
> But it's 'Saviour of 'is country' when the guns begin to shoot.

The presentation of petitions to the House follows a tradition harking back to an age when this was the normal method by which the populace could express their wishes or needs to MPs. A petition must be worded in a very specific, archaic manner, as the Staffords' shows:

> Wherefore your Petitioners pray that your honourable House will not give support to this proposed amalgamation which is unreasonable and ill-judged. And your Petitioners, as in duty bound, will ever pray.

Whereas once petitions formed an important part of the business of the House of Commons, their function nowadays is to harness public support. The ceremony in which the petition is presented represents the culmination of the process of gathering signatures; thus a petition has considerable value in securing public opinion, but little value once it has been presented and placed 'in the bag' (a green baize petition bag behind the Speaker's Chair). Presenters of petitions receive a standard form from the Clerk of Public Petitions which states that 'I have now been told that no Government observations will be issued on the petition.' For a petition to initiate action is very rare; since 1974 the number of signatures on petitions has not even been counted.

Nevertheless, the presentation of the petition was timed to coincide with important Parliamentary business — the debate on the 1991 Defence White Paper (*Statement on the Defence Estimates*), which immediately preceded the petition presentation and continued the following day. It took place only days after the fringe meeting. In this sense, the petition bridged the local and national components of the campaign. This was reflected on 15 October in the copious newspaper coverage devoted to both the petition presentations and the Defence Estimates debate. The regional papers carried the story of the petition presentations as an item of regional interest focusing on the Regiment, with accompanying pieces on the Defence Estimates debate. The national press focused on the debate, while carrying pictures of the delegations of old soldiers with short captions mentioning the regimental campaigns. Among the coverage was a particularly campaign-friendly editorial in the *Independent*; its thrust was familiar:

> Even before the start yesterday of the Commons debate on the Government's proposed defence cuts, skilled Army lobbying and

> representations by angry Tory backbenchers had pinpointed the structural weaknesses of its plans. The critics' arguments are threefold. First, that July's White Paper, *Options for Change*, failed to start with an intellectually coherent review of existing military commitments and their continued relevance in the post-Cold War era. It was therefore difficult for the Services to accept it as anything other than 'Treasury-driven'. Second, that the Army is being disproportionately hit and, if cut as planned, will be unable to fulfil its normal commitments, let alone emergency operations. Third, that the proposed amalgamation of Infantry regiments takes little or no account of local recruitment and retention patterns.

The local campaign was by no means over, but in the completion of the petition it had largely achieved its contribution to Phase One of the overall campaign. Now it was the turn of the national campaign to dominate the attention of the Committee and Westminster Communications.

The Defence Estimates Debate

In terms of the strategy of Phase Two of the campaign, the dramatic success of the Blackpool fringe meeting was an unexpected bonus. Much attention before Blackpool had centred on the Defence Estimates debate, and no decision had been made about the precise shape of the campaign thereafter. The *Statement on the Defence Estimates* (SDE) is an annual White Paper published by the MoD; ideally it should provide a detailed exposition of UK defence policy, giving an overview of spending plans for the coming year, outlining the assumptions on which that spending is based, listing the activities and commitments of the armed forces, describing the international security scene, and setting out procurement decisions. There are several reasons why actuality does not quite fit the ideal. The White Paper is often published in the spring, but debate on it is delayed until the autumn. This happened in 1991, when the White Paper was followed by the July announcement of specific defence cuts, while the Defence Estimates debate did not take place until October. Spending plans can also be altered in a variety of other ways. The Defence Estimates are therefore better seen as a rough guide to the MoD's intentions than as a firm set of proposals.

In his capacity as the most senior Staffordshire MP, Patrick Cormack convened a meeting at the House on the day of the debate, at which John Levey briefed him and his parliamentary colleagues on the issues facing the Regiment and the Infantry. The meeting was also attended by the Chairman and Chief Executive of Staffordshire County Council and the Mayor of Lichfield.

Tom King, the Secretary of State, kicked off the debate with an overview of the rapidly changing situation in the former Soviet Union. This prompted an early intervention by Stephen Day, Conservative MP for Cheadle, who expressed concern that *Options for Change* might not have taken account of those changes. King responded with what was, considering criticisms of *Options for Change*, a strangely worded statement, saying that the Government had taken nothing for granted, and that:

> ... We made no assumption of the collapse of the Soviet centre, and we saw no emergence with such rapidity of the republics or the collapse of central power and of the Soviet Union in the way that seems apparent now. We did take account of the collapse of the Warsaw Pact and of disaffection within the satellite countries. The situation is that events have developed further than the basis on which we planned.

How was this statement to be interpreted? It was precisely such unpredictability that underlay the criticisms of *Options for Change*; yet here Tom King seemed to be using it to justify the level of cuts already envisaged, although he moved on without discussing the implications of his remarks.

This difficulty was compounded by King's concluding remarks and an answer to an intervention by Ann Winterton. King said: 'The issues that we have had to face are set against the background of a full strategic assessment of the defence scene and the most appropriate response that we could make.' Exactly what King considered to be 'a full strategic assessment' is unclear, given his earlier remarks about events in the Soviet Union outstripping the assumptions in Options for Change. Similarly, he left considerable question marks over emergency tour intervals. Ann Winterton asked King:

> Will my right hon. Friend tell the House when the Army's objective of having a 24-month gap between unaccompanied operational tours will come into effect, and how he believes that he can achieve that if the number of battalions is reduced from 55 to 38?

King's answer was vague in the extreme:

> I can assure my hon. Friend that during the exercise I frequently asked about the tour interval and I can give her the answer, which she may not have heard. At present, we do not maintain a reasonable tour interval. We hope to be able to do so in the future.

It has to be said that commending the Defence Estimates to Parliament with such banality was typical of King's style. He displayed a seeming disregard for debate and Parliamentary scrutiny, and his manner conveyed boredom tinged with arrogance. One former Tory Cabinet Minister described Tom King as 'useless' and compared him with 'a rabbit caught in headlights'. King obviously possessed political skill (one does not become a Secretary of State without at least a trace of political nous, and it is said that Margaret Thatcher chose him as a 'safe pair of hands'); he had held a variety of offices, and he was always exceedingly courteous to the author. The trouble was, no one was the least bit convinced by anything he said about defence. In his notorious *Diaries*, Alan Clark, the former Minister for Defence Procurement, shows seemingly mixed feelings about King:

> [Robert Atkins] said that Tom King was a prat: 'a nice chap, but a prat'. This is not entirely fair as Tom King has got a shrewd Willie [Whitelaw]-ish side, but his balls are very weak. He always loses in Cabinet and will not hold out for anything.

Clark goes on to call King a 'loathsome puffball', and to say that:

> I read in the papers that the Defence Secretary after this weekend is going to be Tom King (for God's sake). Any idea that I will do Defence Procurement under that man is OUT. And I will give the Lady [Mrs Thatcher] my reasons.

Clark went on to do Defence Procurement under that man.

It is difficult to know how far Clark's account tells us about King's leadership style and how far it simply tells us that Clark is a malicious gossip and had a disproportionate admiration for Margaret Thatcher. Certainly, however, King's tenure at the MoD is looked back upon by MPs of all parties with great dismay.

Early in the Defence Estimates debate it became apparent that virtually every MP with an interest in defence was concerned that *Options for Change* bore little relevance to the global upheavals of 1989-91. The debate became a symposium on Infantry reductions. Some Members who spoke on this issue supported one or other of the regimental campaigns. Bill Cash, the author, Sir Hector Monro,

Sir Nicholas Fairbairn and Nicholas Winterton all concentrated heavily on the Infantry aspect of *Options*, some emphasising their specific regiments more pointedly than others; Bill Cash, a strong opponent of closer links with Europe, also attacked a common European defence policy. Other MPs who spoke were not directly linked to the campaigns, but sat on the Defence Select Committee or on a backbench defence committee. For instance, Michael Mates, then Chairman of the Select Committee, criticised the secrecy of the amalgamation decisions:

> I have not had a chance to consult my colleagues about this, but I am sure that I speak for them when I say that we shall want to know how these highly controversial decisions were reached. I hope that there will not be a quarrel about this.

He obviously saw a quarrel coming, and indeed it occupied much of the Defence Committee's time. Even former Defence Ministers spoke out against Infantry reductions — Jerry Wiggin, for one, bemoaned the MoD's failure to take account of growing unrest in Europe and suggested that it was 'ludicrous' for the Government not to expect observers to believe that *Options* was a Treasury-led exercise.

Replying to the debate, Archie Hamilton, the Minister of State for the Armed Forces, attempted to deflect the 'Treasury-driven' suspicions of critics:

> This work was conducted under the direction of Defence Ministers and carried out by a team of their military and civilian advisers responsible for policy and programme issues. It was not externally imposed, driven or directed. The work had to take account of resource questions. How could it not, given the other demands on our resources for priorities such as health care, education and social services?

He also parried concerns about overstretch with the argument, to which he repeatedly and strenuously adhered in later debate, that while the Infantry would be reduced by seventeen battalions, Infantry commitments would be reduced by nineteen. No one was convinced by these explanations, and this debate was just the start of a protracted argument.

The debate ended with sixty-six MPs voting against the Defence Estimates. Of those, seven were Tory 'rebels': Sir Nicholas Bonsor, John Browne, Sir Nicholas Fairbairn, Sir Hector Monro, Jerry Wiggin, Ann Winterton and Nicholas Winterton. This 'rebellion' achieved little, other than as a symbolic act, since the Labour Party abstained. The author was one of twenty-eight Labour MPs who defied the party line and voted against the Estimates.

A seven-strong rebellion might not sound significant, but the matter was considerably more complex. Staffordshire newspapers accused Bill Cash of selling out the campaign by voting with the Government. He pointed out that the vote was not simply on Infantry reductions and that he had not felt able to oppose the Government on the wider issue of the defence estimates, which he broadly supported. The Campaign Committee replied to the criticisms of Cash by highlighting his very significant contribution to the campaign. Nevertheless, the seven Tory dissenters highlighted a strong vein of disaffection within their party at *Options for Change* and at the Government's handling of the issue. And, for each of the seven who defied the party whip, there were many others who reluctantly toed the line.

If the final tally served notice on the Government that it had a case to answer, it had further, less obvious repercussions. The negative vote cast by Sir Nicholas Bonsor was instrumental in his selection as Chairman of the House of Commons Defence Committee after the 1992 general election. As we shall see, under the chairmanship of Michael Mates and then of Bonsor, this Committee caused the Government untold embarrassment and had a major influence on the Staffords' reprieve.

Although the Government gave no ground whatsoever, the Defence Estimates debate was a major landmark of the campaign in only the second month of its existence. The Infantry issue was unarguably on the agenda as a result of the efforts of both the SOS and Keep Our Scottish Battalions campaigns and of Simon Nayyar's assiduous behind-the-scenes lobbying. The week of the debate was also remarkable for several events that added to the public profile of the issues of *Options for Change*, the Infantry and the regimental campaigns.

Rumblings in high places

The weekend of 12-13 October 1991 produced two press stories that greatly assisted the SOS campaign. First, a letter from General Sir John Chapple, Chief of General Staff, to Tom King was leaked to the *Sunday Times*. The letter, apparently written in September, was a report on Army morale after the announcement of regimental mergers and the wider reduction in Army personnel from 155,000 to 116,000. Sir John's opinion was that significant concessions would have to be made to regular soldiers to carry through the exercise:

> The fact is that the bulk of those who will have to leave will be officers and senior NCOs in mid-career. We have placed people as our top priority to ensure that their needs are handled properly. This means that we must recognise the worth of our men and women. Living conditions, allowances and housing will all become much more critically viewed if we are to allay the feeling that smaller but better is a bit of a con trick.

Sir John warned that a consensus had developed in the Army that there would not be enough men or units to fulfil its tasks and duties without severe overstretch or 'unacceptable penalty'. What particularly irked the Army, he stated, was the assertion that the *Options* exercise had not been Treasury-led. This was, in his opinion, a public relations disaster; the fault was with the presentation, although he also unwittingly suggested that the actual effects of the exercise were taking their toll:

> The young officers, the [Warrant Officers] and sergeants all express this view in different ways ... they acknowledge that the exercise was initiated for proper strategic and political reasons. It is the final few turns of the screw that have placed their loyalty and commitment under such strain.

Warning Tom King not to get involved in explanations about lack of consultation or particular choices that were made, he said that he wanted the discussion to be closed and for the Army to get on with implementing the changes.

Although the letter was featured prominently and probably helped to elevate the profile of the Infantry issue, contrary to what the accompanying article suggested it was not evidence of dissent within the Army Board. It was a report on the effects on the Army of *Options for Change*, and little more, although it clearly revealed the Army Board's knowledge of the grass roots dissatisfaction in the Army.

The same article alleged that Prince Charles and the Queen were on the *Options* warpath. Prince Charles, according to the story, had written to John Major urging him to order a rethink on *Options for Change*. As Colonel-in-Chief of three regiments facing amalgamation, Prince Charles 'was said to be "astonished, angry and amazed" by the proposals'. According to *Today*, he had scathingly described *Options* as 'an extraordinary state of affairs' and had asked Major to examine the 'implications of rushing into such drastic reductions'. The Queen was alleged to have expressed concern privately to senior Conservatives about the conduct of the 'defence review'.

The *Daily Mail* of 14 October brought The Duke of York into the fight alongside Prince Charles. Charles, it claimed, had taken up the cudgels for the Scottish Division and shown his disapproval for the amalgamations by accepting a request from the Thurso British Legion for a portrait with the proviso that he posed in the uniform of Colonel-in-Chief of The Gordon Highlanders. The *Mail* also alleged that, as Colonel-in-Chief of the Staffords, His Royal Highness The Duke of York was concerned. However, his speech at the 3rd Battalion Presentation of New Colours in September had quite properly remained neutral. But his private support was well known to the Regiment.

The House of Lords

On 16 October, it was the turn of the House of Lords to debate the Defence Estimates, and yet more Staffords' supporters took the Government to task. The Earl of Arran, Parliamentary Under-Secretary of State for Defence, introduced the debate for the Government, and Lord Williams of Elvel replied for the Opposition. The richness of the debate makes it difficult to summarise. Many Peers have considerable wartime experience, and many have occupied senior positions in Government, the Armed Forces or both. This wealth of experience, combined with a less adversarial style than the Commons and the lesser importance of the Government's majority, produced (as is often the case) a frequently incisive and unpartisan debate.

Two speeches stand out in particular. The first, by Lord Whitelaw, was remarkable for its questioning of the Government's intransigence. During his many years in Government, Lord Whitelaw became the epitome of loyalty and adherence to the convention of Cabinet collective responsibility; he has also been very critical of the invective released by former Ministers in the post-Thatcher years. For this reason his words were all the more remarkable.

> ... I simply have to admit that the reduction of seventeen Infantry battalions causes me real anxiety. Fortunately, however, I understand that this reduction will be phased out over a number of years and that some of the regimental amalgamations, particularly the highly contentious Scottish ones, will not be completed until 1994-95. There is, therefore, time for reflection by the Government. I hope, therefore, that there will not blow up in the Ministry of Defence an obstinate determination to cling to the present plans whatever the changes in circumstances.

> Those of us who are anxious about the present reductions in Infantry battalions may well be wrong. But as there are many far more knowledgeable than I am who appear to feel like this, I hope that my right honourable friend the Secretary of State for Defence will be ready at least to accept, and to consider his actions accordingly, that maybe — just maybe — we shall be proved right.

The only English regiments to which Lord Whitelaw referred by name were the Staffords and Cheshires — a tribute to the strength of the arguments for their retention.

One of those 'far more knowledgeable' people to whom Lord Whitelaw referred was Field Marshal Lord Bramall, Chief of Defence Staff from 1982 to 1985. Like so many others in the debates in both the Lords and the Commons, Lord Bramall spoke about a wide range of issues which the White Paper raised, starting with the dubious strategic justification for the cuts. His contribution deserves substantial quotation for two points which he made with far less restraint than other speakers. First, speaking about the feeling in the Armed Forces towards *Options for Change*, he said:

> I do not have to remind your Lordships that there exists in the Armed Forces a widespread feeling that, far from having got it right, those who have served the country so steadfastly in peace and war have been badly let down: and that the cuts, although in many cases inevitable and sensible, have now gone too deep. They especially resent the final few turns of the screw on manpower which they attribute almost entirely to Treasury pressure about which their Ministers and senior officers can of course only advise and have been unable to resist as they would have wished. Over that, they are of course right. If the Minister continues to refute that, I can easily produce chapter and verse.

This last sentence is intriguing, and one can only wish that the Government had taken up his challenge. The forthrightness of the statement, as well as Lord Bramall's former status, render the remark that much more powerful. Likewise, the forcefulness of a later part of his speech added to the incontrovertibility of the SOS campaign's argument:

> Then, with a strong armoured division remaining in Germany, I strongly question — indeed I know it is impossible — whether 116,000 men (which means 104,000 trained men) will be

> sufficient to support both operationally and logistically not only those forces at proper unit strength but all the Army's other commitments. ...
>
> The 116,000 (or perhaps I should say 104,000) figure is now doubly suspect. Not only has the military advice been consistently set at around or just above the original figure of 120,000, with only the Treasury dissenting, but since the reduced figure was released two extra battalions have, for whatever reason, been retained without any extra manpower or money to sustain them. Thus either equally important parts of the programme will have to suffer or all units will have to be made correspondingly weaker. Such cheeseparing over unit strength will greatly reduce motivation as well as efficiency and make a mockery of the 'smaller but better' image.

This was a withering attack on the Government from a former Chief of Defence Staff, with all the experience of defence matters which that position entails.

Not everyone who contributed opposed Government policy, and the odd speaker was somewhat hostile to the regimental campaigns, if only by virtue of loyalty to the Government. For instance, Field Marshal Lord Carver (Chief of Defence Staff from 1973 to 1976) was steadfast in his support for the Government and scathing about the 'opportunism' of the campaigns.

> I congratulate the Government on having stood firm against the clamour. Had they given way they would not only have been favouring those whose eyes are fixed firmly on the past at the expense of those who look to the future but they would also have incurred the resentment of those elements of the Armed Forces — the great majority — which did not try to exploit sentimentality, political sensitivity and connections in high places to preserve their own outfit.

Most speakers, however, were at the very least wary of the Government's policy. Lord Chalfont, a former *Times* defence correspondent, Minister for Disarmament in the 1964 Labour Government and Managing Director of Vickers Shipbuilding and Engineering, makers of the Trident submarine, summed up feelings about the Government's conduct of the *Options* exercise.

> The Government seem reluctant to listen even to their own military advisers or the Select Committee in another place. I

> venture to say that they do not listen to anyone very much except the Chancellor of the Exchequer. Their response to any dissenting voice seems to be the classic reply: 'My mind is made up; pray do not confuse me with the facts.'

Sniper actions

That week the Government must surely have wished that the whole thing would simply go away. Ministers received criticisms from all sides: in debates, through Parliamentary Questions, through ministerial post and through letters from constituents. John Major may have regretted inheriting the dubious legacy of *Options for Change*, and he may well have had less than overwhelming admiration for Tom King. Yet, of the Ministers faced with this onslaught, it was King who must, surely, have wanted *Options* to disappear more desperately than any other, since it was he who so often had to answer the questions, repeating the same bland and smug assurances. On 15 October, for instance, before the Commons started the second day of the Defence Estimates debate, King had to answer an Oral Question from Dennis Turner, the Labour MP for Wolverhampton South East:

> In view of the massive petition that was presented to Parliament yesterday on behalf of the Staffords, and in view of the powerful case that they have advanced, will the Secretary of State please reconsider his unpopular decision? I ask that on behalf of all the people of Staffordshire and the West Midlands — [Hon. Members: 'And Cheshire'] —Yes, and Cheshire.

Characteristically, King's answer sounded like a defence of the indefensible:

> I obviously regret that the famous traditions of any regiment are affected by the changes, but they are inevitable in the proposals that we have announced. ...

Not only did he fail to answer the question; his evasive reply contained nothing whatsoever of substance. It was pure stubbornness.

It was just such evasion that had confirmed the Staffords' and Scottish campaigns in their view and resolve that they would have to conduct a protracted guerilla war against the Government. The Government had been presented with a host of reasons why it should not go ahead with the amalgamations, but nothing had changed; nor, to nearly everyone's chagrin, was any explanation of the contentious decisions forthcoming. It was therefore time to start digging at the

Government's sources of support. One of these was Tory Party funds.

The *Daily Mail* of 14 October 1991 reported the Staffords' and Scottish campaigns' plan to target donations from large companies to Conservative Central Office in the run-up to the general election. The Scots were said to have targeted 200 companies, while the Staffords and Cheshires would target companies in the West Midlands, Staffordshire and Merseyside. Simon Nayyar said:

> Many retired officers not only sit on the boards of the companies, but they also hold important positions in local Tory party organisations. We gave an undertaking that while there was a glimmer of hope, we would not say anything publicly. ... But we are now happy to speak publicly as the Defence Secretary has not given any evidence he is prepared to take on board our objections.

However, the truth of the matter was that the Staffords and Scots were, at best, considering the practicability and desirability of an attempt to staunch the flow of funds to the Conservative Party; they were very far from actually doing so. None the less, this was an effective piece of sabre-rattling designed to put Ministers on the defensive and obtain newspaper column inches.

Phases One and Two of the campaign had turned out to be a qualified success. In a very short time the petition and the formation of a wide-ranging campaign network had raised the campaign's profile enormously in Staffordshire and the West Midlands. Huge numbers of people were ready to assist, and there could have been few people who had not heard of the Staffords' struggle. In Westminster, a bridge-head of supportive MPs had been built who would harass the Government at every turn. Even though the Government had not been defeated in the Defence Estimates debate, there was no denying that its defence policy had suffered a severe loss of credibility. Through a variety of Parliamentary devices, the Conservative Party Conference and relentless media exposure, it had been made clear to the Government that Parliament expected it to be accountable for its actions, no matter how hard it attempted to put a lid on the matter.

After the clamorous week following the Conservative Conference, the campaign settled into a less frenetic timetable. Even before the Defence Estimates debate, active consideration had been given to the parliamentary activity that should be pursued over the following months. Simon Nayyar had identified several specific areas; these included tabling Parliamentary Questions; encouraging a friendly MP to sponsor an Adjournment Debate; soliciting a supportive Peer to initiate an Unstarred Question debate in the House of Lords; and targeting key ministerial advisers, parliamentary Lobby journalists, and the defence journalistic community. The most useful route to follow, however, and the one that the campaign immediately pursued, was the House of Commons Defence Committee.

Chapter 7

The Defence Committee

November 1991 to March 1992

'Making the Right Choice'

An invitation to the Save our Staffords campaign to give evidence to the House of Commons Defence Committee had been conceived early in the campaign, when the links between MPs, the Committee and the campaign were being forged. In October 1991, both the author and Simon Nayyar advised the Staffords' and the Scots' campaigns to prepare written submissions to the Committee for the November inquiry on *Options*. Levey was presented with a challenge of almost biblical proportions: to assemble huge amounts of information into manageable form by the Select Committee's deadline. A flurry of activity involving Levey, Nayyar, Nigel Alderman (Commanding Officer of the 1st Battalion) in Fallingbostel and Ian Freer in Berlin led to a barrage of faxes which Nayyar massaged into a presentable form. The deadline was met, but only just, with a ten-page submission entitled *Making the Right Choice*. In fact, it had to be withdrawn and resubmitted because, as the result of a typographic error, the original appeared to be a submission from The Staffordshire Regiment rather than from the SOS campaign, incorrectly implying regimental involvement. The mistake was spotted by the author after the submission had been sent out; it was withdrawn just in time to make the change.

As already mentioned, the somewhat disingenuous MoD had christened Tom King's proposals *Options for Change*. Because King had denied Parliament the chance to consider the alternatives, it was, as Alan Clark intimated, stretching credibility somewhat to describe them as 'options'. It fell to Nayyar to devise a title for the SOS submission. Trying to find a name that adequately reflected the Regiment's concerns and that was also in keeping with the bogus imagery of King's document proved difficult, but eventually Nayyar came up with *Making the Right Choice*, which the Campaign Committee readily adopted.

Bound in an attention-grabbing electric blue cover, *Making the Right Choice* set out, in ten pages, why 'the wrong decision was reached in proposing this merger.' Beginning with an executive summary, the document contained chapters dealing with the consultation process; overstretch in the Infantry; the implications for morale and future recruitment; regional representation and demography; geography; and a short conclusion. In addition, a set of annexes provided a brief history of the Regiment; an examination of the Northern Ireland requirement; an analysis of whether a smaller future Army would be better than in the past; and a review of the strategic context in which the Infantry reductions had been made.

The chapter on consultation began with a dramatic *crie de coeur*:

> The Staffordshire Regiment received the news of amalgamation with disbelief. It is particularly resentful of the lack of consultation. When a regiment is told, without warning, that it is to be amalgamated, it is not unreasonable to expect some sort of explanation or rationale. When no explanation is given, nor any understandable rationale offered and survival itself is at stake, the result will be a deeply felt grievance among serving officers and soldiers, who will feel that they have been betrayed. After years of loyal service and sacrifice, such treatment is undeserved.

The same chapter concluded, perspicaciously:

> The Regiment would contend that, because its history and public image are not as prestigious as others (although it satisfies all the criteria laid down by the Army Board) and because there are few marginal seats in its recruiting area, there was a general perception by the Army Board, and by others, that an amalgamation between The Staffordshire Regiment and The Cheshire Regiment could be achieved with few military or political repercussions.

The rest of the submission was equally blunt. The analysis was articulate and exhaustive; there were tables and charts; sources were meticulously documented; and absolutely no punches were pulled.

The chapter on regional representation noted, appositely, that 'demographic projections show clearly that The Staffordshire Regiment's recruiting potential from within the County and the West Midlands will ensure its sustainability.' The chapter on geography observed, laconically, that 'the Regimental Headquarters of The Cheshire Regiment and The Royal Welch Fusiliers [ironically, the Cheshires' first preference for amalgamation] are only twenty miles apart', while the RHQs of the Staffords and the Cheshires were as far apart as London and Birmingham — and 'no one would dream of proposing an amalgamation of the Staffords with a London recruited regiment.'

Making the Right Choice concluded:

> The Army Board has failed to provide The Staffordshire Regiment with any plausible rationale for its proposed amalgamation with The Cheshire Regiment.
>
> The Staffordshire Regiment disputes the Army Board's recommendation and believes that it satisfies every criterion laid down by the Director of Infantry that would militate against amalgamation.
>
> The Save Our Staffords campaign, on behalf of The Staffordshire Regiment, invites the Defence Select Committee to consider its submission.

For the first time, the Regiment's grievances were brought together within a single document. To the campaigners it provided a tangible reminder of the legitimacy and multiplicity of their grievances. To the lay reader it provided an easy and engrossing read. To interested politicians it provided a focus of serious concern about the quality of the MoD's decision-making. Finally, for Defence Ministers, it came to provide a source of acute embarrassment for the Government.

Making the Right Choice was, first and foremost, a formal submission from Save Our Staffords to the Defence Select Committee. In this role it served its purpose well; the author was one of several MPs who used the information it contained to question Ministers persistently, a process that eventually helped to wear down the MoD. This was one of the ways that the document vindicated the contact between the campaign and the Select Committee.

Making the Right Choice had a second, almost equally important, role. It was used, with great effectiveness, to mobilise support among those in the county and elsewhere who were still hesitant to offer it; and it served as a powerful weapon to buttress the support of those who had already pledged it. In time, it was also used as a briefing document given to key political influencers who wanted to know more about the Regiment's plight or who needed to be reminded. By the time of the Defence Committee's inquiry into Army manpower, twelve months later, some of the data and observations seemed dated; yet that was largely a tribute to the campaigners' own effectiveness, for during the next year they transformed the debate about the future size and shape of the Infantry. *Making the Right Choice* played a key role in achieving this.

If the proof of the pudding is indeed in the eating, then *Making the Right Choice* proved to be something of a chef's special: the demand for copies in the county and elsewhere was so great that three print runs were exhausted before a halt was finally called.

The Defence Committee's inquiry

A major concern of the SOS campaign, as already discussed, was to avoid accusations of parochialism, at least in the national arena. Contact with the Select Committee brought legitimacy to the campaign through a universalisation of its arguments, which now, via the Committee, reached all corners of the defence world.

MPs had seized on the Select Committee's report on the 1991 Defence Estimates, which made cutting criticisms of the lack of strategic rationale behind *Options for Change*. However, it had been published before the Committee was able to look in detail at the MoD's plans for the Infantry, even though many MPs instinctively felt that the facts did not fit the circumstances. The report promised a further investigation of the implications of King's announcement; the Committee subsequently carried out its work with a vengeance, and produced two scathing reports on the Army and one on the reserve forces.

From the start the Select Committee hearings, during which MPs subjected ministers to a barrage of searching questions, soon began to undermine the MoD's position and to make them realise that this was an issue that just would not go away. The most frustrating and heated parts of the hearings invariably involved Archie Hamilton, the Minister of State for the Armed Forces, who since receiving his knighthood prefers to be known as Sir Archibald. A former Guardsman who served as Margaret Thatcher's Parliamentary Private Secretary, he has been described as a 'hard-Right orthodox traditionalist loyalist'. Hamilton appeared before the Committee on 13 November 1991 and again two weeks later — it was a measure of the Committee's disquiet at his intransigence under questioning that, in an almost unprecedented move, it decided to recall him for a second session.

The heart of the issue was the Army Board's decision that it would not allow itself to be forced to justify any of the decisions integral to *Options*. Hamilton therefore went before his Parliamentary colleagues unable and unwilling to disclose anything that might help the Committee to understand the decision-making process. Hamilton constantly reiterated his refusal to explain in any detail at all why individual decisions were taken. One brief exchange with John McFall, a Labour member of the committee, produced a gem:

> [Mr McFall] The title of the exercise is *Options for Change* [so] it would be helpful to the public if we knew you had a range of options.
> [Mr Hamilton] I am afraid the Committee must take my word for it. ...

Pressed hard on the adequacy of funding for the Army, Hamilton stonewalled: 'I do not think we want to go into details about the development of the decision process.' He did so again in the face of a series of questions from John Home Robertson, Labour MP for East Lothian and a strong supporter of the Scottish regiments' campaign, on the individual criteria used to select regiments for amalgamation; Hamilton's insubstantial responses were supplemented by somewhat more detailed but equally unrevealing comments by Major General Roger Wheeler, Assistant Chief of General Staff. The pattern continued when the author, using statistics from *Making the Right Choice*, confronted Hamilton with a detailed question on the statistical rationale for the amalgamation decision. Hamilton's answer represents a textbook example of foggy imprecision:

> ... the geographical spread is merely one of the considerations we took into account and there were a number of others. All these had to be weighed up and weighed in the balance together before very difficult decisions were made. They were difficult decisions that led to the amalgamation of regiments that would have preferred not to amalgamate. I do not see any point in reopening this issue now. It is very much better if the Army gets on with the amalgamations and looks to the future rather than harping on the past and re-opening the issues. We have taken decisions which have not been easy, a number of different considerations have gone into them. I think it is better that we get on with the job that needs to be done.

Hamilton's dismissive, evasive and occasionally downright rude responses did nothing to help him. Thus, within hours of his second appearance before the Committee on 27 November 1991, Simon Nayyar rushed out a press release noting that 'Mr Hamilton was again quizzed about the proposed amalgamation between The Staffordshire Regiment and The Cheshire Regiment, and again failed to provide adequate explanations for the proposed merger.' The press release concluded with what now seems a prophetic contribution from the author:

> It is disgraceful that a regiment whose origins go back to 1705 should be extinguished without even the courtesy of an explanation. I am outraged at the insensitivity, even stupidity, of the MoD in selecting the Staffords as a candidate for amalgamation — without consultation. I am certain that the decision to reduce to thirty-eight the number of Infantry battalions will eventually be exposed as, at best, misguided and, at worst, endangering national security.

For the Campaign itself Hamilton's appearances, and the subsequent Select Committee reports proved something of a turning-point. Hamilton's uncompromising attitude suggested to the campaigners that the Ministry of Defence's position was far weaker than had been suspected — the MoD had something to hide and, in the words of Michael Mates, the Committee's Chairman, was 'not going to come clean' on the entire *Options for Change* decision-making process, and in particular on the reasons for the regimental amalgamations. The manifest injustice of these decisions, and the MoD's obdurate refusal to justify them in any way or even to recognise that the regiments and wider public opinion were entitled to such justification, provided the fundamental themes for the months of campaigning that now lay ahead.

The first of the Select Committee's reports was released on 6 March 1992. Entitled *Options for Change: Army,* it was the first detailed assessment of the Army reductions. It began by noting that the Committee's appeal, in 1990, for debate on the 'options' implied in *Options for Change* and on the decision-making process had not materialised. Referring to its general report published in July 1990 entitled *Defence Implications of Recent Events*, the Committee noted that:

> In that report, we called for publication of a full and properly considered assessment of various options, for decisions not to be taken in advance of discussion of the conceptual framework within which they were taken, and for full public and parliamentary debate on options rather than mere promulgation of decisions. None of this has happened. Decisions have on occasions preceded even informal agreement on the overall conceptual framework. There have been ample opportunities for Parliamentary debate, but almost without exception these have followed rather than preceded decisions.

This was only the first of several highly critical remarks. Acknowledging the difficulties the Government faced in a constantly changing and uncertain strategic climate, the Committee was nevertheless damning in its assessment of the Government's methods and arguments. Discussing the eventual size of the Army, the Committee said: 'Despite repeated denials, there is a pervasive sense throughout the *Options for Change* exercise that financial constraints have at times overridden purely military considerations.' For a variety of reasons, including training considerations, the deployment of two extra battalions to Northern Ireland and the use of non-Infantry units in Infantry roles, the Defence Committee concluded that the Army was likely to suffer overstretch: it would not be able to meet all its peacetime commitments without excessive strain, and also would not be able to meet the balance of commitments in the event of an emergency.

Discussing the decision-making process which led to the specific amalgamations announced by King, the Select Committee protested that it had not been given sufficient justification for the decisions, and that the accountability of Ministers for the decisions had not been accepted:

> The Minister of State [Archie Hamilton] told us that explanation to the units concerned would simply produce argument and dispute. We cannot wholly endorse that rather bleak view; the absence of information or justification can itself be damaging to morale. We certainly cannot accept that Parliament should also be treated as if it were in the military chain of command, and bidden to shut up and get on with it.

Earlier the report argued that:

> It is our duty to call Ministers to account for the decisions they make. The refusal on the part of Ministers to justify their decisions to the House, to this Committee or to the units concerned, has, however, severely limited the extent to which ministers can in practice be held accountable. On these decisions, we can therefore only report to the House the profound sense of grievance and unfairness which the affected regiments feel; and that such analysis of the decisions as we have been able to make, against the background of published criteria and available objective information, leaves us at best uncertain as to how far the decisions made can be justified as fair.

These comments have been quoted at considerable length to demonstrate how critical the Defence Committee was of the conduct of Army *Options* in substance and in style. While these words were relatively restrained, at least in comparison with what was yet to come, the sceptical tone permeates the entire report. The Select Committee was clearly dissatisfied with the Government's defence policy, but was not prepared to take too adversarial a stance until the Government had had a chance to answer the criticisms.

Nevertheless, Tom King evidently thought that the Committee was indeed straying into the realms of adversity. On 6 December 1991 he wrote to Michael Mates, the Chairman, expressing disbelief at the tone of a letter he had received from the Committee Clerk regarding the help given by the MoD to the Defence Committee's inquiry and claiming that 'so far, the Department's involvement runs to something approximating 1000 manhours.' On the specific issue of regimental amalgamations, he claimed that Archie Hamilton had given the Committee 'a very full explanation of the process by which decisions on regimental changes were taken'.

King also expressed concern over 'misleading reports' in the press attributed to a Committee member, and copied his letter to every Committee member 'so that they can be quite clear about the approach we are taking'. All in all, it seemed to the Committee that, as their report noted, they — and any other critical party — were being 'bidden to shut up and get on with it'.

Perhaps the MoD could justify its claim to have been helpful, in so far as (for the most part) it complied with the Committee's requests for information. In certain areas, however, it was less co-operative, and ministers selectively adopted a discernibly hostile attitude. Part of the problem was stubbornness, a quality often attributed to Tom King. He was adamant that certain areas of information would not be made public, especially on the vexing question of the Army Board's decision-making. Having been repeatedly stonewalled by Archie Hamilton over the issue of the elusive 'other factors' that had supplemented the amalgamation criteria, the Defence Committee met in private session in January 1992 to consider how best to get the information out of the MoD and specifically out of Tom King. They had asked at least five times for the information, and each time had been refused with the customary objection that to divulge such information would be divisive. There was no agreement on how to secure the information. The author summed up the Committee's general feeling:

> The Ministry of Defence has, over the years, been very forthcoming with information requested by us on what is often

> sensitive or classified areas of policy. But when it comes to something that is politically sensitive they often clam up.

As well as being cagey about releasing certain information, King was also less than complimentary about the regimental campaigns, which the Defence Committee had considered authoritative enough to invite to submit testimony. Indeed, on 6 March 1992, the day *Options for Change: Army* was published, King launched a broadside against the regimental campaigners, labelling them 'parochial' on the basis that, in interviews Levey and MacMillan had given to coincide with the release of the Committee's report, they had not mentioned parts of the Army other than the Infantry. One such comment appeared in a press release issued by Simon Nayyar on 6 March, which quoted Levey as saying:

> It just does not make sense to take battalions out of the order of battle, such as the Staffords and those in the Scottish Division, who have proven recruiting records when others who have been retained, do not have the recruiting base to sustain themselves.

It may be fair to add that Tom King almost certainly took exception to the (legitimate) charge contained in the same press release that:

> Ministers at the MoD cannot have it both ways: on the one hand, they have accused us of, wilfully, attempting to distort facts and arguments in an attempt to achieve a review of this proposed amalgamation; on the other hand, they refuse publicly to discuss the arrangement and deployment of the various criteria which they used to arrive at their extraordinary decision to amalgamate The Staffordshire Regiment.

By now, Levey and MacMillan found it very easy to respond to the charge of parochialism. Only hours after King's side-swipe, in the same press release mentioned above, Levey simply pointed out that:

> Had the cuts [in other parts of the Army] been too deep, or their battle efficiency significantly impaired, they would undoubtedly have been making their case, as we are for the Infantry. The reason they haven't is because they don't need to — because they have escaped relatively intact.

MacMillan pointed to another obvious defence:

> Were Tom King willing for one moment to listen to what we have been saying throughout, he would realise that we have

> concentrated on the overstretch which exists now in the Infantry, and the consequences of this overstretch. ...

King would have been all too well aware that the campaigns had been arguing the overstretch case for some time. It therefore seemed to the campaigns and to their supporters on the Defence Committee that economics was the issue, not strategy. This joint rebuttal of King's accusation of petty self-interest concluded with a reminder that:

> The fact that [Field Marshals] Lords Bramall and Carver and many other distinguished ex-General Staff officers share our view shows clearly that Tom King's advisors do not have a monopoly on wisdom.

The opponents of Army cuts continued to argue the strategic case until they were blue in the face, and the Select Committee returned to its inquiry into the Army in the next parliamentary session, after the general election. In the meantime, other developments also helped to maintain interest in the issue of the regiments.

Chapter 8

An Anatomy of the County Campaign

While the first stages of the anti-amalgamation campaign were focused on Westminster, the county was not dormant. A formidable local and regional campaigning organisation was being established to draw on the Regiment's strong Staffordshire and West Midlands roots.

The local authorities

For the most part the local authorities — the county, city, borough, district and town councils of Staffordshire and of those West Midlands boroughs that had formed part of Staffordshire until 1974 — were of enormous help to the Save Our Staffords campaign. Some local authorities had already committed themselves to supporting the campaign either at the launch ceremony at the King's Head or by sending messages of support. Some made their Town or City Hall available as a central point for collecting petition signatures. Many authorities also passed resolutions opposing the merger; these generally instructed the Chief Executive to write to the Secretary of State for Defence, to the Prime Minister, to civil servants or to the campaign. The resolution passed by South Staffordshire District Council on 17 September 1991 is typical:

> a. That this council is saddened and disappointed at the announcement by the Secretary of State for Defence that The Staffordshire Regiment is to be merged with The Cheshire Regiment.
>
> b. That this council acknowledges the close relationship between The Staffordshire Regiment and the Community of South Staffordshire over many years.
>
> c. That the Secretary of State for Defence be urged to reconsider his proposals and to retain The Staffordshire Regiment as a separate Regiment.

Some resolutions argued a case. Staffordshire County Council deplored the potential consequences of amalgamation 'both in terms of its impact on the county's economy and employment position, and in terms of the dilution of the deep rooted links between the County and the Regiment'. The Borough of East Staffordshire (formerly East Staffordshire District Council) noted the Regiment's 'strong recruiting base' and expressed concern at 'the recent attempted coup in the Soviet Union'.

On 10 November 1992, Sandwell Metropolitan Borough Council, meeting in full session, discussed and passed a Notice of Motion to be sent to Malcolm Rifkind and the Borough's four MPs. In line with Council procedures, the Notice was circulated in advance with supporting evidence, which was provided by the Campaign Committee. Councillor John Sullivan, the Council Chairman and a strong Staffords supporter, masterminded the exercise. The Notice pledged the Council's support for the Regiment and drew attention to the facts that 'many families in the Borough could be adversely affected by the loss of The Staffordshire Regiment' and that 'the soldiers concerned are unable to defend themselves publicly'. The effect on the Borough's MPs was electric, and all four responded immediately with assurances of support for the campaign.

Local authorities often sent their Chief Executives or Mayors (nicknamed the 'Chain Gang') to important campaign events, such as the initial launch and, later, the launch of the Campaign Control Centre during the 1992 general election campaign. These public personages provided something of a media focus for events that otherwise were not very media-friendly. Mayors in their chains and robes of office were reasonably photogenic, especially when combined with Watchman and Sergeant Bowers.

The civic receptions that followed the Regiment's Freedom Marches were ideal venues for the campaigners to discuss objectives with civic dignitaries, canvass their support and, of course, to photograph them with Watchman. They also provided ideal opportunities to demonstrate publicly the close links between municipality and Regiment, for it was the local authorities that conferred the freedom the Staffords celebrated in the Freedom Marches. Coinciding with the campaign's initial efforts, the Marches served to raise the profile of the Regiment and provided innumerable signatures for the petition. Jeanette Cox of the Wolverhampton Gulf Support Group, for one, realised the value of the Freedom Marches for the petition and followed each one, gathering many signatures.

Some councils and mayors were quicker off the mark than others. For instance, even before Tom King's announcement Sandwell managed to initiate its opposition to amalgamation. The Mayor, Councillor Albert Handley, held a reception for ex-servicemen in the week before Tom King's statement in the House of Commons. At the reception a photograph was taken of Mayor Handley and the former soldiers holding 'the Borough's most prized Staffords' item, a copy of the last battle order given to the 2nd Battalion South Staffords at the Battle of Arnhem'. The possibility of the Staffords' amalgamation was raised then, and the Mayor was asked to pledge to the Staffords the support of the entire ex-service community should the Regiment be targeted. On 22 July, the day before the Secretary of State's announcement, the Mayor's Officer rang RHQ in Lichfield. Thanking the Mayor and the ex-servicemen for their support, RHQ suggested that the Staffords were in little danger because they were well recruited, met the required criteria, and had heard nothing. When Tom King's amalgamation plan turned that optimism into dismay, the Mayor's letter of opposition was in that evening's post.

In addition, mayors, chief executives and councillors often worked in their own capacity to help the campaign; several were affiliated to it as members of the Regimental Association or the Friends of the Regiment. Ann Johnson, then Mayor of Lichfield, offered to put up campaigners from outside Staffordshire during the general election campaign; several mayors and chief executives wrote to the Secretary of State for Defence or to the Prime Minister or both; and Councillor Mrs Constable of Lichfield District Council wrote to HRH The Duke of York, Colonel-in-Chief of the Regiment. Stewart Titchener, the Chief Executive of the City of Stoke-on-Trent, who was also Secretary of the Friends of the Regiment, gave interviews in the press and on local radio.

Local authorities helped in many other ways. For instance, the Campaign Control Centre (see Chapter 11) was sited in Lichfield, with its strong connections with the Regiment, and the Chief Executive of Lichfield District Council also provided great assistance in acquiring the former Dudley's furniture shop as its base. Lichfield District Council franked all its outgoing post with the Save Our Staffords logo, which Pitney Bowes produced in rapid time.

Some local authorities on the edge of the Staffords' recruiting area were not active in the campaign, reflecting weaker links with the Regiment. The Chief Executive of Dudley Metropolitan Borough Council told the author that 'the Council had very little involvement with the Campaign to save the Staffordshire Regiment'. Nevertheless, most local authorities — too many to list here — were active, and the help this provided to the campaign cannot be overstated.

The regimental network

A network of Regimental supporters provided an army of volunteers to carry the campaign to every corner of the region. They collected petition signatures, distributed information on the campaign, and produced literature, stickers and badges. During the general election campaign they also provided information on candidates' public appearances, attended meetings to grill the candidates on their support for the Staffords, and monitored the media. The list of tasks is almost as long as that of the supporters' names; unfortunately it is impossible to acknowledge everyone here, and there is space only for some highlights. The Campaign Committee was well aware of the depth of support the campaign enjoyed and of the unquestioning commitment of so many people. The Regimental Association; the Friends of the Regiment; the Warrant Officers and Sergeants Past and Present; the Royal British Legion; ex-soldiers; impromptu organisations, such as Mrs Cox's Gulf Support Group; friends and families — all gave selflessly in the struggle to maintain the Regiment, which became a bond between them all.

Of these organisations, the two largest were the Regimental Association and the Friends of the Regiment, some of whose members can trace their loyalty to the Regiment as far back as the First World War. The Regimental Association extends over a wide area. Locally there are branches in Burton-upon-Trent; Fenton; Hednesford; Lichfield; Rugeley; Stoke-on-Trent; Stourbridge; Tamworth; Walsall and Bloxwich; West Bromwich; Willenhall; and Wolverhampton. The list spreads further, to Nottingham, Chesterfield and Colchester; until 1992 there was also a London and Home Counties branch. The branches vary in size and in regularity of meetings, but most took an active part — even a mischievous one, as in the case of the Wolverhampton branch, which reported in the 1992 *Stafford Knot* an alliance with the Wolverhampton Support Group:

> Every member of the alliance did their bit but a special thank you must go to certain people, to the 'Hit Teams' who staked out the strategic points of the town which resulted in being evicted from the Mander and Civic Centre on more than one occasion.

The Stourbridge Branch was very active. Formed in 1988, it soon found a role for itself in defending the Regiment. Its members collected 10,000 signatures for the petition — although not all the potential signatories were clear about what was being asked of them. One young woman, approached to sign the petition to help save the Staffords, enquired whether, 'if you save them, will you save me a couple for Saturday night?' — a deal which some soldiers might have found highly acceptable!

Sid Gibbons, Secretary of the Stourbridge branch, alone collected 800 signatures in the Lower Gornal British Legion Club, delivering them personally to Dr John Blackburn, MP for Dudley West. This example serves to highlight that the many connections between organisations, groups and individuals fundamentally underpinned the campaign. Former Staffords also belonged to such organisations as the Airborne Forces Association (which has a branch based on the 2nd Battalion South Staffords) and the Normandy Veterans; the involvement of these groups must not be undervalued. Nor should we forget the contribution of less soldierly organisations. The Women's Institute, for instance, provided many supporters. Wishing to preserve its political neutrality, the WI did not 'affiliate' to the campaign, but many members became active individual supporters.

During the 1992 general election campaign (to which we shall return shortly), every branch kept a close watch on the movements of candidates. Whenever possible they attended meetings, always asking the same question: 'If you are elected, will you support the campaign to save The Staffordshire Regiment?' John Gash, the President of the County branch, and Tony Clarkson, the Chairman of the County Friends, appeared in Patrick Cormack's election literature, with the caption 'Discussing tactics'. This was repeated in Labour and Liberal Democrat literature elsewhere in the county. On the eve of the election a dozen members telephoned each candidate in the area seeking pledges of support and reminding them that, as far as the many supporters of the Regiment were concerned, this was not a transitory campaign.

Every branch mounted a letter-writing campaign to ministers, MPs and the press. The Lichfield branch advertised its opposition in the local press and one of its members, Ray Clarke, enlisted the support of Birmingham taxi drivers, persuading them to display Save Our Staffords stickers in their cabs. Ray Clarke also thought to write to the Queen; he was not terribly surprised to receive a less than forthright response. The Walsall and Bloxwich and the Willenhall branches benefited from having the author as a core supporter of the campaign, and so were largely freed from having to lobby their MP, although they did benefit from campaign photo-opportunities. Walsall also had a supportive Mayor and Council, for the town has supplied countless recruits to the successive regiments that now form The Staffordshire Regiment; at the Town Hall, the names of all the soldiers of those regiments who died in the First and Second World Wars are listed, and two large murals depict the Regiment in action during the First World War. Like, it seems, every other branch, Walsall had some remarkable stalwarts. Ernest Blincow served in the Normandy campaign with the 59th Staffordshire Division and came from a family with regimental ties dating to the First World War; he was responsible for producing 50,000 of the stickers that found their way on to many Staffordshire and West Midlands taxis — indeed, on to any suitable surface, including VDUs at the House of Commons and Bill Cash's lapel during his Adjournment debate. And Jack Keenan collected 4,600 signatures for the petition — no mean feat for a 79-year-old.

The two Stoke branches, co-ordinated by Alf Hordell and the late Bert Knight, fully utilised opportunities presented by the *Stoke Sentinel* and BBC Radio Stoke-on-Trent. Both were fed copiously with news of the campaign. BBC Radio Stoke-on-Trent was particularly helpful with its phone-in programmes, on which branch members and their partners and friends aired the Regiment's grievances.

The Friends of the Regiment were equally busy, with branches in Burton-upon-Trent, Leek, Lichfield, Sandwell, South Staffordshire, Stafford, Stoke on Trent, Tamworth, Walsall, and Wolverhampton and Dudley and, to extend the campaign's influence to further shores, the United States. Whether working as individuals — Councillor John Mellor, Chairman of the Sandwell Friends, wrote individually to 210 Peers — or in groups, they were indomitable.

County Councillor Michael Dale, a former Royal Marine Commando, revived the Stafford Friends after his mayoral year in 1981. They persuaded local businessmen to sponsor regimental plaques that were donated to pubs that displayed collecting boxes, so raising significant amounts of money. The Burton Friends joined forces with the Burton Regimental Association, co-ordinated by Sam Hutchings, to raise £300 for the campaign, as well as collecting 28,000 signatures for the petition, saturating the *Burton Daily Mail* with letters, lobbying MPs and attending meetings.

George Taylor, the Secretary of the Burton Friends, was a classic example of the interconnections which made the campaign network so strong; he also illustrates the Regiment's roots in the region. A member of the Regimental Association since 1938 and of the Friends of the Regiment 'since its inception', he served in the 5th/6th North Staffords (TA) between 1930 and 1939, and re-enlisted from 1947 until 1951. He was Escort to the Colours in 1939, when they were laid up, and again in 1947. In 1971 he was awarded the British Empire

Medal for services to the local community. His pride in taking part in the SOS campaign was inseparable from his long and distinguished association with the Regiment.

Former soldiers — 'the Old and the Bold' — were an indispensable source of support, within the Staffords-based organisations, in other ex-Army groups, and acting individually. The Government was relentlessly bombarded with letters from former soldiers, mostly as an orchestrated tactic by groups, but many from individuals who knew where the weight of opinion counted. Letters arrived from as far away as the USA and Brunei (where a former Commanding Officer was living). Colonel Jeremy Swynnerton OBE, who spent forty years in the Staffords, was Colonel of the Regiment between 1977 and 1985, and whose father had been Colonel of the Regiment of the North Staffords, mounted a personal letter-writing campaign to Douglas Hurd, the Foreign Secretary. Unfortunately for Hurd, Colonel Swynnerton lived in his constituency, and so he was bound to reply to the correspondence himself, rather than pass it to a Junior Minister to answer. The Foreign Secretary dutifully adhered to the Government's position, but Colonel Swynnerton pressed him hard, on one occasion writing that 'I am at a loss to follow the argument of your letter.'

Nor did Norman Lamont, the Chancellor of the Exchequer, escape interrogation. Major Tom O'Hara demanded, by letter and in person at his constituency surgery in Kingston-upon-Thames, that he justify the Regiment's appearance in *Options for Change*. Similarly, Andrew MacKay, the Conservative MP for East Berkshire and then Parliamentary Private Secretary to Tom King, came in for close questioning, by mail and in his constituency, from Major Brendan Donnellan.

Reg Abberley, a former Warrant Officer with twenty-three years' service in the Staffords and now Managing Director of Universal Commercial Security, enlisted the support of his eighty-four-strong workforce and their families, even though they were based in Middlesex. They made 250 telephone calls to Conservative Central Office, and the company's vehicles displayed signs publicising the campaign.

This overview of the activities of groups and individuals supporting the campaign represents scarcely the tip of the iceberg. The author can only acknowledge the fine service that all these people rendered to their Regiment, and request leniency if any exploits have been omitted.

Lobbying politicians

Since the Staffords' catchment area included all Staffordshire and parts of the West Midlands, several West Midlands MPs were drawn into the SOS campaign or joined it wholeheartedly. The geography created some confusion. For instance, Archie Hamilton, the Armed Forces Minister, invited Staffordshire MPs to discuss the amalgamation issue, but excluded relevant West Midlands MPs; this did not go down well either with the author or with Nicholas Budgen (Conservative MP for Wolverhampton South West), among others. This was not a matter of pride; it was felt that the full force of regional opposition to the amalgamation would not be conveyed if several of the region's MPs were excluded. There remains a strong residual identification by West Midlanders with Staffordshire — many people still write 'Walsall, Staffs' on their envelopes, for instance. Nor has there been the slightest diminution of regimental loyalty in Walsall, where the historical connections, particularly with the 38th/80th (South Staffordshire) and the Staffordshire Regiments, have remained as strong as ever.

MPs' affiliations resembled a series of concentric circles, with some moving, under pressure, from outer circles towards the centre during the campaign. In the inner core were, in alphabetical order, Bill Cash (Conservative, Stafford), Patrick Cormack (Conservative, South Staffordshire), and the author, Bruce George (Labour, Walsall South). These were more or less continuously engaged at both Parliamentary and constituency levels. The second circle consisted of the largest group, genuine and enthusiastic supporters who readily made speeches, attended debates and submitted Parliamentary Questions. The third circle was made up of MPs who either gave grudging support or displayed sporadic and limited enthusiasm. Several in this category moved up from the fourth tier; they did the right things, but the campaign was far from central to their Parliamentary or constituency activities. The final, fourth tier, consisted of the minimalists; despite repeated invitations to meetings and lobbying during the general election campaign, they remained indifferent and unresponsive both inside the House and out.

By and large, the vast majority of MPs could be counted as supporters, though some experienced conflicting loyalties. Not all Labour MPs see themselves as rabidly pro-defence, though the Party has long since shed what might be characterised as its anti-defence stance of the early to mid-1980s. Conservative MPs were in a quandary; after all, their Government had initiated the proposed merger and, right until the very end of the campaign, resisted pressure to reverse the decision. No MP (other than Government Ministers) explicitly opposed the campaign, though in one instance it was a 'damn near-run thing'.

Anyone familiar with British politics could reasonably suspect that problems might haunt a campaign seeking support from the two main political parties. However, the nature of the SOS campaign was such that little party political capital could be made by using the campaign as a platform. An MP might lose support by failing to back the campaign, but the MPs involved generally regarded the issue as transcending partisan politics and pooled their influence to promote the campaign rather than their own political careers. This self-denial, sacrificing party political advantage for the higher goal of saving the Regiment, was maintained with only a few exceptions. The most serious of these was when a Conservative Prospective Parliamentary Candidate attacked the Labour Party over defence policy at the campaign launch. Little came of this incident, which illustrated the cross-party consensus created by the campaign.

Another potentially damaging incident, which threatened not the party consensus but the general co-operative framework of the campaign, occurred at the Presentation of new Colours to the 3rd Battalion, when there was the distinct risk that an MP would report a Territorial Army officer to the MoD for distributing a notice to MPs requesting a 'photo-opportunity' on behalf of the campaign. Had this been done, and the young man been disciplined, considerable ill-feeling would have been created among other MPs of both parties, which could have damaged campaign unity. Fortunately party politicking and disruptive behaviour were kept to a minimum, even during the general election campaign.

If most MPs in the area supported the campaign, they did not all have universally cordial relations with their campaigning constituents or with the various campaigning organisations. Remarkably, one MP complained on national television that no one in his constituency had lobbied him on the Staffords, provoking the considerable ire of those who had indeed done so. They wrote a 'stiff' letter to the local newspaper complaining of his indifference to the campaign.

The Campaign Committee also encouraged local people to put pressure on the political parties through their constituency and their national offices. Captain Patrick Baron was one of several people who used these tactics, getting up the noses of several prominent Tories by telling them that he would refuse to vote Conservative at the general election. He received a curt, albeit beautifully scripted, reply from Lord Hailsham, who suggested that, although he shared the view that the cuts were ill advised, the other parties would cut deeper; Jeffrey Archer and Lord Whitelaw also replied in this vein.

For its part, the Campaign Committee became highly skilled at putting the Regiment's case to key political decision-makers at the heart of the Government. John Levey, for instance, talked to people such as Perry Miller, then special adviser to the Secretary of State for Defence; Richard Normington, Conservative Party desk officer on defence; and Edward Bickham, special adviser to the Foreign Secretary. He also met regional businessmen who were in contact with the Government, in one case briefing a Staffordshire businessman who was to lunch with the Prime Minister.

Brigadier Sir Louis Hargroves was also assiduous in using his considerable contacts. For instance, he arranged several meetings with Government and Conservative Party grandees, including one with Norman Fowler, then the Party Chairman. The Campaign Committee agreed that such approaches would be useful, but that they should be handled carefully in order to avoid the 'nuisance' label. This thoughtfulness characterised the Committee's plans for approaching influential people. For instance, as one of the Deputy Speakers until the 1992 general election and Speaker thereafter, Betty Boothroyd, MP for West Bromwich West, had to remain neutral about all controversy; the Campaign Committee therefore decided that any lobbying should be done by one of her constituents who was also a member of the Regimental Association. Hardly anyone in a position of authority or influence was disregarded by the Committee, which almost always identified the appropriate approach to take with each individual as well as the most effective means of reaching them.

The local elite

From the outset the Campaign Committee had great support from senior local figures. Among them were the Earl of Shrewsbury and Waterford (who initiated a House of Lords debate, see page 128), and Sir Arthur Bryan, the Lord Lieutenant of Staffordshire and patron of the Friends of The Staffordshire Regiment. Shortly after the amalgamation announcement, he wrote personally to all local MPs complaining that 'for the Staffords who fought so gallantly in the Gulf just four months ago to be treated in this cavalier manner is little short of shabby and disgraceful'. Equally influential, particularly in Conservative circles, were Sir Eric Pountain and Sir Anthony Bamford, two other patrons of the Friends and leading Midlands industrialists. The view taken by these men was that, should the

Regiment disappear, so too would a potential pool of young, well trained labour. Recruitment to large employers such as Tarmac and JCB could well have been adversely affected.

These senior figures were far from passive supporters. As well as being prominent Tories, and wielding considerable clout in Smith Square and even, in some circumstances, with the Cabinet, they also were very willing to help in practical ways. Sir Anthony Bamford, for instance, laid on a reception at his Mayfair offices on 29 January 1992, which boasted all the regular attractions of the campaign, including soldiers from the 3rd Battalion and Watchman III standing sentinel on the door. Unfortunately the event was poorly attended, mainly because of a vote in the Commons, but that neither dampened the spirits of the campaigners nor lessened the commitment of important industrialists to the cause.

If the event was less successful than it should have been, it was nevertheless important in helping to maintain the momentum of the previous three months. In December 1991 certain voices in the SOS suggested toning down the campaign, fearing that its prominence could jeopardise its credibility. The Committee rejected that proposed change in approach, sensing correctly that the outspokenness of its representatives was generating nothing but good publicity. Any event that carried the campaign forward was more than welcome.

In addition, the campaign could count on the support of what might be termed the 'county set' — ex-senior officers, an elected elite, industrialists and the rural upper middle class — connected in a social, economic and professional network and by their readership of *Staffordshire Life*. The September/October 1992 edition carried a generous feature on the SOS campaign, to which we shall return.

Chapter 9

Campaign Co-ordination

The campaign and the media

No account of the SOS campaign would be complete without acknowledging the media's hugely supportive role; at a time when the media tend to receive more criticism than praise, it is refreshing to be able to bestow a few compliments. The media were vital to success, not only because they reported news of the campaign, but also because of the supportive policies adopted, explicitly or implicitly, by editors. The geographical extent of the campaign, together with its dual regional and national strategy, meant that a vast network of media could be utilised, including local radio (both BBC and commercial); television; national, regional and local newspapers; and freesheets. Most local newspapers were immensely supportive, providing editorials, a regular stream of mostly uncritical news items, and photo stories.

The broadcast media also were of great help in publicising the campaign's activities. There were regular news items on regional events, as well as more substantial programmes such as the Central Television documentary broadcast in December 1992, to which we return in Chapter 13.

Regional media provided excellent coverage of events, whether local actions or national debates. As Jeanette Cox discovered when she organised a public meeting of the Wolverhampton Gulf Support Group at Whitmore Reams Working Men's Club, sometimes the media were more supportive than the general public. Mrs Cox was incensed that only fifty people attended, a majority of whom were media representatives or the organisers themselves. In a subsequent article Mrs Cox — whose son, Graham, and son-in-law, Mark Banks, were in the Staffords — stated indignantly that 'the response of the general public was almost zero — they should be ashamed.'

National TV and radio coverage tended to feature the issues underlying the national campaign and the arguments being advanced in Parliament and by the Ministry of Defence. There was some overlap between national and regional coverage, such as the presentation by ex-soldiers of the anti-amalgamation petition to MPs. For the Staffordshire and West Midlands media, this was a newsworthy event, which received prominent coverage. For the national media, the pomp surrounding the presentation was a decorative border around the main attraction — the defence debate in which there was some ruffling of feathers over a possible backbench Tory rebellion. It was therefore in this context that reporters and photographers from *The Times* and the *Daily Telegraph* attended the launch ceremony at the King's Head.

Generally speaking, local and regional editors look for angles on stories which appeal to a sense of local community. Since the Staffords are the local Regiment, it is plain common sense for them to take a specific emotional interest in its fate. National editors, by contrast, seek to transcend local or regional interests, so that, for instance, they tended to feature the issue of Infantry cuts rather than the specific case of the Staffords. Furthermore, the editorial policies of the national press, particularly the tabloids, are rather more explicitly political than those of regional newspapers. One journalist on a major national tabloid told the author that the newspaper would be most unlikely to oppose the Government's decision by giving favourable coverage to the Staffords' campaign. He also explained that, the paper's political stance aside, the policy was to treat the campaign on the normal assessment of news value. 'Newspapers love personalities, and the more eccentric or vocal they are the better. A few noises or grunts from people in high places would go unnoticed.' So it is not surprising that the national press tended to pick up newsworthy events along those lines; the threat of a Tory rebellion involving recognised personalities such as Bill Cash, Patrick Cormack and Nicholas Budgen would be infinitely more appealing than the arguments of the relatively unknown campaign leaders.

During the SOS campaign the local media — from regional TV and press down to seemingly innocuous publications such as specialist magazines and football club programmes — proved to be superb conveyors of information. The value of football programmes was immense, given that football and other sports clubs generate intense local loyalties. There are many examples of local media support for the campaign. For example on 18 September 1992 the *Cannock Chase Chronicle* featured a number of advertisements by local businesses supporting the retention of the Regiment. On another occasion the *Chronicle* very generously donated a free two-page feature to the campaign. On 30 October 1992 the *Tamworth Herald* published a full-page 'advertisement feature' in support of the campaign, urging readers to write to the Defence Secretary; all the advertisers in the feature supported the SOS campaign, including a pub, Tamworth Borough Council, several used car dealerships, the Tamworth Co-op and Mates condoms. The close link between the *Herald* and the Regiment was perhaps not too surprising since a *Herald* reporter, Louise

Budd, was an officer of the 3rd Battalion. She produced a series of excellent articles following a visit to the 1st Battalion in Northern Ireland, and also wrote occasional short 'local boy' features. She also guaranteed that every letter to the editor from former members of the regiment would be published — and so a rota of supporters was organised to write. Sometimes the media's support for the campaign was more subtle. For instance in January and February 1992 the *Staffordshire Newsletter* produced an excellent series on the Regiment highlighting achievements such as Passchendaele and the heroism of the Regiment's Victoria Cross recipients.

There was also considerable support from the regional media. The September/October 1992 edition of *Staffordshire Life* carried a double-page feature on the campaign, explaining its origins, strategy and arguments, illustrated with a photograph of Staffords campaigners with the petition outside Parliament. Philip Thurlow-Craig, editor of *Staffordshire Life*, explained the decision to carry the feature in terms of a moral responsibility.

> It was something the magazine wanted to get involved in. The Regiment forms part of the heritage of the County, and if there are more threats to the fabric of our history people will take up the cudgels again. Some people thought it was a lost cause, but we believed that if it was right then it should be done — everyone was proud to be associated.

This extremely favourable coverage also carried supportive statements from a number of personalities. There were messages of support from four Staffordshire MPs (Bill Cash, Llin Golding, Sir Ivan Lawrence and Tony Wright), Ann Johnson, Mayor of Lichfield, and County Council Chairman John O'Leary, as well as from Stan Clarke CBE, Chairman of St Modwen Properties, Richard Cartwright, Chief Executive of Hourds (publishers of *Staffordshire Life*), and Peter Coates, Chairman of Stoke City Football Club, whose pride in the Staffords must approximate his pride in his team. His message captured something of the intense feelings towards the Regiment and its impending amalgamation:

> Many thousands of soldiers from the Regiment have supported us at the Victoria Ground — hundreds of former members still do. This is a fine Regiment with strong links with this city. As a one-time member of the Parachute Regiment it grieves me that a Regiment with such distinguished connections with Airborne

> Forces forged in Sicily and Arnhem, should be treated in this way. The campaign is showing all those characteristics which make British Infantry admired the world over: guts, discipline and a strong will to win. With continued support I'm sure it will. This troubled world needs more peace-keepers, not less.

The second significant feature appeared on 1 October 1992 when the *Birmingham Evening Mail*, which has a much wider readership than other Midlands papers, carried a two-page feature with a banner Staffords headlines on the front, a colour photograph of the Regiment, and messages of support from civic leaders, MPs, industrialists and mayors. It also included a message from 95-year-old George Heath, one of the oldest Old Comrades and a corporal in the North Staffords during the First World War. Apart from the subtly placed picture of The Duke of York, the Colonel in Chief of the Staffords, which subliminally implied his endorsement of the campaign, the contents of this feature reflected fairly accurately the make-up of the regional campaign. The Campaign Committee bought 10,000 copies which were distributed free of charge in shopping precincts in Dudley, Oldbury and Warley.

The Campaign Committee's shrewd media-targeting was assisted immeasurably by Jim Guthrie of the *Birmingham Evening Mail*, who agreed in August 1991 to co-ordinate a Staffordshire/West Midlands press campaign on the Regiment's behalf, and by a large number of sympathetic and helpful editors, such as Philip Thurlow-Craig. Specifically designed advertisements were placed in specialist magazines. For instance, an advertisement in the 1 December 1992 edition of the magazine of the Institute of Supervisory Management demonstrated the Staffords' cause by adopting a corporate analogy:

> Companies insure against business risks. Likewise our Country needs insurance against loss of overseas markets caused by international unrest. Overseas stability is maintained by soldiers on the ground.

The Campaign Committee took careful account of the different media audiences. For instance, when the *Staffordshire Life* feature was being planned, it decided that it should be short and simple so that people would not be put off and therefore miss the message. The Committee also listened to professional advice on media relations. When preparing for Phase Three of the campaign, Mike Mogridge (of whom more in Chapter 10) met Steve James, Press Officer of Stoke-on-Trent City

Council; he advised Mogridge to ensure that enquiries from journalists, who have urgent deadlines to meet, were dealt with immediately. This meant that the 'watchkeepers' in the Campaign Control Centre (see also Chapter 10) would have to be thoroughly briefed before being allowed to answer the telephone, and as individuals would have to be capable of swift, decisive thinking. This proved to be very valuable advice.

The campaign organisation kept a comprehensive list of nearly 50 media contacts, including the regional reporters of national newspapers. These contacts were utilised to great effect, so producing almost instantaneous coverage of the campaign's activities across Staffordshire and the West Midlands. As well as having a deep understanding of the value of the news media, the Committee was also shrewd in seizing one-off opportunities such as the launch of Nicholas Benson's book *Rats' Tales* in February 1993. The launch itself was held in Lichfield Guildhall, thanks to the astute Ann Johnson, and complimentary copies of the book were also sent to individuals and organisations 'who could be beneficial from a Regimental profile point of view'.

John Levey also proved to be very telegenic. Fitting central casting's stereotype of the retired officer, he was a regular and extremely capable performer on radio and television. An apt combination of knowledgeable insider, loyal soldier and eloquent critic, he proved a hot potato for the Government, neither conforming to Margaret Thatcher's image of the 'enemy within' nor being an obsequious, unquestioning loyalist. The combination of an eager press and a shrewd Committee was an important aspect of the campaign.

The Cheshires' campaign

Little has been said so far of the Cheshires' campaign, entitled 'Cheshires Challenge the Cuts'. While the Staffords were creating their campaign organisation in August and September 1991, the Cheshires were thinking along the same lines, and it was natural for the two Regimental HQs to keep in touch with each other. However, there were considerable differences between the two campaign structures. First, the Cheshires did not create a Campaign Committee, but instead relied on an *ad hoc* group consisting mainly of Brigadier Keith Prosser, Colonel of the Regiment; Major General Peter Martin, a former Colonel of the Regiment; Colonel Dick Peel; and Brigadier Bill Bromley Davenport, Commanding Officer of the 3rd Battalion (and, later, Lord Lieutenant of Cheshire). Second, the Cheshires seem not to have allocated the same level of resources to the campaign as the Staffords did from the Regimental Trust. The Eric Butler bequest was considerably larger than was revealed to the press, so that later stories of funds drying up were very much pieces of disinformation; the Trust was used to underwrite the Regimental Fund, with plenty left over at the end of the day.

There were some obvious differences between the two campaigns. The Cheshires could not boast the same regional publicity as the Staffords. There were fewer MPs within their catchment area, and the lack of a formal campaign organisation, and the paucity of funds, meant that the Cheshires could not run high publicity 'sub-campaigns', such as SOS's Phase Three during the general election campaign. The Cheshires had hired Westminster Communications in September 1991, and an account executive called Susannah Jowitt (who later became a successful author) took up the case; however, Keith Prosser wound up the campaign at the end of October 1991 after the Defence Estimates debate. The Cheshires were clearly thinking along the same lines as the Staffords until then, but lacked the resources to continue the campaign into 1992. In the opinion of Nicholas Winterton, Conservative MP for Macclesfield, the value of the consultancy to the Cheshires lay in the priming of otherwise reluctant MPs. There was a core of MPs committed to the Cheshires, including Nicholas and Ann Winterton (Conservatives, Macclesfield and Congleton), Gwyneth Dunwoody (Labour, Crewe and Nantwich) and Gyles Brandreth (Conservative, City of Chester), and awareness of the campaign was probably boosted by the early efforts of, for instance, Bill Bromley Davenport, who organised meetings between MPs and supporters of the Regiment. The fact that MPs continued to fight for the cause was testimony to the consultancy's, and the campaign's, early achievements. So is the fact that, even without the cross-regional publicity of their neighbours' campaign, the issue was nevertheless prominent during the general election of 1992. The issue came up frequently on the doorstep, and one Cheshire MP recalls stories of individuals' obstinate refusals to support a Government bent on destroying their Regiment.

After October 1991 the main feature of the Cheshires' campaign was an informal relationship in which Peter Martin briefed Cheshire MPs and carried out, on a slightly less demanding scale, the same functions that John Levey, Simon Nayyar and the Campaign Committee were performing across the densely populated Staffordshire and Black Country. These included liaising with the regimental organisations, briefing MPs, feeding the press, and constantly issuing questions and letters for campaigners to use.

It is remarkable that, without any formal campaign organisation, the Cheshires' campaign did not collapse completely. There were national and regional aids to the campaign, of course. The national media were fed a steady diet of *Options for Change* and Infantry stories, which old soldiers would be bound to pick up. And the Staffords naturally lent whatever assistance they could because of their shared objective — there were in any case old links between the campaign leaders.

There were other coincidental links as well, such as Nicholas Winterton's dual allegiance to the two Regiments. As MP for Macclesfield, he owed The Cheshire Regiment his professional loyalty; as a native of Lichfield (his grandfather had been Mayor) he grew up around Whittington Barracks and used to go hunting around the barracks, so he felt a strong pull towards the Staffords. His own regiment, The 14/20 King's Hussars, was also selected for amalgamation, but, because the case for the Cavalry was not quite as strong as that for the Infantry, it failed to put up a fight, despite the best retention record in the Cavalry. The 14/20 King's Hussars knew they were going down. Thus it was not difficult for Winterton to concentrate on the Staffords-Cheshires merger.

'Keep Our Scottish Battalions'

The relationship between the Staffords and the Keep Our Scottish Battalions campaign was much more formal and functional. The two campaigns were similar in organisation, resources, population base and regional appeal; hence an alliance created a much broader front to the MoD. Early on, the two campaigns had realised that co-operation and information-sharing were not only mutually advantageous but increasingly necessary as the MoD pulled up its drawbridges and refused to consider the views of any party opposing the amalgamations, however logical their arguments.

Keep Our Scottish Battalions and Save Our Staffords were not competitive. Their horses were hitched to the same wagon: the Infantry. Early on Simon Nayyar identified that there was a political *quid pro quo* involved in reprieving Scottish regiments, which could be made to benefit the Staffords and Cheshires. It would be politically expedient for the Government to reprieve one or more of the proposed Scottish amalgamations (The Royal Scots with The King's Own Scottish Borderers, and The Queen's Own Highlanders with The

Gordon Highlanders). To balance matters, an equal number of reprieves would have to be enacted south of the border. Keep Our Scottish Battalions ran an equally good campaign aided, again, by a capable board of former senior officers. Its campaign may have lacked the political weight of the Staffords', who could lobby twenty-six MPs, but they compensated in other areas; for instance, a number of senior Ministers represented constituencies within the recruiting areas of the battalions targeted for amalgamation. The symbolism and emotional appeal of a kilted soldier and bagpipes were particularly useful to the Scots' campaign, and Lieutenant General Sir John MacMillan and his supporters were certainly not afraid to exploit the politics of Scottish grievance.

Connections between the two groups were reinforced by the long-standing personal friendship of John Levey and his counterpart John MacMillan. The two campaigns co-operated from the very beginning — the Scots were instrumental in the selection of Citigate and Westminster Communications as the SOS's lobbyists, in as much as they had already engaged the two consultancies, and the petition presentation and the fringe meeting at the 1991 Conservative Party Conference were organised jointly. After the 1992 general election, MacMillan, Levey and Nayyar met Sir Nicholas Bonsor, the new Chairman of the House of Commons Defence Committee to outline their concerns about Infantry overstretch and its policy implications. Further joint action included the simultaneous submission of evidence on Infantry overstretch to the Defence Select Committee.

Chapter 10

Keeping up the Siege of Whitehall

November 1991 to February 1992

Between November 1991 and February 1992 the legion of Staffords supporters in both Houses of Parliament continued to use every Parliamentary device open to them to keep the issues alive, maintain pressure on the Government and, later, to prevent the campaign's public profile sinking as the Defence Select Committee's *Options for Change: Army* inquiry tailed off after January 1992. Several unplanned developments helped to give heart to the campaigners.

Parliamentary Questions

Early in the campaign, Nayyar had identified the importance of encouraging supportive MPs to table Parliamentary Questions (PQs). These were intended to achieve several objectives. First, they would raise the Regiment's profile with Ministers at a time when they would be hoping that the campaigners were running out of steam or out of funds. Second, PQs would force the MoD to address the awkward issues regularly raised by Save Our Staffords, since Ministers are generally bound to supply reasonably plausible answers to Questions. Third, seeing local MPs tabling regular PQs gave local campaigners faith that the campaign was moving forward clearly and constructively. Finally, each PQ and its corresponding ministerial reply provided a hook on which to hang crucial local — and occasionally national — media publicity. In addition, there was always the chance that an answer to a PQ might reveal some hitherto unknown and useful information, although this did not happen very often.

All the significant PQs asked were based on information and briefings supplied by John Levey and Simon Nayyar. Nayyar wrote to Sylvia Heal and Bill Cash on 11 November 1991, encouraging them to table Written Questions on 'key issues where Ministers have failed publicly to provide substantive information', and providing them with comprehensive briefings. (Written Questions, the answers to which are published in *Hansard*, are designed to elicit factual information; typically Oral Questions, which Ministers answer on the floor of the House, have the effect of eliciting a not very helpful political point.) In the early stages of the campaign, Archie Hamilton's answers

— carefully crafted by his civil servants — offered very few insights into the MoD's decision-making processes. Take, for instance, Hamilton's reply to the following question from Sylvia Heal:

> Mrs. Heal: To ask the Secretary of State for Defence why he decided not to consult or warn the Colonel of the Staffordshire Regiment of the likelihood of amalgamation; and if he will make a statement.
> Mr. Archie Hamilton: All regimental Colonels were invited to express their views about how the reductions were to be achieved, but none were told of the Army Board's decisions before the day of the announcement.

Likewise, Hamilton's reply to Bill Cash's more detailed question was as evasive as possible:

> Mr. Cash: To ask the Secretary of State for Defence (1) what are the Director of Infantry's current guidelines on amalgamation of regiments in respect of the relative priority for amalgamation of those regiments which have already been amalgamated since 1945 and those which have not; (2) if he will list the order of preference for amalgamation submitted by The Cheshire Regiment to the Army Board.
> Mr. Archie Hamilton: The detailed basis on which the Army Board came to its decisions about regimental amalgamations is an internal matter. The Board took account of all relevant factors.

Archie Hamilton was not the only person ducking and diving. Responding to an Oral Question from Patrick Cormack on the floor of the House of Commons in March 1992, Tom King chose to avoid the issue by evading and trivialising it:

> Mr. Cormack: Does my right hon. Friend accept that the anxiety that still persists in Staffordshire about the fate of The Staffordshire Regiment is not mere local and parochial concern but is based on a wider concern for the strength of the Infantry? Can he say anything this afternoon that will enable me to reassure my very worried constituents?
> Mr. King: I entirely sympathise with the feelings described by my hon. Friend. I was met by a very respectful group of Gordon Highlanders when I visited Aberdeen recently, when I said that I would have been on the line as well had I been in their position. …

The Adjournment Debate

Nayyar knew that an Adjournment Debate would provide an effective vehicle for taking the campaign forward at Westminster. (An Adjournment Debate, the last business of the day in the Commons, offers MPs a means of putting on record their interest in an issue of personal, policy or more usually constituency concern.) MPs eager to initiate an Adjournment Debate enter a ballot and hope for the best. Although the debate lasts for only thirty minutes, its crucial value lies in the fact that, no matter how late it begins, a Minister from the relevant department of state must be present to provide an official reply on behalf of the Government. (Not all MPs, it must be said, believe that Adjournment Debates are useful, because they relegate the issue under discussion to an empty Commons in the depths of the night. But when one is faced with a limited number of options, it is wise to exploit every possibility.)

The only question was: who would initiate the debate? Bill Cash, Llin Golding and the author had all told the campaigners that they were willing to do so. Acutely aware that a general election was approaching, all three MPs put their names into the ballot to increase their chances of success — preferably sooner rather than later. They did not have to wait long. On 30 January, Nayyar learned from the Leader of the House's weekly Business Statement that Bill Cash had been successful. An Adjournment Debate on 'the Future of The Staffordshire Regiment' was to take place on the following Wednesday, 5 February, just four Parliamentary sitting days away. There followed a frantic call from Cash to Nayyar asking for comprehensive and easily digestible briefing notes. Nayyar immediately rang Levey, who began work. Now the SOS campaign was truly on a war footing, as a major set-piece battle loomed large on the horizon.

Together, Nayyar and Levey prepared detailed briefing papers, drawing upon *Making the Right Choice*, but updating the material to include changes in opinion and in the strategic environment after it was written. Nayyar fired off letters to all the local MPs, and to others known to have a policy or personal interest in the Staffords or, more broadly, in the Infantry reductions, encouraging them to attend. On the day itself, Nayyar buttressed his approach with personal telephone calls to each of these MPs, reminding them of the debate and imploring them to be in the Chamber that evening. Levey, Nayyar, Lieutenant General Sir Derek Boorman and Bill Cash met that evening at Green's (later re-named Shepherd's), a well-known restaurant in Westminster frequented by politicians (and equipped with a Division Bell, to warn MPs that a vote is being held in the Commons), where a final briefing was given and outstanding issues were resolved. To John Levey's consternation, Bill Cash reckoned that the Staffords' chances of securing a reprieve were approximately 12 per cent!

The MP who initiates an Adjournment Debate is entitled to permit other Parliamentary colleagues to intervene. Because the debate is so short, interventions are usually very brief, and can be curtailed or prevented by the sponsoring MP or by the responding Minister. Even before the debate began, Archie Hamilton let it be known that he was not disposed to permit more than one contribution from each Opposition party. Although this procedural device is not without precedent, it is rarely invoked and in the circumstances many MPs felt that it was peculiarly ungracious. As it was, the debate was extraordinarily well attended. Besides Cash, Hamilton and a Government Whip, there were seventeen MPs on the Government and Opposition benches, including most of the Staffords' key supporters and several of the Cheshires' and Scots' as well. (This may not seem many, but almost qualifies as a packed House by the standards of Adjournment Debates.) As the forty or so serving and retired officers sitting in the Strangers' Gallery above could clearly see, many Staffordshire and West Midlands MPs had come equipped with copies of the bright blue *Making the Right Choice* document, which Nayyar had circulated earlier.

The debate began at 12.16 am. From the outset, Archie Hamilton made it perfectly clear that he found his attendance in the Chamber, at this late hour and on this particular subject, wholly disagreeable — an attitude that perhaps contributed to the vociferousness of the debate. MPs on each side of the House found themselves sitting on the edge of their green leather benches, ganging up on the unfortunate Hamilton who must surely have wished that the whole issue would go away and that he could be home in bed.

Bill Cash rose to make what was later agreed to be a memorable speech. He went through the Army Board's published criteria for retention, yet again demonstrating that the Staffords met all these criteria. He delivered a succession of devastating salvoes at the exposed ministerial flank: 'Just because a decision may have been ill-judged and might prove embarrassing to review is insufficient reason to refuse to review it.' Cash focused on the political responsibility for the Army Board's decision-making process, and challenged Hamilton directly:

> It is not acceptable for [Hamilton] or his officials to hide behind the pretext that because decisions on amalgamation have now been made, they cannot be considered because that would open a Pandora's Box and lead to every regiment clamouring for a review of its own case.

Cash had hit upon the crux of the argument, for the 'Pandora's Box' to which he referred was the centrepiece of the MoD's defence that it dare not reconsider its previous decisions.

An exchange between Cash, Nicholas Winterton and Nicholas Budgen deserves quotation as a summary of the debate from the regimental perspective, not least because all three MPs are Conservative colleagues of Archie Hamilton:

> Mr. Cash: ... It would be a tragedy if The Staffordshire Regiment were to be re-amalgamated at a time when other regiments have not been amalgamated since 1945, when the regiment has an outstanding record of service to the county and to the country, when its recruitment and retention are good, when demographic trends show clearly its sustainability, while other regiments' demographic projections do not, and when the geography and regional representation arguments simply do not stand up to examination.
> Mr. Nicholas Winterton (Macclesfield): Will my hon. Friend confirm that the crux of his very excellent argument is that both The Staffordshire Regiment and The Cheshire Regiment entirely meet the criteria of the Army Board for retention as they are, while many regiments that have remained unamalgamated and unmerged do not meet those criteria, and that is the unfairness of the situation?
> Mr. Cash: That indeed is the case, combined with the total inadequacy of consultation before the decision was taken.
> Mr. Budgen: It is all very well talking about fairness, but a political decision was taken and, therefore, the politicians ought to explain it.
> Mr. Cash: Indeed, we shall wait to hear what the Minister has to say. I urge the Minister to consider the fact that The Staffordshire Regiment was never given a chance to put its case to the Army Board, because of a breakdown in the military hierarchy. That is where the problem lies. I also urge my right hon. Friend, in the strongest possible terms, to look again at the rationale for that amalgamation.

Before Archie Hamilton responded, the author intervened to add a note of strategic caution concerning Infantry overstretch, as well as to warn the Minister that the issue would not quietly disappear. Arguing that the 'smoking gun' of the Treasury was there for all to see, he pointed out that the 'strategic rationale' was wrong, and would be exposed as folly if the cuts were allowed to go ahead undiminished:

> The key question is whether an Army of the size proposed by the Government will prove sufficient in peacetime, let alone crisis and war. I am certain that it will not. ... The decision to merge The Staffordshire and Cheshire Regiments is bizarre and has not been explained. The Minister hopes that the issue will go away, but it will not. I guarantee that it will return to haunt him, his colleagues and the members of the Army Board who endorsed it.

A plainly needled Hamilton rose at 12.33 am to respond for the Government. He spoke from notes that contained passages identical to those that would be used by the Earl of Arran in the House of Lords a week later — unsurprisingly, since the speech notes were prepared by the same civil servants. Hamilton proceeded to pay virtually no attention to the concerns of the MPs who had spoken; nor, for that matter, did he spend much time talking about the plight of the Regiment. Instead he elected to talk in global strategic terms that were wholly inappropriate to the debate. When Cash finally forced Hamilton to give way, he said what everyone in the Chamber was thinking:

> What is the relevance of what my right hon. Friend is saying? We understand the basic arguments in relation to *Options for Change*, but fail to understand the relevance of the arguments that my right hon. Friend the Minister is now advancing have to the decision taken last July.

When Nicholas Budgen asked why the merger of The Royal Welch Fusiliers and the Cheshires had turned into the Staffords-Cheshires amalgamation, Hamilton simply stated that he was 'not prepared to comment on the process of the decision-making'. Likewise, when he turned to the issue of the amalgamation criteria, he bluntly asserted that it was not in anybody's interests to examine them in detail:

> If my hon. Friends and hon. Members think that it is good for the Army to reopen the whole issue, and to have the whole thing thrown back into the melting pot, they are totally and utterly

> wrong. The best thing we can do is to accept the decisions that have been made, unpalatable to some as they may be.

Not only did Hamilton say that the issue was not open to discussion, he also accused the opponents of amalgamation of deploying 'inaccurate figures'. He then set out to demonstrate the 'truth', although he merely reiterated the argument he had already made to the Defence Select Committee, namely that a cut of seventeen Infantry battalions would be more than offset by a cut of nineteen Infantry commitments. As the Committee's report pointed out the following month, this simplistic argument failed to take into account such factors as unit manning levels. Attempting to deflect any argument on that point, he suggested that the Army's prevailing overstretch problem was caused by undermanning of units, and that a reduced number of battalions brought up to strength would eliminate the problem and satisfy the target twenty-four month emergency tour interval. That assessment was itself questionable, and also did not satisfy the Staffords' supporters, who pointed out that the Staffords were one of the best-manned units in the Infantry. The increasingly acrimonious argument culminated in this gem:

> Mr. Hamilton: ... Following amalgamation with the Cheshires, the new regiment should be able to achieve full strength, thus eliminating the cause of overstretch -
> Mr. Nicholas Winterton: They are over-recruited now.
> Mr. Hamilton: They are not over-recruited now. The Staffords are not over-recruited, but under-recruited now.
> Mr. Winterton: They are.
> Mr. Hamilton: They are not. This is an absurd conversation. I am telling my hon. Friend that the Staffords are under-recruited.

A second exchange between Winterton and Hamilton showed that the issue was undermining the usually formidable Conservative Party unity.

> Mr. Hamilton: One of the arguments being proposed is that, in practice, we shall not have enough Infantry battalions to do the jobs that we are being asked to do.
> Mr. Nicholas Winterton: There will not be enough.
> Mr. Hamilton: My hon. Friend clearly has not listened to what I have been saying.
> Mr. Winterton: I do not believe it.
> Mr. Hamilton: If he does not believe it, that is a different matter. It is up to him to decide whether he believes me or not.

When the debate concluded at 12.46 am, Hamilton and Alastair Goodlad, the Government's defence Whip, stormed out of the Chamber. For the Regimental supporters, including the Earl of Shrewsbury, watching from the Strangers' Gallery, it had certainly been a lively debate. But it was hardly encouraging as, yet again, Archie Hamilton had stuck to his script and made no real response to the many points put to him. On the other hand, while the debate did not produce any concessions or explanations, it was at least the first opportunity for the specific issues of the SOS campaign to be properly debated in Parliament. The campaign's dissatisfaction with the conduct of the *Options* exercise was restated, and the Government was served notice that, Hamilton notwithstanding, the issue was far from closed.

The House of Lords

A similar result was achieved when the Earl of Shrewsbury and Waterford — England's premier earl, a Conservative Peer and a Patron of the SOS campaign — secured an Unstarred Question debate in the House of Lords on 10 February, just one week after Bill Cash's Adjournment Debate in the Commons. An 'Unstarred Question' takes the form of a fairly short debate on a topical issue, generally lasting about an hour; crucially, however, there is no time limit and no restriction on the number of speakers. The 'Unstarred Question' asked whether the Government was 'satisfied that their plans for the future of the Infantry provide adequate reserves for likely contingencies'.

Lord Shrewsbury had been profoundly dismayed by the quality of the argument that the Ministry of Defence had deployed in the Adjournment Debate. Shrewsbury, who was president of the Wolverhampton branch of the Soldiers' Sailors' & Airmen's Families Association, already had a fairly detailed understanding of contemporary military strategy. Wishing to be as confident as possible that he had minimised the risk of Ministers skirting the key issues or losing him in a smokescreen of irrelevant and opaque statistics, he and Nayyar discussed the issues at length. Levey and Nayyar also scrutinised Shrewsbury's draft speech notes, meticulously revising right up to the day of the debate. Every statistic that Shrewsbury planned to cite was painstakingly checked and double-checked. The aim was to ensure that no flank was exposed, and no quarter conceded, to Ministers.

The day of the debate dawned less than auspiciously for the MoD, for that morning it was obliged to announce that an Infantry battalion from The Queen's Regiment was to be despatched to Northern Ireland to deal with a sudden escalation in sectarian violence. For the Earl of Arran, the Junior Minister who was to defend the Government's record, this announcement could not have come at a more embarrassing moment. And, of course, that evening Shrewsbury was swift to draw attention to the decision, noting acidly that 'if nothing else, history has surely taught us that the unexpected invariably happens.' Shrewsbury went on to point out that the decision meant that 'more than a third of the proposed thirty-six Infantry battalions (less the Gurkha battalions) are presently deployed to Northern Ireland.' Field Marshal Lord Bramall joined in this beating of the Government with its own stick, saying that:

> Whatever one may have thought of *Options for Change* and however well it may generally seem to have been accepted, Northern Ireland has driven a coach and horses through the military arithmetic.

Before the onslaught began, Shrewsbury and Nayyar took time out to have dinner at Green's. Last-minute modifications were made to the speech notes, and Nayyar talked Shrewsbury through some further refinements of the arguments.

No sooner had Shrewsbury returned to the House — and before he reached the Chamber — than he was set upon by Government colleagues urging him not to pursue the debate because of the embarrassment it would cause; he could assert, instead, that he had had a change of heart because of the lateness of the hour. This sounded like the perfect excuse because as a rule their Lordships do not like being kept sitting up unreasonably late. It was also the clearest indication of the significance Ministers and Government Whips attached to the debate, and it steeled the Earl of Shrewsbury's determination to proceed.

It was also a reflection of the extent to which Ministers were out of touch with the views of their Parliamentary colleagues that during the debate Lord Swinfen, a Conservative Peer, dispensed with the usual courtesies and revealed the lengths to which the Government had gone in its desperate (and ultimately futile) attempt to prevent Shrewsbury airing his legitimate — and widely shared — grievances. Swinfen revealed the Government's motivation:

> I congratulate my noble Friend Lord Shrewsbury upon tabling this Question and also upon not being derailed by attempts to

> make him postpone it owing to the lateness of the hour. I suspect that if it had been postponed it would not have been heard at all, certainly not before an election.

That, of course, was the point. Ministers hoped that, by promising Shrewsbury that they would reschedule the debate within weeks, they would none the less be able to forget their promise when the now imminent general election was called.

The debate began at 9.35 pm. Shrewsbury leisurely reviewed the strategic environment in which the *Options for Change* decisions had been made. At this time, the Government still clung to the belief that it would not have to send troops into warring former Yugoslavia as part of a multinational United Nations force. It was therefore extraordinarily prescient for Shrewsbury to observe that 'I have no doubt that a United Nations peacekeeping force will be wanted there shortly', and that Britain would be expected to play its part. Time would prove him right on this and the Government wrong.

Shrewsbury analysed the impact of overstretch on serving officers and soldiers and their families. This, he considered, led to 'undermanned battalions, poor morale among those who remain, additional recruiting effort, more expense for the taxpayer and a less well-trained and thus less effective Infantry'. The simple and unassailable logic of what he said had the House listening with rapt attention. He also noted the Government's spectacularly optimistic assertions that a twenty-four-month gap between emergency tours — which had not been achieved even with fifty-five battalions — would soon be possible, despite having seventeen fewer battalions to draw on. He lingered fondly on the British command of the ACE Rapid Reaction Corps (ARRC), pointing out that, given the double-hatting of Infantry battalions — in other words, tasking them with being available for two separate roles simultaneously — our command of the ARRC 'would be comic if it were not quite so serious'.

Finally, Lord Shrewsbury turned to the plight of The Staffordshire Regiment. He reiterated the lack of rationale for the proposed amalgamation, the absence of consultation, and the Regiment's excellent recruiting record; and he challenged the Earl of Arran to provide evidence that the Staffords' case had been put to the Army Board, concluding: 'I am, however, confident that he will not. He cannot, because there never was a presentation to the Army Board of the Staffords' case'.

The speech lasted thirteen minutes. When he sat down, one could have heard a pin — certainly a rifle cartridge — drop between their Lordships' richly upholstered red leather benches. By then, all — including the Earl of Arran — sensed that the House had been disquieted by what he had disclosed, and was in an unforgiving mood.

Shrewsbury's stirring call to arms brought a sustained and damaging cannonade down on the Government. Peer after Peer, predominantly Conservative, underscored Shrewsbury's reservations about the MoD's calculations. Leading the charge was Lord Bramall, a Crossbencher (independent). Congratulating Shrewsbury on initiating a debate about the Infantry, and commanding all the authority of his former Service position, he went straight for the jugular:

> On the subject of Army manpower, with its special impact on the Infantry, the Government clearly have it wrong, and I strongly suspect that everyone in the MoD knows that they have it wrong, have overdone it and are wondering how they will get off the hook.

There could hardly have been a more scathing and authoritative indictment of the Government's defence policy. Lord Glenarthur, a former Conservative Minister, believed that the unseen hand of the Treasury was at work:

> All my experience leads me to the conclusion that if the exercise was wholly a Ministry of Defence proposal, it must be a fascinating historical achievement. It would be the one occasion on which the Ministry of Defence demanded more of itself than the Treasury demanded of it.

Glenarthur concluded, ominously, that 'the Government would not be wise to discard as irrelevant, or as just plain busybodying, the anxieties that have been raised.'

Next to open a fusillade against the Government was Lord Harmar-Nicholls, an elderly Conservative Party loyalist and former MP, generations of whose family have been born and bred in Staffordshire; his family kept a pub in Darlaston in the author's constituency. The author had briefed him, thus becoming one of the relatively few MPs of one party to advise a Peer of another; our Darlaston and Staffordshire Regiment connections, as well as our love of the Victorian music hall, make us good friends. In a stirring appeal to emotion, Lord Harmar-Nicholls paid homage to the Regiment and noted ruefully:

> Whether or not it is before the next election, … Staffordshire will insist on rectifying this grievous undermining of the

> contribution of one of the most outstanding Regiments of the Line that this country has ever had.

At the time many Peers, on both sides of the House, were inclined to discount his contribution as rather too long on emotion and relatively short on substance. But in time Lord Harmar-Nicholls would be proved right.

Lord Mayhew, the Liberal Democrats' defence spokesman in the Lords, warmly supported Lord Shrewsbury's 'powerful criticism of the handling of the merger of the Staffords by the Army Board'. Speaking for the Opposition, Lord Williams of Elvel also urged the Government to take on board Shrewsbury's concerns.

Many powerfully expressed points that undermined the Government's case were made during the debate. The speakers pressed for direct answers, but none were forthcoming. Replying for the Government, the Earl of Arran carefully restated the MoD's position on the strategic context of the reductions in the armed forces. Noting that many Peers, including numerous Conservatives, had referred to the plight of The Staffordshire Regiment, he attempted to draw a veil over the issue of the proposed amalgamation:

> I have every sympathy with those units which were selected for disbandment or amalgamation, but I do have to say that the time for brooding has now passed. Furthermore, I should like to add that it is not particularly helpful to the Army as a whole — and certainly not to those units most affected — to have the uncertainty that prolonged discussion of such matters inevitably creates when my colleagues and I, both here and in another place, have repeatedly made clear that this Government see no grounds for altering the decisions that have been made in relation to both the future size of the Army and the units it will comprise.

Lord Shrewsbury immediately rose to intervene. He asked Arran whether it was true that, having last been amalgamated in 1959, the Staffords had been given to understand that they would not be amalgamated again 'in the foreseeable future'. Arran refused to answer the question and tried to change the subject. This prompted Lord Williams to pose the question a second time. Arran, clearly irritated by the unusual and unseemly persistence of Peers from all sides of the House, retorted:

> My Lords, I make it quite clear to your Lordships' house … that

> it serves no useful purpose or point in going into further considerations and details about the decisions and how they were made.

Arran sat down, and the debate ended. Once again, the Government's final word was a point-blank refusal to answer not only this, but the many specific questions put to it in the debate.

Political manoeuvring

Ministers' intransigent refusal to discuss the individual amalgamations in either the Commons or the Lords clearly indicated that they had been taken aback by the widespread and well informed criticism of their amalgamation proposals. During the Commons debate, Archie Hamilton had offered a fascinating insight into the laager mentality that the Staffords' campaign had by now engendered. He made what many regarded as a low blow, clearly targeted at the SOS campaigners: 'Regrettably, many inaccurate figures have been quoted by those who seek a reprieve.' This was a low blow because Hamilton was privileged, on the one hand, to know how the decision-making process had unfolded (three years after the reprieve, the Staffords campaigners can still only speculate about the amalgamation decisions) and to be in a position to refuse to justify or explain it in Parliament. On the other hand, he happily used that knowledge to wrongfoot the campaign whenever possible, but without paying the campaigners the courtesy of explaining where and how their concerns were misplaced. Nevertheless it is a supreme tribute to the campaigners' political judgment and professionalism, and that of their advisors, that Ministers were not able to make such remarks more often.

In addition to this apparent obduracy — which was fast convincing campaigners and military alike that the MoD not only would not, but could not, justify its behaviour — the Unstarred Question debate contained a 'ticking time-bomb' that exploded beneath the Government a few months later. This was Lord Arran's seemingly innocuous observation that 'the current indications are that the 1993-1994 emergency [tour] plot will allow a minimum twenty-four-month tour interval for most battalions.' The Government's argument rested on the satisfactory attainment of this goal — it had claimed all along that once the turbulence of restructuring had settled, and despite indications that overstretch existed with fifty-five battalions, the thirty-eight battalions of the new 'smaller but better' Army would enjoy the benefits of the twenty-four-month tour interval. Morale, and therefore efficiency, would improve, and the campaigners would be shown to be the parochial 'moaning minnies' everybody knew them to be. Within seven months, however, this estimate was revealed as wildly optimistic. In evidence to the Defence Committee on 22 September 1992, Archie Hamilton admitted that in 1993-94 the tour interval would be some seven months short of the target — that is, an average seventeen months instead of twenty-four. This did not cause a public storm, but to the defence community, and especially to the campaigners, it was a landmark admission.

While campaigners harried away at the MoD at the end of 1991 and the beginning of 1992, the high profile of the Infantry campaigns, assisted immeasurably by their media friendliness, was achieving considerable success with the voting public. In a Market and Opinion Research International (MORI) poll of 1,100 people, quoted in the *Sunday Times* in early November 1991, 63 per cent of respondents opposed regimental mergers, while 25 per cent supported them and 12 per cent were undecided. This remarkably high figure probably reflected not so much the success of the campaigns *per se*, but also the public's general support for the Army. It was this natural bedrock of support that made the SOS campaign increasingly confident.

That the Government was undeniably aware of the vote-losing potential of the issue was shown by a frantic damage-limitation exercise conducted in response to remarks made by two senior Scottish Cabinet Ministers just before the Kincardine and Deeside by-election in November 1991, in which the Conservatives faced a strong Liberal Democrat challenge. The identical nature of their arguments made the implications of the incident relevant to both the SOS and the Keep Our Scottish Battalions campaigns. The same *Sunday Times* article that carried the poll findings also reported considerable fall-out within the Government following remarks made by Ian Lang (Scottish Secretary) and supported by Malcolm Rifkind (Transport Secretary) during the by-election campaign. Interviewed on Grampian TV on 24 October 1991, Lang had stated that:

> These amalgamations will take place over a period of years, during which there is time for reassessment, and any changes in the military circumstances will be fully taken into account. I will make sure that that review will take place. ...

Lang repeated these assurances in an interview with the *Scotsman* on 25 October, and was also reported to have told Scottish Tories that he would be demanding a review of the Scottish battalions' cases.

Furthermore, according to the *Independent* of 29 October, campaigners for The Gordon Highlanders withdrew their plans to run an Independent candidate in the by-election when Lang assured them that the amalgamation would probably be reassessed.

John Reid, junior Labour defence spokesperson and also a Scottish MP, called for Lang's resignation.

> Either he was expressing a political view which has been rejected by the Prime Minister as well as being rebuffed by the Secretary of State for Defence. Or he was well aware that his public assurances about a review of the regiment decisions did not have the backing of the Cabinet but used them merely to buy-off opposition in Kincardine and Deeside.

Certainly something seemed to be amiss within the Cabinet; although the Scottish Office tried to put a favourable gloss on Lang's words, there were reports that the incident produced a 'back me or sack me' ultimatum from Tom King to John Major. According to the *Sunday Times*:

> Cabinet Ministers were initially understanding about [Rifkind's and Lang's] need to sound hopeful in the face of the Kincardine campaign and for most of last week Ministers accepted that 'vague promises' had to be made in an attempt to hold the seat.

However, Tom King was said to be furious and, although Downing Street denied that King had delivered an ultimatum, he was said to have told colleagues that he had 'taken all the flak he intended to take'. Despite Reid's call for Lang's resignation, the row never boiled over in public. However, a senior Tory backbencher with strong military connections confirmed that there was ferment in the party and the Government: 'for obvious reasons we are conducting our rows in strict secrecy ... but they are savage.'

The episode says little about the process of decision-making, but it did reveal that the Government was far from unanimous in its views on *Options for Change*. It was unlikely that anyone in Government explicitly opposed the amalgamations. However, it required the full use of the convention of collective Cabinet responsibility to prevent the policy disintegrating.

What this episode did demonstrate is that if two battalions could be used as a political football in one by-election, then the broader and more complex issues of the Infantry and regimental amalgamations could have considerable political potential. The Government staunchly maintained that the decisions concerning the Services were strategically motivated, but the suspicion was that the Infantry issue was driven by political rather than strategic considerations.

Archie Hamilton added to the campaigners' suspicions when he stated on 27 January 1992, in another *Scotsman* interview, that it was not 'politically acceptable' to have a large number of regiments in one part of the United Kingdom and fewer in another. As far as the SOS campaigners were concerned, this statement confirmed that the amalgamations had been based on 'hidden criteria', and that these were why the Government refused to discuss the decision-making process. Although Hamilton had been talking in the context of the Scottish Division, his words were clearly relevant to the Staffords. How could the sudden substitution of the Staffords for the RWF be explained except as the result of political calculations that found it too risky to go ahead with an amalgamation of a Welsh and an English regiment? Furthermore, as Bill Cash pointed out in his Adjournment Debate, the logic of the amalgamation still made no sense when one compared, for instance, the region of England north of the Humber-Mersey line with the Midlands. Cash argued that, in direct contradiction to Hamilton's words, there was an unjustifiable concentration of battalions in one part of the country at the expense of another.

Needless to say, there was no reply to these accusations. The SOS campaign could do little more than it had already to get the Government to comment. There was a similar difficulty with the figures which the SOS campaign used to challenge the MoD. For instance, when John Levey wrote to Archie Hamilton on 21 April 1992 about the MoD's assessment of the Staffords' manning levels, he could only hope that his figures did not arouse too great a curiosity at the MoD. His argument itself was watertight, as is demonstrated in a letter to Archie Hamilton:

> As a professional infantryman with over thirty years' experience, I am, of course, aware of the manning differentials between types of battalions; of the current fifty-five battalions, only six were, at the time of the Gulf War, at the large establishment of an Armoured Infantry Battalion. It is entirely consistent with a seven-year posting to Fallingbostel and the subsequent need to move to an Infantry Type B Battalion that The Staffordshire Regiment should have experienced a short period of variation in manning patterns. At the same time, and perhaps more significantly, I understand that you have told Bill Cash that your

> officials predict that undermanning in 1 Staffords will worsen (by 1.5 per cent) between February and May this year. My understanding is that the situation will improve dramatically (up 3.38 per cent, to an almost negligible 0.85 per cent below establishment). I am, therefore, at a loss to understand how your officials could have arrived at so fundamentally different an assessment.

What worried Levey a little was the source of his figures. Clearly, to present such a detailed argument on the subject of manning levels required intimate knowledge of the subject, which was not difficult for a former Commanding Officer to claim. But such up-to-date information could have raised a few eyebrows. According to John Levey, the SOS campaign was 'sailing very close to the wind' over the information it used to debate with MoD. Levey describes a letter from Archie Hamilton to Bill Cash of 24 February 1992, just before the letter quoted above, as a 'watershed document'. It was the first recorded occasion on which the MoD had supplied accurate information about any of the claimed decision-making criteria on amalgamations. Meanwhile, MoD continued to supply the Defence Select Committee with old, inaccurate information. This made building arguments relatively straightforward for the SOS campaign — but only because the Campaign Committee had copious access to regimental sources.

Thus the campaign could only press certain matters so far. On the issue of the politics behind the regimental mergers, the campaigners could only ask, but had no access to the sources that would indicate the criteria that had really been applied. On the protracted argument over manning, recruitment and retention, the campaign could not push too far without raising questions about the possible sources of its information.

Chapter 11

Back to the County

March 1992 to April 1992

By March 1992, the national component of the campaign was losing importance as the general election became imminent. In February, Steve Johnson, a former North Staffords officer, had invited Levey and Nicholas Budgen MP, also a former North Stafford, to dinner at the Horse Guards Hotel, just off Whitehall in London, to discuss future plans for the campaign. Budgen's advice, to go back to the county, happily coincided with a letter to John Levey from Major Mike Mogridge. Mogridge, who was now living in Sidmouth, Devon, had been a company commander in Berlin in 1969 when Levey was battalion second in command and had retired from the Regiment at thirty-eight and taken up a second career. Mogridge argued that, despite the Campaign Committee's herculean efforts over five months, the MoD had not shifted its stance, and it was difficult to see what more could be achieved without a radical change of tack. The announcement of a general election could not be delayed much longer; in his view, if the Committee failed to exploit that brief window of opportunity the campaign's momentum could be jeopardised. The window was soon flung open by the announcement that the general election would be held on 9 April. Mogridge was deemed to be right and was asked to put his ideas for a regional campaign to the Campaign Committee.

The key to Mogridge's proposal was the axiom that MPs must always be sensitive to the wishes of their constituents, and that the nearer a general election, the more susceptible they become. Similarly, a groundswell of opinion in individual constituencies could goad candidates into extravagant promises of support. Orchestrating such support in all twenty-six constituencies within the Staffords' recruiting area could produce a grouping of up to twenty-six sympathetic MPs in the new Parliament, providing clout that the campaign had previously lacked.

Accepting Mogridge's premise as a basis for immediate action, the Committee noted that the cause needed to be simplified so that everyone could understand it. The Committee adopted a regional theme — the injustice arising from the Regiment's selection for amalgamation when it had met all the published criteria for remaining independent. The MoD had compounded the apparent injustice by refusing to account for the discrepancy, its silence breeding suspicion that something untoward had occurred. Mogridge was co-opted on to the Committee and designated manager of this new campaign phase. Initially, the Committee had anticipated that the election would be called for Thursday 2 April. Planning and preparation therefore had to begin immediately. The announcement of 9 April gave Mogridge and his team a very useful extra seven days.

Mike Mogridge left Sidmouth in late February and was away almost continuously until 11 April, when the intense local campaign was wound up. To raise the level of public awareness from Biddulph in the north to Stourbridge in the south, from Wolverhampton in the west to Burton in the east was a daunting task — but someone had to do it.

Mogridge decided that he had four instruments directly at his disposal:

1 The twelve local branches of the Regimental Association: seven in the county and five in the West Midlands Metropolitan Boroughs
2 The civilian support groups in Stoke-on-Trent and Wolverhampton
3 The Friends of The Staffordshire Regiment
4 Territorial Army members of the 3rd Battalion acting in a private capacity and controlled by Bill Mottram, their second-in-command.

In addition, Mogridge and the team could count on the support of the local media, who were already well disposed to the Regiment for a variety of reasons. These included the Campaign Committee's cultivation of contacts, old friendships, journalists with prior military experience or current service in the 3rd Battalion, and an element of natural sympathy towards the county Regiment, especially after local lads had gone off to fight in Iraq. Nine local radio stations, some twenty-four local newspapers, one regional magazine and two regional television stations (Central Television and BBC Midlands, known as 'Pebble Mill') were available; some were more friendly than others but all had the potential to transmit the message to every corner of the region, and beyond.

Mogridge, who put an enormous amount of effort into pre-planning this local phase of the campaign, foresaw that a secretariat of sorts would be required to manage and coordinate his anticipated campaign network. He sought help from retired officers and warrant officers of the Regiment. His round-robin letter, principally to his contemporaries, elicited a dozen firm offers of assistance on the ground and a large number of good-luck messages (important, he says, for his own morale at the time). Mogridge realised that Regimental Headquarters could not perform this function: it was too isolated; given its everyday duties it was not authorised, or able, to tackle the huge amount of extra administration that would be generated; and, conclusively, it had insufficient civilian telecommunications.

Mogridge stayed with Councillor Ann Johnson throughout the campaign, and her hospitality enabled him to take her advice about where to spend his time most effectively and to benefit from the introductions she gave him. While Mogridge was looking for offices to rent as an HQ in Lichfield, Ann Johnson, John Thompson (chief executive of Lichfield District Council) and Peter Robinson (senior partner of the estate agents George Robinson and Partners) intervened to drop premises into Mogridge's lap. George Robinson were agents for St Martin's, a Kuwaiti-owned property company, which, hearing of the campaigners' search for accommodation, offered them a choice of retail sites in Lichfield, rent-free. For St Martin's this was an opportunity to thank the Staffords for their efforts in the liberation of Kuwait. The campaign gratefully chose the largest and most prominent site, Dudley's furniture shop at 20/21 Baker's Lane.

With the premises secured, much work had to be done and much support had to be counted on to turn it into the control centre Mogridge envisaged. John Levey contacted Wendy Gordon, who had family connections with the Regiment, and asked her to assist Mike Mogridge and the Committee by managing Baker's Lane — designated the Campaign Control Centre (CCC) — during the general election campaign. The launch of CCC was set for 16 March, and the team had its work cut out.

Having found out about the CCC, many people and organisations seemed to drop all else and hurry to help, frequently without recompense. The City of Lichfield, the District and County Councils, British Telecom, Midlands Electricity, Pitney Bowes, Bass, Staffordshire Office Services and a host of local traders all pledged help or support. Wendy Gordon recalls that, as Lichfield is only a small city, people and businesses were only too pleased to help. Viking Office Supplies lent all the office furniture, which filled the large showroom downstairs and the even larger control room above. At one stage, all the chairs were sold from under them, and were immediately replaced with a fresh supply! Before the opening, CCC was cleaned by Dusters and Flusters, while flowers and plants were borrowed from Lichfield District Council for the day.

British Telecom's quick response was vital. Good communications were essential to control such a large area and so many agencies. Wendy Gordon and the Control Room Duty Officers (note the military precision of the terminology) needed their own lines, as did Levey, who was forced to divide his time between the CCC and Westminster with consummate professionalism. The media were allotted a dedicated number, so that they could always get through, and a fax was installed to receive Simon Nayyar's communications from London; subsequently it was also used to issue the many press releases to the hundred or so recipients. Finally, by far and away the most important line was the Freephone, which was intended to allow Mogridge access to a stream of information on the candidates' movements and general feedback from everyone involved in the groundwork of the campaign.

While the CCC was being prepared under the supervision of Wendy Gordon and Major Jim Ellison, Mogridge continued to brief the branches of the Regimental Association. He asked branch secretaries for a Scale A attendance — the military equivalent of a Parliamentary three-line whip. He was never disappointed. There is no substitute, Mogridge observed, for face-to-face briefings. He managed to brief ten of the dozen branches, visited Mrs Cox in Wolverhampton, and met the Committee of the Friends. Each meeting followed the same format: a resume of the campaign so far; a reiteration of the campaign's determination to win; a broad outline of the general election phase; and a discussion of the role of the branch.

The function of branches was to locate the constituency election headquarters of the three principal parties, to obtain details of candidates' itineraries, and to organise branch attendance at meetings or walkabouts involving candidates. On meeting a candidate, a branch representative would invite him or her to state what was to be done about the Regiment's predicament. These meetings were to be non-confrontational and 'non-irritating' to other people in the audience. Any information from these meetings was to be passed to the CCC by the Freephone; if the branch member experienced any difficulty with the meeting, the Freephone could also be used to get help or advice. Old soldiers they might have been, but the branch members, according to Mogridge, 'relished the task and behaved like men half their age'.

Of course, the emphasis may have been on old soldiers, but there were scores of women on hand to help, and Mogridge urged branch members to involve wives, daughters and sisters. Women had votes, and would undoubtedly be 'glad-handed' by passing candidates. There was no reason why they should not also ask questions to put candidates on the spot. Women understood the trick being pulled on the Regiment and joined the campaign in large numbers.

At the Campaign Committee meeting in the Baker's Lane premises on 10 March 1992, just before the local launch, Mogridge set out SOS's general aims during the general election campaign:

> Through the twelve county branches of the Regimental Association to ask Prospective Candidates for Parliament to commit themselves to saving the Regiment using the criteria set down by the Ministry of Defence. This is to be done in a clear but pleasant manner — it is imperative that we are not labelled as a 'Bloody Nuisance'.

The first offer of help came from the five professional football clubs in the area (Wolverhampton Wanderers, Stoke City, Port Vale, Walsall Town and West Bromwich Albion), with an offer of advertising space in their match programmes. As a result of this offer, Mogridge designed the memorable logo of a goalkeeper stretching out to save the regimental badge with the slogan 'The Staffordshire Regiment — Worth Saving'. John Levey was delighted with the design and authorised its use for the entire local phase on posters, leaflets, badges, newspaper advertisements and notepaper — in fact, every form of publicity material.

The launch of the Campaign Control Centre

The launch of the Campaign Control Centre marked the opening of Phase Three of the SOS campaign, which focused on the general election contest as it was fought out in the constituencies of Staffordshire and the West Midlands. The Control Centre opened its doors on 16 March with a media briefing attended by reporters from national and local newspapers, regional television news and local radio. The Chairmen of Staffordshire County Council and of the Metropolitan Boroughs (Dudley, Sandwell, Walsall, Wolverhampton) within the Staffords' recruiting area, together with those of the Freedom Towns, turned out in force. Hospitality for the large gathering was provided by serving and retired regimental wives led by Helen McLean and Irene Ellison.

John Levey introduced Mike Mogridge, his Phase 3 Manager, who explained the theme underlying this phase of the campaign. This was the deceit and secrecy that seemed to surround the Regiment's selection for amalgamation and the strong suspicion, fostered by MoD's continuing silence, that the Regiment was a late substitute for another. This was the first public airing of an argument that everyone would readily grasp and with which candidates in all twenty-six constituencies would soon be bombarded.

John Levey could justifiably be satisfied with the launch. It was a public relations success. Both Central Television and BBC Midlands gave it good coverage, and in local newspapers it occupied many column inches, accompanied by an array of photographs.

Watchman III and Sergeant Bowers were also present to hear John Levey announce the aim of Phase Three. This was to secure an undertaking from each parliamentary candidate that, should they win on 9 April, they would actively campaign to ensure that the amalgamation plans were derailed. Levey introduced his Campaign Support Board — a visual aid enabling the media and visitors to Baker's Lane to keep track of each candidate's performance. The board measured 10 feet by 8 feet and featured a map of the region sectioned into Parliamentary constituencies. Around the edge was listed each candidate's name and address. Beside these were the all-revealing symbols. A green sticker represented pre-election support, a gold star signified that if elected the candidate would actively campaign to retain the Regiment.

The military discipline of the Campaign Committee has already been mentioned. What more salient evidence can be offered of the military minds plotting this offensive than this board, with its potent resemblance to a Headquarters campaign map? There are no records of the effect the board and the CCC had on MoD morale, but one can safely assume that they shook in their foxholes.

The more astute candidates realised the PR potential of the CCC and the Campaign Board for their own campaigns. Many made a pilgrimage to Baker's Lane, accompanied by their own photographer, to have a picture taken in front of the Board, preferably with John Levey or Wendy Gordon — and definitely Watchman — in attendance.

John Levey was systematic in securing candidates' support. An initial letter was despatched between 9 and 11 March, describing the present level of support for the Regiment both in the region and at Westminster, and outlining the reasons for the campaign itself, notably the lack of consultation. With the first letter was sent a copy of *Making the Right Choice*, the SOS submission to the House of Commons Defence Committee. In the last paragraph the letter asked for support and a clear commitment from the candidate. If a response was forthcoming, a second letter was despatched, thanking the candidate for his or her message of support and asking for help in promoting an effective opinion-forming programme at Westminster. Enclosed in the second letter was a questionnaire, devised by the author.

Long-serving members of Parliament, veterans of many election campaigns, are wise in the ways of avoiding commitments demanded in the run-up to an election. This questionnaire, however, made obfuscation or evasion very difficult. Deliberately designed to minimise the likelihood of an equivocal answer, it listed a range of parliamentary devices available to MPs and asked which would be the most effective to deploy on the Regiment's behalf. The options ranged from a Parliamentary Question to a private meeting with the Secretary of State for Defence. Had the questionnaire contained vague or unspecific questions, the answers would have been correspondingly unsubstantial or irrelevant. The questionnaire promised confidentiality for those who completed it.

One candidate (in this case a former MP standing again — MPs lose their status when an election is called, and are merely candidates for the duration) steadfastly refused to respond, not only to this but apparently to all other past and potential future questionnaires, despite repeated requests from the CCC. Another candidate, David Lightbown, MP for Staffordshire South East and a Government Whip until his death in 1995, told his local newspaper, the *Tamworth Herald*:

> I think it is very foolish of the Campaign Committee to do this at this time. ... I am certainly not going to be screwed against the wall by people saying do this or else. ... I have always supported the Staffords and I will continue to do so should they behave responsibly.

Lightbown's attempts to avoid commitment did not last long. Initially, he was one of the third-level MPs (see page 109) who sought to remain independent, but he soon realised that this was impossible in the face of the campaign, which only accepted utter dedication. Staffords' supporters reacted with outrage in the *Herald's* letters' pages. The following is typical:

> He [Lightbown] intimates that he will give support only if they [the SOS campaigners] behave responsibly, as if addressing a classroom of children. The Staffords have always behaved responsibly, eg in Africa, Sicily, Burma, Anzio, Arnhem, the Gulf and N. Ireland, to mention but a few occasions.

> Mr Lightbown goes on to talk of his profound and deep love for the Regiment after having called its campaign committee fools and refusing to commit himself unconditionally to its support.

As a Whip, David Lightbown was certainly not in a position to voice any criticism of Government policy on the amalgamation issue or indeed any other topic. Towards the end of the campaign he paid a fulsome tribute to John Levey, remarking that his 'high intelligence, faith and great personal charm' made him an effective campaigner.

Pressure from the campaigners made candidates either give in out of necessity or genuinely awaken to the intensity of popular feeling about the Regiment's future.

Most candidates were enthusiastic. Some were too enthusiastic; when the questionnaire asked what actions they would be prepared to undertake, some ticked the box offering to initiate a debate in the House of Lords. A thoughtless reply, perhaps, or maybe someone else filled in the form; perhaps some candidates were not fully aware of the limits to an MP's powers! Some candidates simply avoided ticking any affirmative response in an attempt, it seems, to avoid commitment. Unfortunately for them, the campaign was much more single-minded than they were; the replies were meticulously categorised and recorded, and a poor answer did not long escape the campaign's attentions. The dates of outgoing and incoming post were recorded, and promises, or the lack of them, were displayed prominently on the Campaign Support Board. If a candidate made a half-hearted reply, or, for that matter, any reply that the campaign considered less than wholly supportive, it stood out on the Campaign Support Board. Within hours of CCC receiving such a reply, campaigners in the candidate's constituency knew about the lukewarm response and were preparing to challenge the candidate at his or her next public appearance, aided by the constant flow of intelligence about candidates' movements.

If there was no response to the initial letter, a follow-up was sent, explaining that the Committee was aware of the many issues facing the candidate and summarising the arguments for the Staffords once again. Levey concluded that if he received no response to this 'reminder', the candidate did not support the Regiment's retention. Failure to respond was probably not the wisest decision during an election campaign, when a considerable interest group, as well as the weight of local public opinion, lay behind the questionnaire.

Support for the campaign was bipartisan, and there was no question of targeting candidates according to their political party. In any event, the issue of defence policy was remarkably subdued in the general election campaign, notwithstanding sporadic efforts to force it on to the political agenda.

Yet, as might be considered natural in a political campaign, some politics slipped into the mix. On the whole, this was apparent not in cross-party attacks but in internal party considerations. For instance, in marginal constituencies the support of disenchanted Conservative voters could prove crucial to Labour candidates. Equally, less than wholehearted support for the campaign by one or two candidates on the left of the Labour Party could have been decidedly unhelpful to their prospects. Similar considerations were at work within the Conservative Party. Intelligence passed to the CCC by a retired officer indicated a dilemma posed by 'arch Conservatives' who were pressuring Tory candidates to adhere to Government policy at the expense of SOS. One former secretary of a Conservative Association was quoted as saying that he wanted 'nothing more to do' with such right-wingers.

Where candidates were unsympathetic to SOS, the effect of party dilemmas could have been to undermine their own support. Yet the real effect was to pull those on the wings of their parties towards the centre, benefiting the campaign. In many cases candidates and constituency party organisations who knew the importance of the SOS campaign in the election exercised a moderating influence.

The Campaign Control Centre at work

The workload of the CCC was tremendous. Wendy Gordon, the office manager, worked a six-day week, assisted by two paid secretaries from Staffordshire Office Services and a constant stream of volunteer help. She devoted much of her time to the public relations aspect of the CCC, arising in particular from candidates' and press visits. As the media took an increasing interest, so attendance by members of the public swelled.

The showroom had two large windows where photographs and newspaper articles about the Regiment were displayed. There were more inside, together with videos of the Regiment in action; the video players were lent by Bradshaw's. The main attraction, however — the one that pulled the most people into CCC — was Watchman III. During his numerous visits he sat in an armchair, in full view of passers-by, obstinately refusing to parade outside when the weather was poor. There were always ex-serving members around to help, many staying locally with friends while they did their bit for their Regiment. They were also joined by members and wives of the Lichfield Branch of the Royal Naval Old Comrades Association, co-ordinated by Joe Brown, their Secretary, who assisted the old soldiers in their duties — and whose generosity was greatly appreciated.

Wendy Gordon soon realised that the public visiting the CCC, having given tremendous support to the petition six months previously, was now asking for practical ways to work with the campaigners. Three sample letters were placed in the CCC so that the public could come in, choose a letter, sit down at one of the desks and use the outline letter to write to their parliamentary candidates. The CCC staff then sent the letters on their behalf. The first three letters soon had to be augmented — visitors were asking for slightly more sophisticated versions, so the sixth specimen became a very erudite, well-reasoned and lengthy case. Soon there were so many letters that a brown buff envelope was reserved for each candidate, and sealed and mailed at the end of each day. Even this eventually became unworkable, and instead candidates were informed each week how many letters had been collected for them at CCC.

In the meantime, from the upstairs control room, Mike Mogridge continued to orchestrate the campaign throughout the West Midlands and the county. His earlier letter to former members of the Regiment now paid dividends. A stream of retired officers and warrant officers — Captain Pat Baron, Warrant Officer II Nobby Clarke, Major Brendan Donnellan, Major Jim Ellison, Warrant Officer II Bill Harper, Sergeant Phil Kidd, Major David McAllister, Major Jim Massey, Major Gene O'Neill, Major Duncan Reeves, Warrant Officer I Pete Settle and Major Paul Whelpton — gave a few hours or a few days to the cause. Some 100,000 publicity items were despatched in a three-week period to the twenty-six constituencies, mainly to branch secretaries or to the Friends for display locally; to library services; to schools; and to local free newspapers to be taken round by delivery boys and girls. The 'old and bold' rolled their sleeves up and got on with a complicated and demanding motorcycle despatch system.

As watchkeepers, the volunteers also had to assist with the press and public. They were well briefed by Simon Nayyar on the lines to take with the media and the public throughout the campaign. He produced an easily digestible sheet — known as a 'Q & A' in PR and advertising circles — suggesting answers to the most common questions about consultation, rationale for amalgamation and support for the Staffords, as well as more detailed information to give if questioners pushed. This meant that anyone helping at CCC, whether on the telephones or in the showroom, knew exactly where the campaigners and the Regiment stood on the issues, and that the clarity and consistency of arguments were maintained. The supply of reliable watchkeepers allowed Mogridge to get out on to the ground to broaden the Regiment's support base still further. And broaden it he did.

For many years there was a strong affinity between The South and North Staffordshire Regiments and the local mining communities. In Phase Three, Mogridge received generous personal help from Joe Wills, Secretary of the National Union of Mineworkers (Midlands). His request to members and retired members produced another surge of letters to candidates, principally in Stoke, Newcastle-under-Lyme and Cannock. Partly to help the candidates deal with this surge, Levey gave a private briefing to four Labour candidates, Llin Golding, Joan Walley, Mark Fisher and George Stevenson, at the North Stafford Hotel in Stoke. The meeting was also attended by Councillor Les Sillitoe and members of the Stoke Support Group.

Similarly, through the efforts of Vera Houldcroft, its chairman, and Sheila Slaney, the general secretary, the Staffordshire Federation of Women's Institutes, although by its Charter unable to support the Campaign corporately, encouraged individual members throughout the County to take whatever action with candidates they thought necessary. This led to another surge of letters.

Another piece of good fortune came via Stan Clarke CBE, the chairman of Uttoxeter Race Course. He invited the campaign to use the Spring Meeting as a publicity platform, and endorsed the campaign in his personal message of welcome on the race card. With further assistance from Major David McAllister a special advertisement was included in the race card, and a few thousand leaflets were distributed during the day. Some 10,000 race-goers went to the Meeting, giving it considerable publicity potential, so the assistance was most gratefully received.

Phase Three — the final few days

In early April, with polling day looming, it was clear that the grass roots campaign had begun to generate its own momentum. Letter-writing by the public under Wendy Gordon's direction at the CCC; the broadening of the campaign's regional base of support; the activities of Regimental Association branches, the Friends and support groups at candidates' public meetings and appearances; the wide-

Watchman III, the 3rd Battalion mascot and, for the duration, the SOS campaign mascot. *(Sally Ann Thompson Animal Photos)*

Sergeant Bowers with Watchman prepares to lead the Scots Campaign Parade in Edinburgh on 11 December 1992. *(Scotsman)*

(Left) 1st Staffords march past Lichfield Guildhall on 9 September 1991 in celebration of the Regiment's part in the Gulf War victory. At this time – less than 2 months after the amalgamation announcement – it was feared that this march might be the Regiment's last in Lichfield. *(Stafford Knot)*

(Below) 'Save Our Staffords' Committee members at the official campaign launch at The King's Head, Lichfield, on 9 September 1991, the very pub where the Regiment was founded in 1705. John Levey, the Campaign's central personality, sits behind the microphone. *(Staffordshire Sentinel Newspapers Ltd)*

'Save Our Staffords' Committee (left to right) Major Mac McLean (Secretary), Colonel Tony Griffiths, Brigadier John Levey (Chairman), Colonel Jimmy Baines, Lieutenant Colonel Doug Bridges, Brigadier Sir Louis Hargroves. Inserts (left) Major Mike Mogridge, (right) Colonel Walter James. *(Sandy Willmore)*

Regimental Association Members presenting the 100,000 signatures at the Houses of Parliament on 14 October 1991 in the company of supporting MPs Patrick Cormack, Bill Cash and Bruce George. *(Stafford Knot)*

Regimental Museum

Sergeant Bowers, Watchman and Supporters.

Brigadier John Levey addresses Staffordshire and West Midlands VIPs at the launch of the County Campaign in Lichfield on 9 April 1992. *(Stafford Knot)*

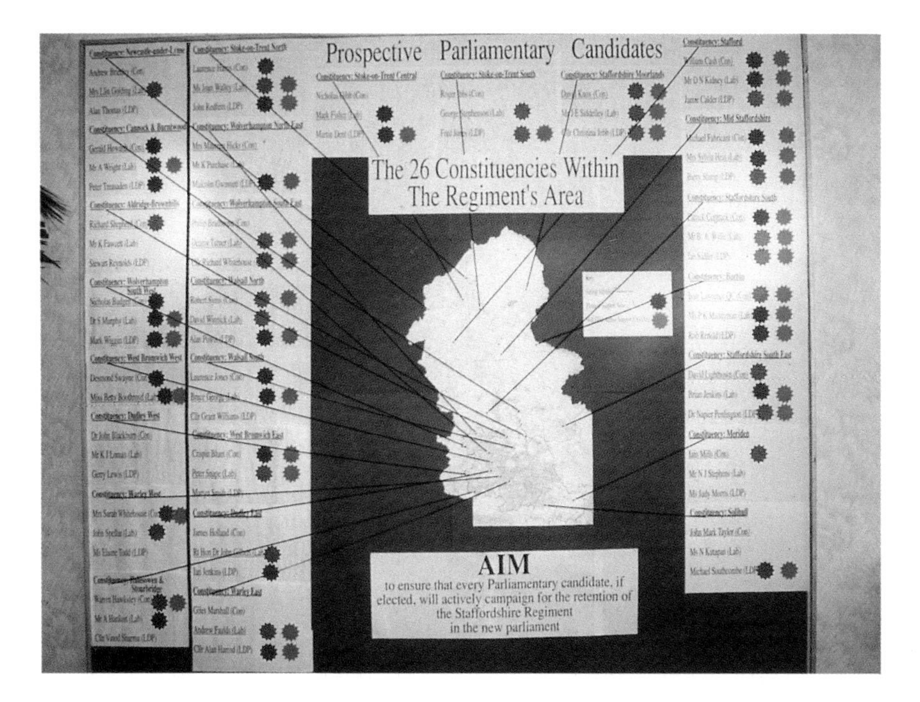

The Campaign Support Board at the Lichfield Campaign Control Centre. The Board displayed the pledges of support for the Regiment given by candidates in the 1992 general election. *(Stafford Knot)*

Councillor Ann Johnson, Mayor of Lichfield 1992-1993 and a staunch Staffords' supporter, and members of the 1st Battalion celebrate the publication of *Rats' Tales*, Nicholas Benson's book about the Staffords' Gulf War exploits. The launch was held on 9 February 1991, just six days after the Regiment's reprieve. *(Stafford Knot)*

Campaign logo used in newspapers and football programmes.

The postal franking stamp used by Lichfield District Council and the Campaign Control Centre.

Campaign Badge.

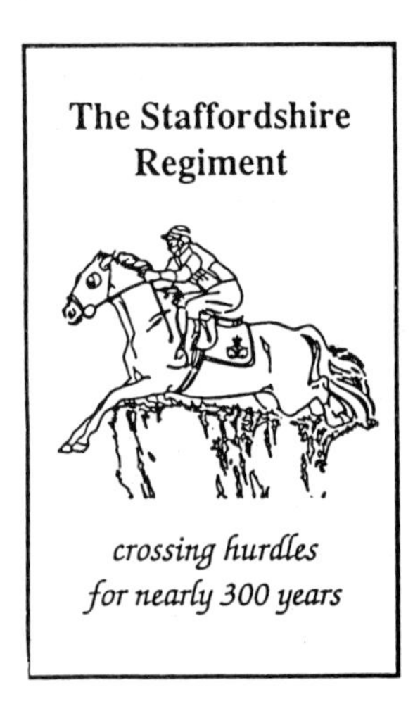

The design used by Uttoxeter Race Course.

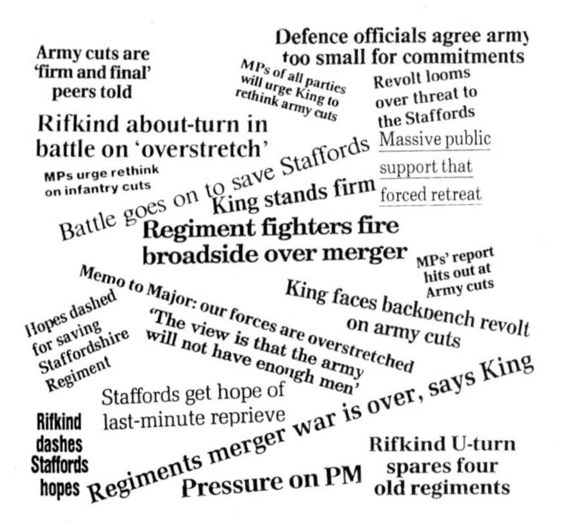

Just a few of the many hundreds of newspaper and magazine headlines generated by the campaign.

Left to Right: John Levey, Mrs Janette Cox, Major General Ian Freer, Sergeant Malcolm Bowers, Watchman III and Bruce George MP at Walsall Town Hall on 29 April 1993. *(Birmingham Post and Mail)*

"QM says to tell you it's all off . . . and no need to start on the new signs!"

This advertisement and the one shown overleaf were used as part of the Regiment's efforts to put right the under-manning caused by the threat of amalgamation. Fortunately the position has recovered after much hard work by all concerned.

Stoke on Trent
36/38 Old Hall Street
Hanley
ST1 3AP
Tel: 0782 212070/281780
Burton on Trent
181 Station Street
Burton
DE14 1BN
Tel: 0283 68172
1st BATTALION THE STAFFORDSHIRE REGIMENT
(The Prince of Wales's)
CONTACT YOUR LOCAL ARMY CAREERS
& INFORMATION OFFICE
During out office hours please leave your message
on Stoke on Trent - 0782-212070
JOIN
YOUR COUNTY REGIMENT
Wolverhampton
43a Queens Street
Wolverhampton
WV1 3BL
Tel: 0902 23892/20340
Birmingham
46 The Pallasades
Birmingham
B2 4XN
Tel: 021 633 4963
IT IS RECRUITING MEN LIKE YOU NOW!!

spread distribution of posters, leaflets, stickers and badges; and a sympathetic and enthusiastic media — all had mobilised constituents who, in turn, applied intense pressure on candidates.

The author can readily attest to these pressures. Alan Griffin, secretary of the Walsall and Bloxwich branch of the Regimental Association, ruthlessly pursued the candidates in his constituency — one in particular; and he kept steady telephone pressure on Smith Square and Walworth Road, the national HQs of the two main parties. The clout that individuals could wield is illustrated by Norman Champ, a 28-year veteran of the North Staffords, who, having received a 'weak reply' from his candidate (the former MP), wrote to his local newspaper. The number of people who undertook this kind of action made the campaign devastatingly powerful. In none of the twenty-six constituencies was the campaign's case unknown, and it would have been a particularly thick-skinned candidate who claimed ignorance of the Regiment's plight.

Some candidates, taken up with matters seemingly more profound, reacted irritably to the relentless campaigning, and a few telephoned complaints to the CCC. Gerald Howarth, standing again for the Conservatives in Cannock and Burntwood, telephoned to say that letters generated by visitors to the CCC and sent to candidates would be counter-productive. Levey had to point out that letters were unsolicited and that the public was keen to let its views be known to parliamentary candidates. A candidate in the same constituency approached a front door. Before he could knock, it flew open; an irate elderly woman appeared, wagging her finger in his face and saying: 'I'm not voting for you until you've done something about the Regiment!' The door promptly slammed shut before he could utter a word. John Levey dealt with the candidate's subsequent complaint that the campaign was over-zealous by pointing out that the momentum the campaign had created was seemingly self-generating. It was, Levey suggested, obvious that many other voters felt as strongly, and it was also perfectly obvious what the candidate was expected to do.

The final offensive was to co-ordinate telephone calls to Conservative Central Office and Labour Party Headquarters in London. All the Regimental Association branches took part, and the aim of a hundred calls to each HQ was probably achieved. Until the last days, individuals also found opportunities to press home the case. When Tom King appeared on the very popular Ed Doolan show on BBC Radio WM (the West Midlands regional station) a week before polling day, Westminster Communications alerted CCC to this publicity opportunity. Jeanette Cox of the Wolverhampton Support Group submitted a question in advance, ensuring that King's day in the Midlands became a reminder of the Staffords' campaign.

In the end, the general election results rewarded the persistence of the local campaigners. Of the twenty-six MPs elected from the region, twenty-three had pledged their support for the Staffords' fight for survival. Phase Three had been an immense success, yet as Wendy Gordon recalls there was a feeling of deflation as CCC closed down on 10 April, its job complete. Mogridge wrote a final letter to the branches of the Regimental Association, the Friends, the Support Groups and the TA thanking them for their support, persistence and ingenuity. He asked for further 'gentle pressure'. Now that the new MPs were known, campaigners were advised to maintain momentum by organising rosters for visits to their surgeries, to continue pressing the Regiment's case. This, at least, would ensure that MPs would not forget that the fight for the county Regiment was not over. Throughout the first three months of the new session, and on into the summer recess, MPs were reminded of their promises to the Campaign Committee during the campaign, and returned to London with the issue in the forefront of their minds.

This had truly been a People's Cause — 'democracy at work', as one campaigner put it. The Campaign Committee and Mike Mogridge deserve accolades for their perceptiveness, recognising the opportunity and grasping it with vigour, securing victory when it was so badly needed. However, they would agree that it was the foot soldiers of the campaign who made it all possible: the branches of the Regimental Association and the Friends, the Support Groups, individuals from the TA and from the WI, and countless other groups and individuals who had some personal connection with the Regiment or who simply knew its worth. Their concerted efforts were vindicated by the MPs' campaign promises, and particularly by messages such as that from one MP who had, it seems, previously been ignorant of the SOS campaign:

> It has been brought to my notice that the Regiment's problem is a matter of great importance to a significant number of my constituents. Rest assured, I will do all I can to assist the Campaign because that is what my constituents expect of me.

No matter what MPs' personal views might be, on this issue they were forced to drop campaign rhetoric and put their money where their mouths were. Of course, some would be less vocal and less supportive than others, but it would be a foolhardy MP who would go back on his or her commitment. This groundswell of public opinion, directed through Parliament, was to give the Government real headaches in the months to come.

Chapter 12

Battle Rejoined at Westminster

April 1992 to September 1992

On 10 April 1992, the day after polling day, the fatigued campaigners felt more than satisfied that their intensive and sophisticated campaigning had won such extensive support from the newly-returned MPs, both fresh faces and old hands. None the less, Save Our Staffords was soberly aware that, although they had won an important battle, they certainly had not won the war. The campaign now returned, with a fresh mandate and renewed strength, to Westminster; the Committee rightly decided that pump-priming in the county should continue, under Mogridge's able direction, but at a lower intensity.

During the general election campaign, Simon Nayyar had been seconded from Westminster Communications to work at Conservative Central Office as a media relations adviser to Ministers. He had also kept in close touch with Levey to offer advice on how best to position SOS with candidates reluctant to offer fulsome support; to alert him to important issues; and to identify further opportunities for profile-raising or opinion-forming. So great was the paranoia of Defence Ministers about SOS that, on the instructions of Ministers, Nayyar was asked to take twenty-four hours' leave from Central Office when the Party devoted one day's campaigning to defence and foreign affairs. Even within Central Office, there was much mirth at this latest example of the absurd lengths to which Ministers were prepared to go to ensure that they got their way.

The Hamilton-Levey dialogue

The first thing that Levey and Nayyar agreed to do was to pick up the correspondence in which Levey had been engaged for several months with Archie Hamilton, Minister of State for the Armed Forces. The correspondence had begun on 30 January 1992 when Levey, in his capacity as Chairman of the Campaign Committee, wrote to Hamilton, setting out the Regiment's case; requesting a meeting with the Minister; and enclosing a copy of *Making The Right Choice*.

On 12 February — an unusually swift response from a department of state — Levey received a closely argued, evasive and extremely lengthy letter, signed by Hamilton himself. It must be remembered that in the interim Hamilton and his colleague the Earl of Arran had run the gauntlet of many unhappy Conservative MPs and Peers, whose hostility to the decisions on amalgamations had become clear during

Bill Cash's Adjournment Debate and the Earl of Shrewsbury's debate on the Infantry. Hamilton's personal response should be seen in this light. The Minister prefaced his response with a gracious compliment to the 'professional presentation' of the campaigners. Thereafter, he embarked on a policy defence that had very little to do with the plight of the Regiment and a great deal to do with reaffirming the fundamental tenets of the *Options for Change* decision-making process.

Hamilton wrote that 'the Staffordshire Regiment has itself been consistently under strength for a number of years.' This charge particularly angered SOS, and Levey would soon return to the issue. Hamilton ended on a depressing note:

> I have been pressed on numerous occasions to embark on explanations of judgements as they affect individual regiments, including how and why they were made. But the Army Board have concluded that to do so would be divisive, painful and altogether unproductive, and I concur with this view. While I recognise the work that has gone into your campaign I do not see that a meeting to discuss it further would be constructive.

Here was the crux of the problem so tellingly demonstrated during Bill Cash's Adjournment Debate. Archie Hamilton was seeking to put the onus of the decision-making on to the Army Board, without acknowledging that Ministers and officials were a major part of it, and that officials, by precedent and practice, always voted with Ministers. In other words, it was a political decision not to discuss the rationale behind particular amalgamations.

Twelve days later, on 24 February, with an election now seeming imminent, Levey replied to Hamilton's defence of the impact of *Options* on the Staffords:

> You state that: 'the Staffords' wish to avoid amalgamation was fully taken into account.' I am afraid that this causes me some dismay. For the Colonel of the Regiment was never able to put The Staffordshire Regiment's case against amalgamation to the Army Board. We would, of course, be happy to drop this particular issue, were we to receive a categorical assurance from you that the Army Board did see the Colonel of the Regiment's submission. Surely the best way of discovering the true position on this would be for you to request that the submission be given to you by your officials?
>
> Secondly, you say that 'The Staffordshire Regiment has itself

> been consistently under strength for a number of years.' But the Regiment will be up to strength when it begins its tour of duty in Northern Ireland, in May [1992]. As for its past record, as you know, few Infantry regiments have, in the recent past, been up to establishment strength; the Staffords have, however, been consistently better recruited than most Infantry regiments, and by a significant margin.

On 10 March, the day that John Major announced the election, Hamilton fired back a short reply that contained a very significant admission, the first that SOS had succeeded in extracting from Ministers. Hamilton grudgingly conceded that, 'the Staffords have recruited at a level above the average for the units in the Prince of Wales Division.' Levey, Nayyar and their colleagues were amazed by this admission. Hamilton was now accepting that the Staffords had met one of the Army Board's key determinants that ostensibly underpinned the selection of regimental amalgamations. Moreover, in doing so Hamilton had accidentally granted the campaigners what he had been unwilling to entertain in Parliament, namely discussion of the amalgamation criteria. Hamilton also took this opportunity to point out that the Battalion was now up to strength only because it had moved from an armoured infantry battalion role to that of a Type B battalion based in the United Kingdom, which involved a reduction in establishment of over 100 men.

Now the general election intervened. Soon after the Conservatives had won their fourth consecutive victory, Levey, who like Hamilton had been out on the campaign trail, took up the cudgels once more. On 21 April, Levey suggested to Hamilton that, if any doubt continued about whether the Staffords' case had been put to the Army Board, 'you ask your officials for the Colonel of the Regiment's submission [to the Army Board] to be given you'. The campaigners were of course confident that this was impossible, because no such submission existed.

The second issue was so fundamental that it threw the entire *Options for Change* decision-making process into question. Indeed, it is no exaggeration to say that the 21 April letter proved to be a watershed in the history of the Save Our Staffords campaign. In an earlier letter of 24 February to Bill Cash, Hamilton had provided projections on undermanning in the 1st Battalion between February and May 1992. These appeared to show that undermanning would worsen by as much as 1.5 per cent during this period. This was in clear conflict with the

Regiment's own projections on future manning levels, direct from the Manning and Record Office; these showed that, far from deteriorating, manning levels were likely to improve dramatically, and rise by 3.38 per cent to just 0.85 per cent below establishment. Levey hurled these projections back at Hamilton, adding that, 'I am, therefore, at a loss to understand how your officials could have arrived at so fundamentally different an assessment.' If MoD's data, on which important strategic decisions were reached, could be so out of date, there was no reason to believe that its data on any of the Army Board's other criteria would be more accurate.

Levey went on to remind Hamilton that twenty-three local MPs had offered the Regiment 'explicit support', and concluded:

> The decision to amalgamate The Staffordshire Regiment is wrong. I am clear that the Secretary of State is aware of the issues as they affect the Infantry because of the concerns of his own constituents, and the dialogue in which they have engaged with him over many months.

This last sentence alluded to the fact that Malcolm Rifkind, the new Defence Secretary and MP for Edinburgh, Pentlands, had been lobbied hard during the preceding months by supporters of his local — and the oldest — regiment of the line, The Royal Scots. (With a meticulousness worthy of the Civil Service, Keep Our Scottish Battalions had copied to SOS all the correspondence between Rifkind and The Royal Scots.)

By now it was clear that the Ministry of Defence had no intention of conceding any further information that might be used to heighten Ministers' discomfort. Indeed, Ministers had nothing to gain and everything to lose by prolonging the dialogue with the campaigners. Under Levey's and Nayyar's tutelage, Save Our Staffords had become a finely calibrated and extremely effective campaigning machine, able to identify errors and omissions in Ministers' briefings and draw them to the attention of the defence media community, most of whom the campaigners now knew well. Thus it was that, on 6 May 1992, Hamilton returned a terse letter to John Levey, noting Levey's comments about the lack of consultation but repeating that 'it remains the view of the Army Board that it would be damaging to the Army as a whole to go into details about how individual decisions were made.' With dramatic finality, he concluded: 'I am sure it would not be in the wider interests of the Army to re-open the decisions taken last year.'

The campaigners were by no means disheartened by this letter — they had not been expecting Ministers suddenly to cave in, and Simon Nayyar and the author had advised Levey all along that if the Regiment were to win it would be the result of a progressive campaign rather than because of a single dramatic event. The regimental campaigners of Keep Our Scottish Battalions, and many defence media specialists, had exuberantly welcomed Malcolm Rifkind's appointment as Secretary of State in succession to Tom King. During the Kincardine and Deeside by-election campaign in November 1991 (see page 134), Rifkind had appeared to support a re-assessment of the amalgamation of The Queen's Own Highlanders with The Gordon Highlanders. It seemed to some that Rifkind's appointment would lead — and, perhaps, was even intended by the Prime Minister to lead — to a reassessment of the *Options for Change* reductions. Levey and Nayyar regarded this as ill-judged speculation and a distraction from the work in hand: neither was convinced of the likelihood of an imminent further review. Both fully recognised the financial constraints under which the Ministry of Defence was operating, and were also aware of rumours circulating in Whitehall that, far from reprieves, the MoD was already sniffing around to see what further departmental savings it could make.

Nevertheless, the style of the Secretary of State was different from that of his predecessor. Initially, many people were unsure what to expect from Rifkind, although few thought that his tenure would be worse than the posturing and evasion of the MoD under Tom King. A welcome change of attitude soon appeared and, although there was little public acknowledgment that *Options* needed a second look, a few encouraging signs were given privately.

A minor illustration of Rifkind's different temperament was his attitude towards a meeting with Sir John MacMillan and several Scottish MPs on 17 December 1992, also attended by Archie Hamilton. According to MacMillan, just before the meeting broke up Rifkind stated that, although there were prospects of improvement in the strategic situation, he would nevertheless ask his officials several questions as a result of that day's discussions. Neither Tom King nor Archie Hamilton would have been prepared to offer this. This more courteous and seemingly more flexible attitude encouraged both the Staffords and Scots campaigners to fight on, even if official MoD statements continued to leave little room for hope.

Through their unstinting efforts in the preceding six months, Levey and Nayyar had placed The Staffordshire Regiment four-square on the political agenda, whether Ministers liked it or not. The campaign organisation had by now established a reputation with the regional and national media for speaking with authority, cogency and conviction. Having achieved this powerful public profile, the campaign could now afford to spend time polishing the arguments it would deploy in the coming months to its key political audiences. Levey and Nayyar now put together a programme of carefully co-ordinated and sustained lobbying of key political influencers who would be likely to carry weight with Ministers and their closest advisers. They were assisted in one subtle, but peculiarly important respect: the recent general election had slashed the Government's majority over all other parties from eighty-nine to just twenty-one. The Government was now obliged to pay heed to all its backbenchers all the time, in a way that had not been necessary before the election.

Driving the campaign forward

It is easy to view the period from April 1992 until January 1993 as one of limited SOS activity, and indeed Ian Freer described the summer months as 'the doldrums'. It is true that there were not the same opportunities to capture the kind of national publicity that had characterised the earlier stages of the campaign. There were no significant photo-opportunities, because there were no high-profile events, such as the earlier petition delivery. By and large the post-election phase of the campaign was conducted much more discreetly than the previous phases. Continuous and concentrated streams of correspondence, private meetings, further rigorous activity by the Select Committee, and Parliamentary Questions (rather than full-scale debates) kept the campaign surging ahead but remote from the public eye. The deceptive appearance was of a campaign that had thrown its all into the previous high-intensity, high-profile phases and whose vitality was now spent. The reality was altogether different: the campaigners' concerns were becoming well known and understood in Whitehall and Westminster, even by those who tried hard not to listen. This was entirely the result of the superior battle tactics the campaigners employed to prosecute their war against MoD Ministers.

John Levey and Simon Nayyar continued their meetings with crucial political advisers to Ministers, Conservative Party policy officers and a raft of leading defence and Lobby correspondents including Phil Johnston of the *Daily Telegraph*, John Keegan and Christy Campbell, defence editors of the *Daily Telegraph* and the *Sunday Telegraph*, and Michael White, the political editor of the

Guardian. Simon Nayyar's meeting with Michael White serves as a reminder of just how incestuous and parochial a community Westminster is: of all the restaurants in London where they might have dined, they inevitably found themselves in Green's — seated at the very next table to Archie Hamilton. Needless to say, Nayyar spent the evening talking in whispers.

There continued to be two core strategic objectives. First, SOS had to make the Infantry overstretch case so compellingly at Westminster that political pressure on Ministers to look again at overall numbers would become irresistible. The second objective, flowing from the first, was to ensure that, when global figures were reappraised, The Staffordshire Regiment's credentials for reprieve were so unarguable and widely recognised, that it, and not some other regiment, would win through.

There was a sub-text to these core objectives. From the outset, the Scottish regimental campaigners could — and did — exploit the peculiarly Celtic characteristics of their case, the so-called 'Tartan factor'. This was a politically powerful dynamic, with seventy-two Scottish MPs to be strong-armed into offering their support. Equally, concern within the Conservative Party, and particularly at Number 10, about protecting the Union ensured that the Scottish campaigners would receive a hearing at Westminster, whatever the quality of their case (although, it must be said, its quality was always very high). To many English MPs, the Staffords were just another worthy English county regiment. So it was essential that the campaigners, first, created a belief throughout Westminster that it would be politically unacceptable to set aside a regimental amalgamation in Scotland without doing the same in England. Only after this had been achieved could the Staffords be positioned as most worthy of a reprieve. Indeed, only in this way could the Staffords create a situation in which their case would be heard at all.

The messages that Levey and Nayyar used to influence political opinion were constantly remodelled. Nayyar minutely analysed every meeting, every conversation, every letter and noted subtle shifts in the individual policy positions of key targets. They took inordinate care to burnish the campaign's image and to manage this single-issue cause in a way that maximised its impact. The campaigners used agreed forms of words to deliver their messages as effectively and persuasively as possible. For example, they made a point of always referring to 'the proposed amalgamation', as though the Ministry of Defence had still not absolutely made up its mind; gradually, this form of words gained currency throughout Westminster and, in time, politicians and journalists only ever talked about 'the proposed amalgamation'.

Another good example of how Nayyar and Levey carefully tailored their messages to suit their recipients' concerns came shortly after the general election. Nayyar decided to cost the reprieve of the 1st Battalion. He had realised that, if politicians were to be won over to the cause in the tight fiscal climate of the early 1990s, they needed to know just how much public money was at stake. Quick calculations were made, and it became clear that the 1st Battalion cost the taxpayer a maximum of £15 million a year. Nayyar then went out into Westminster and Whitehall, wryly observing to anyone who would listen that 600 infantrymen's jobs could be protected at the cost of just one RAF Tornado. Nayyar and Levey knew, of course, that the RAF had come out of the *Options* review relatively unscathed, and that seasoned Services observers had considerably less sympathy for the Air Force than for the Army. (Subsequently, and perhaps not coincidentally, the RAF found itself bearing the brunt of personnel reductions in the Front Line First review that Malcolm Rifkind announced to Parliament on 21 July 1994.) More than that, the prospect of retaining 600 highly skilled soldiers, with their uniquely flexible and mobile operational capabilities, at the cost of a single fighter aircraft was guaranteed to find favour in many political quarters.

Parliamentary Pressure Grows

Even before the SOS campaigners got underway at Westminster after the general election, Professor Sir Michael Howard, the eminent military historian and Emeritus Professor of Modern History at Oxford, fired a shot across their bows. In a *Times* article on 24 April, he scornfully claimed that it was only 'retired officers with golden memories' who 'clamour for the retention of ancient regiments'. In one sense, it was flattering that such a famous military historian should take time out to cast aspersions on the motivations of the Staffords and Scots campaigns. It showed, too, how the campaigns were disturbing the professional military *cognoscenti*, who arrogantly supposed that they had a monopoly on military wisdom. Nayyar was adamant that the Staffords should respond at once. Not only was the charge unfair, but — given that it came from a well-respected military historian and had appeared in a prestigious newspaper — key political opinion-formers and decision-makers would read it; if no repudiation were forthcoming from the Staffords, it would be assumed to be true.

Levey's reply, which *The Times* published several days later, prominently positioned under the title 'Soldiering on', contained a point-by-point rebuttal of Howard's article. Levey drew attention to the effect of overstretch and shortened tour gaps on soldiers and their families. He regretted Howard's view and retorted:

> We, and those others who are campaigning to achieve a review of the rationale for the proposed regimental amalgamations, have always framed our respective cases in a serious and substantive way. We have not been, nor would we ever be, a party to seeking a reprieve by dwelling upon maudlin and wholly irrelevant appeals to emotion.

Levey concluded his letter on a cautionary note: 'too much is being asked of today's Infantry soldier, and ... he is, as always, being taken for granted for reasons of political expediency.' Over the next weeks, it became clear that politicians had read it. As a direct result of the letter, the Conservative Peer Lord Wedgwood wrote to John Levey offering to help. A meeting was arranged and Wedgwood at once agreed to take up the Regiment's case in the House of Lords.

It was at about this time that Archie Hamilton brought his correspondence with Levey to a peremptory close. But intelligence from other sources confirmed the need to continue the political dialogue and not to place particular reliance on military lobbying of the Ministry of Defence. For example, Colonel Hugh Willmore, a Stafford working at the MoD, was warned during spring 1992 by a bellicose senior staff officer (who had been intimately involved in constructing *Options for Change*): 'The Staffords haven't a chance of being saved. The plan will not change. You're wasting your time.' This sort of moral intimidation had, of course, precisely the opposite effect to that intended. Far from frightening the Staffords into submission, it strengthened their resolve and helped them to formulate their strategy. While it would help to establish a watertight military rationale for retaining the Regiment, the military case for retention would have to seep slowly into the MoD's calculations and consciousness through continuous and careful positioning. The most important people to lobby were not resentful senior officers from other regiments, Arms or Services, but Ministers who needed to be constantly bombarded with reminders of the political unacceptability of amalgamation.

The two strands would combine into an irrefutable case at the point at which military and politicians meet — at the level of the Defence Council, which includes the Army Board. Here the Army would be able to highlight its overstretch problem and the relative leniency of the cuts in the RAF, in this way permitting Ministers to consider the Scottish regiments-English regiments question. If this 'pincer' movement worked to plan, Ministers and Service chiefs would be unable to deny the logical necessity of restoring at least two Infantry battalions. The question then would be whether to reclaim the additional costs from other Arms or Services, or to reduce the savings flowing from *Options for Change*.

On 7 May, an indisputable authority on defence policy unexpectedly came to the aid of the campaigners and gave them fresh heart. Lord Bramall, stalwart of earlier Lords debates, spoke on the Infantry during the Lords' Debate on the Address on 7 May 1992, stating that:

> There is now scarcely an informed observer who does not believe that without an injection of between 3,000 and 5,000 extra men the Army will not be able even to carry out its day-to-day commitments without intolerable overstretch.

He also wrote to the press. In a later letter, which appeared in the *Daily Telegraph* on 23 December 1992, he argued:

> *Options for Change* has been shown to have serious 'fault lines' in it, and the Army's manpower ceiling is now manifestly inadequate and unworkable. ... Mr Major can now appreciate for himself that any further extension of operations [in Bosnia] must be based on military reality on the ground, and on what can actually be done to improve the situation. It should not be influenced unduly by what is financially convenient and would fit in with the over-optimistic paper plans drawn up more than three years ago, when the world scene looked very different.

Field Marshal Lord Bramall played a hugely important role in the parliamentary part of the campaign. He was not allied to any one campaign, but his deep specialist knowledge, gained from a career's experience (much of it in the Royal Green Jackets), culminating in three years as Chief of Defence Staff, placed him in a uniquely well informed position from which to comment on the military implications of political decision-making. He used this position to challenge the Government relentlessly over its plans for the Infantry. The MoD might try to fob off the campaigners with half-baked self-justification and occasional 'red herrings', but the Government could not easily deny the authority of experts of Lord Bramall's stature.

Lord Wedgwood, who together with his fellow-Peer Lord Shrewsbury deserves much respect for his work for the campaign, tabled a Starred Question (the Lords' equivalent of a Commons Oral Question) on the Army, asking the Government 'Whether they are reconsidering *Options for Change* and their plans for the future strength of the Army'. Answering for the Government, Viscount Cranborne, the Under-Secretary for Defence, told their Lordships that Malcolm Rifkind was keeping firmly in mind the requirement 'that future force levels are appropriate to the demands placed on the armed forces'. This answer sounded more flexible than the oft-repeated statements in the King era which said that what was done, was done; on the other hand, it also sounded non-committal. In the short discussion that followed the Question, all the Infantry's standard-bearers in the Lords were present, including Lord Bramall.

Immediately after the election, Levey, polite to a fault and never one to miss a trick to position SOS favourably with local MPs, fired off letters of congratulation to each newly elected MP. This simple act, and many other similar gestures during the campaign, raised the Regiment's stock with MPs, and underlined the sheer professionalism of the campaigners.

It seemed appropriate that the first MP to take up the cudgels in the new Parliament was Bill Cash, given that his Adjournment Debate had been one of the final and most memorable Parliamentary assaults before the election. On 15 May, following approaches from Levey and Nayyar, Cash sent Malcolm Rifkind a three-page letter about the plight of the Regiment. In this definitive exposition of the case, Cash addressed exhaustively all the areas of concern that he, other MPs, the Regiment, its supporters and its advisers identified about the proposals for amalgamation. He tackled the issues in three parts: consultation, the Army Board's own criteria, and the public position of Ministers.

Cash reminded Rifkind that Archie Hamilton had, 'despite repeated requests to do so', failed to produce any evidence that the Colonel of the Regiment's case against amalgamation had been considered by the Army Board. He repeated the Staffords' competitive position on demography, present manning patterns and appropriate regional representation. He reminded Rifkind that Ministers had been trying to play it both ways: on the one hand, they had 'implied that campaigners have, knowingly, used incomplete or inaccurate material to achieve a reprieve', and, on the other, they had refused to discuss the arrangement, deployment, or weight attaching to the Army Board's individual determinants. He drew attention to the 100,000-signature petition to Parliament; his own widely-reported Adjournment debate; the Earl of Shrewsbury's Unstarred Question, in which, he observed, 'none of the Peers on the Government benches sought to support the government's position on the proposed amalgamation'; and Lord Bramall's most recent remarks in the Lords. Finally, he highlighted the fact that pledges of support for a review of the amalgamation had been elicited from twenty-three MPs from Staffordshire and the West Midlands and sixteen from Cheshire (including Ministers). He concluded:

> What we are seeking is the most marginal re-evaluation, in the light of significantly changed geopolitical circumstances, of the global figure for the Infantry and, within that, of the validity of the decision to amalgamate the Staffords. The military value of a re-appraisal far outweighs the minimal capital costs involved in their retention. *Options for Change* is largely right; it is only in the margins that the balance needs to be re-defined. To review the rationale for the proposed amalgamation of The Staffordshire Regiment and The Cheshire Regiment would go a long way toward restoring regional confidence in our willingness to listen to the electorate.

Within days, Malcolm Rifkind had agreed to meet Staffordshire MPs. The date of the meeting was fixed for 4 June 1992. It would take place in the Secretary of State's own office in the Ministry of Defence Main Building in Whitehall.

Dialogue with the Defence Secretary

Two days before this meeting, Malcolm Rifkind and his ministerial team ran a gauntlet of hostile Questions about the Infantry reductions and the regimental amalgamations at the monthly Commons Defence Question Time. Archy Kirkwood, a Scottish Liberal Democrat MP, asked Rifkind when the Government intended to respond to the Defence Select Committee's third report on *Options for Change*, in particular, in relation to the Infantry. Kirkwood and others, including Bill Walker, a Scottish Conservative MP, followed this up by reminding Rifkind of the views he had expressed during the Kincardine and Deeside by-election, when 'he wrote a letter expressing his hope at that stage that some of the proposed amalgamations for the Scottish regiments could be reconsidered'. In a significant departure from everything that Defence Ministers had said until then, Rifkind replied that, 'if the Government ever came to the view that force levels needed to be reviewed that is what they would do.' The sentence was lost in a longer statement about the wider strategic environment. But this important change in tone and substance did not escape Save Our Staffords. It was now clear that the door was ajar. The question was whether it could be flung wide open in the time before the amalgamation was due to take place. Ann Winterton immediately made a direct appeal to Rifkind on behalf of the Cheshires. Would Rifkind consider 'the excellent case for the retention, as a single county regiment, of The Cheshire Regiment, which is well-recruited and well-retained'? Rifkind dodged the Question. In a sense, this was irrelevant. The SOS campaigners had achieved a vitally important objective: a pillar of the temple — or rather, of the Ministry of Defence — was beginning to crumble before their eyes.

The scene was now set for the meeting organised by Patrick Cormack, as the senior Member for Staffordshire, between Staffordshire MPs and Rifkind. Beforehand Levey hosted a lunch for some of the MPs at l'Amico, a well-known Westminster restaurant frequented by politicians and lobbyists. The meeting itself was attended by Bill Cash, Patrick Cormack, Llin Golding, and three new MPs (Michael Fabricant, Conservative, Mid Staffordshire, who had defeated Sylvia Heal; George Stevenson, Labour, Stoke-on-Trent South, a former MEP; and ex-academic Tony Wright, Labour, Cannock and Burntwood). The cross-party nature of the delegation increased the importance of the MPs' views. The ministry had neglected — whether purposely or not is difficult to ascertain — to include West Midlands MPs, despite the fact that almost a third of the Regiment's recruits are drawn from these constituencies. It was for this reason that the author and two Conservative MPs, Nicholas Budgen and Richard Shepherd (Aldridge Brownhills), who had supported the Regiment as vigorously as their Staffordshire colleagues, were unable to lend their weight to this important meeting.

Malcolm Rifkind listened politely, and with increasing interest, to the delegation's concerns. He emphasised his commitment to ensuring that force levels were equal to the tasks expected of them, and he indicated again that he would soon respond to the Defence Select Committee's report into *Options*. For their part, the MPs repeatedly urged Rifkind to look again at overall Infantry numbers in the light of recent international developments, to recognise the detrimental effects of overstretch on Service life, and to reprieve The Staffordshire Regiment. This, said Patrick Cormack, would do justice to 'a Regiment with a distinguished history, an impeccable recent record, and one of the most heavily populated recruiting areas in the country'. Perhaps the most encouraging aspect of the meeting was the fact that it was taking place at all. Unlike Tom King, here was a Secretary of State who was prepared to invest the time to hear his colleagues' — and the campaigners' — concerns.

John Levey subsequently sent a letter to Patrick Cormack in which he set out, in the starkest terms, the serious impact of overstretch on the Infantry once the rundown was complete. Levey observed that service in Northern Ireland was 'for the ordinary Infantryman ... a continuing drain on his dedication and loyalty'. A high turnover of men, induced by an eighteen-month tour gap, created 'the unedifying situation of an Army that is working ever harder just to stand still'; 'short-term trimming of the Army can, therefore, easily lead to long-term problems.' Levey also touched on the issue of the Reserves and reaction times. Unsurprisingly, he devoted rather more attention to the future of the Regiment, again demonstrating the 'clear lack of equity in that the combined Staffordshire-Cheshire regiment will have a population base of eleven million and will return forty-five Members to Parliament', while other regiments that were to be retained had, in contrast, tiny recruitment reservoirs and few constituency MPs. He re-examined the issues of the Ministry's obsessive secrecy, manning levels, the fulfilment of each of the Army Board's criteria, and the lack of consultation. All this, he concluded gravely, had 'motivated the Staffords to campaign nationally with the Scots on behalf of the Infantry, and in particular, on behalf of the long-suffering Infantry soldier who has for too long been taken for granted'. Cormack dutifully passed on Levey's extremely authoritative appreciation of the current military position to Malcolm Rifkind for his comments.

The meeting also led to an unexpected exchange between the campaign and Michael Fabricant, one of its strongest Parliamentary supporters. After the meeting with Rifkind, Fabricant told the *Lichfield Mercury* that he was 'astonished' that the Regiment had not submitted its opposition to amalgamation with the Cheshires in writing to the Army Board, and that he was 'not surprised now that the Staffordshire Regiment was one of those picked on for amalgamation'. The *Mercury* also carried John Levey's amazed response:

> Everyone in Staffordshire has known and all the MPs have known that we weren't able to make a submission because we did not know we were under threat until it was too late. For him

> to make that comment after arriving late for the briefing I gave to MPs before the meeting and not being aware of the facts is a bit silly. Obviously we would have put in a submission if we had been on the list of regiments being considered for merger. … That has been the basis of our whole campaign.

It was clear to Levey and Nayyar that they were winning the war hands down on the purely intellectual level. Rifkind's response to Cormack, on 7 July 1992, devoted unprecedented space to personal attacks on Levey, and rather less to addressing the concerns that Levey's letter to Cormack had contained. In an extremely defensive letter, which appeared to suggest increasing irritation at the persistence and obduracy of Save Our Staffords, Rifkind began:

> The points raised in Brigadier Levey's letter are not new. Most have already been addressed by Archie Hamilton in previous correspondence; some were raised during our discussion on 4th June.

This was simply not true; much of what Levey's letter had set out was the result of recently commissioned, meticulous research. Rifkind continued that 'the Brigadier's dismissal of our calculation of future commitments is a little too easy.' And on the issue of the deployment of other Arms, in an Infantry role, to Northern Ireland, Rifkind declared: 'I do not agree with Brigadier Levey that this is a wasteful and inefficient policy.' Only on the issue of the Reserves did Rifkind demonstrate concern about the way ahead and implicitly heed Levey's cautionary words. But the most curious aspect of the letter, and the most poignant, was the complete absence of any reference to the future of the Staffords. Past experience had left SOS in absolutely no doubt that, whenever the campaign revealed an opportunity for counter-attack, the Ministry of Defence was swift to pounce. The fact that the MoD had not attempted to take issue with the detail of the campaigners' carefully constructed case provided the clearest possible evidence that Ministers were unable to.

In due course, Levey provided Cormack with a critique of Rifkind's letter which Cormack, in turn, passed to the Ministry of Defence. On 18 August, Malcolm Rifkind replied. Rifkind recognised the Staffordshire MP's belief that, 'if the Government ever judged that there was a case for reviewing Army manpower levels, then the Staffordshire Regiment had a strong claim to continue as an independent regiment.' He went on to declare, 'I would be the first to acknowledge that since the Government announced its proposals last July [1991], a great deal has happened in the world.' However, he did not accept that this would necessarily place a greater burden on the Infantry. Then, in an even more vigorous restatement of the subtle policy shift which he had revealed to the House on 2 June, he commented: 'If I felt there was ever a need to reconsider the overall manpower levels of the Army, I would have no hesitation in doing so and in making any changes which I considered necessary.' He concluded on the sourer note that the decision to amalgamate the Staffords and Cheshires 'was taken, along with other painful decisions, in the interest of the Army as a whole'. But the key point had been made. There could now be no doubt that its new political master had instructed the MoD to soften the position on manpower, while Ministers took stock of the situation.

On 28 August, Levey sent back a letter to Patrick Cormack, expressing horror at the failure of Ministers to do the simple mental arithmetic of matching battalions to commitments. He observed sagely:

> I cannot believe those advising Ministers have the slightest idea of the strain on the Infantry or they would not draft such a naive response. If they do, and some rumours suggest they do, they are then proving unwilling to present Ministers with unpalatable (military and political) home truths.

He noted acidly that the decisions on amalgamations 'were taken, as is always the case, as a result of Service lobbying and other Service interests', and concluded: 'I believe it is obvious that [Malcolm Rifkind] is being constrained primarily on financial grounds.' And that, of course, entirely accorded with the view of the Defence Committee and of most independent observers and commentators.

In parallel with the work that a significant number of Staffordshire and West Midlands MPs were undertaking for their regiment, some of The Cheshire Regiment's MPs were working hard for their regiment's cause. On 2 July, Gyles Brandreth, the TV celebrity who had been elected for the City of Chester for the Conservatives in 1992, led a delegation of Conservative MPs to meet Malcolm Rifkind to put the Cheshires' own case for retention. At the time, the Staffords were garrisoned at the Dale Barracks in Chester. Just before Brandreth's meeting with Rifkind, Nayyar arranged for him to visit the Dale to meet the wives of serving Staffords officers and soldiers. Nothing could be more appropriate than that the MP for Chester should meet his constituents — albeit that they were only temporary constituents and they were also Staffords! The Regiment deployed the wives of two privates, two corporals, two senior NCOs and two officers for the breakfast meeting with Brandreth on 24 June. Nayyar explained to Brandreth that this should provide a useful opportunity for 'a wide-ranging discussion of the issues attending on the Infantry reductions in general, and the Cheshire-Staffordshire regimental amalgamation in particular'. (It was not, of course, lost on Nayyar that a ringing third-party endorsement from the Chester MP about the Staffords' own grievances would carry due weight when the Cheshire MPs met Rifkind.)

By now John Levey of the Staffords and Sir John MacMillan of Keep Our Scottish Battalions were almost universally regarded as the two leading military authorities on the Infantry aspect of *Options for Change*. The Defence Select Committee and its new Chairman, Sir Nicholas Bonsor, knew this well. In early September, Levey, MacMillan and Nayyar were invited informally to lunch with Bonsor at his grand country seat, Liscombe Park, near Leighton Buzzard. For three hours, Levey and MacMillan briefed Bonsor on how overstretch really affected the Infantry, as a whole, and infantrymen in particular. They also advised Bonsor on the sort of questions the Select Committee should ask Defence Ministers and officials and how it might best identify when the Ministry was leading it up the garden path. When they left Liscombe Park, Levey and MacMillan felt entirely satisfied with the way this unofficial briefing had gone. They had played their part in setting the agenda for the forthcoming Select Committee inquiry, and they knew that they could look forward to another period of intense activity when Parliament reconvened in October.

Chapter 13

The Clock Ticks On

October 1992 to December 1992

Two significant events occurred at the start of October, just before Parliament resumed after its long — but, from the Staffords' point of view, eventful — summer recess. First, The Cheshire Regiment was deployed to Bosnia, just eleven months before it was due to amalgamate with the Staffords. It seemed to the campaigners that no other single event could have demonstrated more starkly the shortage of military resources than this decision to commit a regiment, earmarked for imminent amalgamation, to serve in a war zone. The second event, which underpinned the significance of the first, was a speech by Douglas Hurd, the Foreign Secretary, to the Royal United Services Institute on 13 October. Hurd warned that Britain might soon be faced with sending many more troops abroad on peacekeeping duties:

> If boils keep breaking out around the world, our commitments could well increase, providing that is, that we wish to maintain our position as a medium sized power with a developed sense of international responsibility

As soon as they emerged from their summer siesta, MPs took up the cudgels again, assisted by Levey and Nayyar. Patrick Cormack invited John Levey to brief MPs before he took a delegation of Staffordshire MPs to see Archie Hamilton. Excluded from that group as a 'non-Staffordshire' MP, the author organised his own meeting with Hamilton, accompanied by Nick Ryan, his new research assistant, for whom this was the first taste of the Staffords' campaign. In a letter dated 20 October, Levey and Nayyar brought MPs up to date with the latest developments and provided them with ammunition to use when writing to Ministers. The letter concluded, firmly: 'the need for an urgent and realistic reassessment of the Infantry requirement is now beyond question, and is absolutely vital.' This new round of correspondence was most effective, with MPs adding their own information. The Minister was bombarded with letters from about twenty to twenty-five MPs of all parties, including Cheshire MPs, of whom Nicholas Winterton was the most prominent.

The monthly Defence Question Time, when Defence Ministers are obliged to answer Parliamentary Questions relating to their department's work, occurred seven days later. During a discussion of the housing needs of redundant servicemen — itself occasioned by

Tom King's defence review — Patrick Cormack valiantly raised the issue of the future of The Staffordshire Regiment with Archie Hamilton, Minister of State for the Armed Forces.

> Cormack: Does my right hon Friend realise that he could solve the problem [of housing for ex-Servicemen] at a stroke if he would do the decent thing as regards The Staffordshire Regiment, and have regard to the needs of the Infantry? If he would think again about reprieving the Staffordshires and the Cheshires, we would not have so many redundant servicemen.
> Hamilton: I do not quite follow my hon Friend's logic when he says that if we did not amalgamate the Staffordshire and Cheshire regiments, we would have no redundancy problems. The fact is that we have made decisions about the amalgamations and there is no reason to believe that they will not go ahead.

It was clear from what he said, and from the pained expression on his face as he said it, that by now Hamilton was heartily tired of the issue of the proposed amalgamation. Moreover, he fundamentally failed to grasp why so many Members, from both sides of the House, persisted in their quest to right the significant wrong the Ministry of Defence had done to the Regiment.

Nayyar was concerned by Hamilton's chosen form of words. 'There is no reason to believe that [the amalgamations] will not go ahead' appeared much less positive than Rifkind's comment, just two months earlier, that, 'if I felt there was ever a need to reconsider the overall manpower levels of the Army, I would have no hesitation … in making any changes which I considered necessary.' The campaigners were uneasy. A change in the form of words could indicate a hardening of policy within the MoD against the campaigners. Was the window of opportunity now closing?

However, some small comfort could be derived from the letter that Archie Hamilton now wrote to the Staffordshire and West Midlands MPs who had passed John Levey's letter of 20 October on to him. In his replies, Hamilton repeated, practically verbatim (itself no surprise, since the same officials would have drafted this and previous letters), the form of words that Malcolm Rifkind had used in August:

> We are not inflexible; if we felt there was ever a need to reconsider the overall manpower levels of the Army, we would

have no hesitation in doing so and would make any changes we considered necessary.

But there was a sting in the tail, for the letter concluded: 'I have to say at the moment though that nothing in recent events casts serious doubt on the judgments we have made.'

To Levey and Nayyar, it seemed that the window was still open, but risked being slammed shut before their eyes. More precisely, they felt that a war of wills was being waged within the Ministry about whether or not to addback regiments in order to meet increasing commitments at home and abroad. While this wrangle, at the heart of the debate on manpower levels, continued, Ministers — caught in the cross-fire of this conflicting professional advice — were publicly hedging their bets. This appeared to confirm what Nayyar and Levey were picking up elsewhere. For example, at a drinks party given by Westminster Communications during the Conservative Party Conference in October, a Cheshire MP had warned Nayyar that Defence Ministers were in a dilemma about whether or not to retain more regiments. A week or so later, after Parliament had resumed, a senior Conservative MP (and former Guards officer) similarly warned Nayyar that intelligence he had gleaned from contacts in the Ministry suggested that a decision was about to be taken; but the MP was unwilling to quote odds on the outcome.

On 16 November 1992, amid these swirling uncertainties, Nayyar attended a political meeting addressed by the Secretary of State for Defence. The meeting was curious for a number of reasons. Malcolm Rifkind was accompanied by his special political adviser, Perry Miller. Also present — but now a fellow lobbyist — was John Gardner, Tom King's defence special adviser at the time of *Options for Change* and, as such, privy to the *Options* decision-making process. Rifkind opened the meeting, clearly believing that his audience would broadly, if not enthusiastically, support his record at the Ministry of Defence. Instead, he faced a barrage of questions about whether the Conservatives had moved away from their traditional position of firm support for the Armed Forces; whether manpower levels were equal to existing, and possibly unforeseen, needs; and whether the criteria relating to the selection of individual regiments had been met. Rifkind looked visibly startled.

Nayyar knew that he would get only one opportunity to put his concerns to Rifkind; Miller and Gardner both knew how much grief he had personally caused their political masters on behalf of the

Staffords and the Scots. Neither would countenance his speaking to Rifkind for long. Nayyar used this opportunity to pursue a line which Sir John MacMillan had used for the first time at the meeting with Sir Nicholas Bonsor in September. He asked Rifkind how confident he was that, when he met serving officers and soldiers in his capacity as Secretary of State for Defence, the men were really frank with him about the effects that manpower reductions had on their morale and operational efficiency. Surely, said Nayyar, it was most unlikely that professional soldiers would be willing to let their ultimate boss know in exactly what stressful, under-resourced and over-committed conditions they toiled? In this way, he concluded, it was most unlikely that the Secretary of State would ever be permitted to gain the first-hand evidence that would undermine the calculations of Army and MoD policy-makers and, ultimately, call into question the decisions of the Army Board itself.

It was clear that Rifkind knew that Nayyar had an armoury of facts and figures at his fingertips, and so he was careful in his reply. He said he recognised that this was always a real problem. He very much hoped that he and his ministerial team had struck the right balance, but that changes in the strategic environment might force a re-think. Although the answer could not be tied down specifically, Nayyar was left in no doubt that Rifkind possessed the political will to effect change if he was convinced of the correctness of that change. In addition, Nayyar was confident that the tenor of the meeting had taken Rifkind by surprise, that it would be remembered, and that some of the questions put to Rifkind would, in due course, find their way back to relevant policy officials at the Ministry of Defence.

To the lay reader, it may well seem that Save Our Staffords had become embroiled in extremely technical and abstruse discussions, and that it was engaged in intellectual and verbal gymnastics remote from securing a reprieve for the Regiment. Nothing could be further from the truth. The fact that Defence Ministers and civil servants spent their time sniping at the campaigners provided the clearest possible evidence of the extent to which SOS, not Ministers, was shaping the political agenda on manpower levels. Between them, the Staffords and the Scots had created a siege mentality at the Ministry of Defence.

The letters Hamilton sent to MPs in November illustrate something of this siege mentality. They began with the by now obligatory side-swipe at John Levey, whose 20 October letter MPs had sent on to Hamilton. Without reservation, Hamilton declared Levey to be 'mistaken' in his belief that the target twenty-four-month tour interval 'is now unattainable'. In making this routine jibe, Hamilton's officials blundered. Levey had said no such thing. What he had said was that the twenty-four-month tour interval 'was now unsustainable'. The difference was much more than semantic. Hamilton was claiming to MPs that Save Our Staffords believed that it was impossible ever to achieve this target tour gap. In reality SOS was simply maintaining that it could not be achieved continuously for any length of time. As a result, on 3 December John Levey sent a terse letter to Staffordshire and West Midlands MPs drawing attention to this ministerial error, noting that it 'is simply not true', and suggesting that 'you may ... feel that you wish to go back to the Minister to make this point.'

Batting policy points to and fro with Ministers, directly or through MPs, was the key to getting them to explain their past decisions on the strategic context of the Infantry reductions and on the selection of individual regiments for amalgamation. It was also vital to try to elicit from Ministers a meaningful understanding of the future commitments they envisaged for the Army, and how the Army was expected to meet them. It is a fundamental part of the way Whitehall and Westminster work that Ministers continually make statements and publish policy papers which, if unchallenged, pass inexorably from theory into practice. If this decision-making process is to be thwarted, even slowed, it is vital to deploy cogent and widely-publicised counter-arguments as soon as possible in the face of the oncoming Whitehall juggernaut. This is particularly important when taking on a department as perennially secretive about decision-making as the Ministry of Defence — where even staff canteen menus are allegedly classified as restricted documents. From the campaign's earliest stages, Save Our Staffords, advised by Nayyar and run by retired professional infantrymen who between them boasted dozens of years' experience of working at the Ministry of Defence, fully understood this and rose to the challenge.

Save Our Staffords had fought the Ministry of Defence to a standstill, as was evident from Archie Hamilton's Answer to a Written Question on 24 November from Michael Fabricant. He had asked Rifkind 'if he will now reconsider the proposed amalgamation of The Staffordshire and Cheshire Regiments'. Hamilton responded thus:

> No. The amalgamation of The Cheshire regiment and The Staffordshire regiment is due to take place in August 1993 and there is currently no reason why it should not go ahead.

Meanwhile, a number of MPs who received John Levey's letter stating that Hamilton had misquoted him passed it on to Hamilton. In due course, Hamilton responded. The reply sent to Llin Golding, the Labour MP for Newcastle-under-Lyme, on 22 December — the last from the Ministry of Defence before the historic reprieve just six weeks later — ran:

> There is, I am afraid, little I can add to my previous reply. The arguments have all been very well rehearsed and what it now boils down to is a simple difference of opinion between us and the Brigadier.
>
> I can only reiterate that we believe the changes which are now in hand to be workable. Despite some short-term difficulties, which I have made no attempt to deny, I remain satisfied that the restructuring will deliver a balanced force that is well-matched to our future needs and able to meet the challenges of the mid-1990s and beyond. Should circumstances change, and we are faced with new long-term commitments, as I have already indicated, we will have to look again at Army manpower levels. Nothing in recent events, however, convinces me that this is yet necessary.

Built into this important letter was the Ministry's implicit recognition that every policy avenue that it had explored in a bid to outwit and outmanoeuvre the campaigners had been blocked. As Hamilton acknowledged, what was at issue was 'a simple difference of opinion' between the Ministry and the regimental campaigners. But, as the campaigners knew, this innocuous sounding 'difference of opinion' belied the fate that awaited their Regiment. The finality of the last paragraph of Hamilton's letter obscured the Ministry's use of one important but modest word — 'yet'. With the benefit of hindsight, it is now possible to see that the Ministry slipped this unobtrusive extra word into the final sentence of Hamilton's letter for a very good reason.

Autumn Offensive in Staffordshire and the Black Country

In late August, fearful that the long Parliamentary recess could dull some MPs' enthusiasm for the renewed campaign in Westminster, John Levey had once again called on the services of Major Mike Mogridge. He was given the task of maintaining the campaign's purpose and profile by means of a series of events and articles that would keep the Regiment's name and plight before the public and local MPs. Between September and November Mogridge frequently visited the area, and even when at home in Devon found himself constantly on the telephone, pushing and shoving, encouraging and demanding efforts from editors, Regimental Association branches and other supporters.

The meeting of Branch Chairmen and Secretaries just before the Old Comrades Annual Dinner on 5 September gave Mogridge an ideal opportunity to remind just how important it was to maintain constant pressure. The effects were immediate. The *Cannock Chase Chronicle* ran a favourable feature on the campaign later that month. West Bromwich Branch wrote to all twenty-six MPs in the Regiment's recruiting area and eventually found itself in protracted correspondence with eighteen of them. Councillor Les Sillitoe, a Friend and Normandy Veteran, arranged for an article to appear in the free monthly newssheet put out by Stoke-on-Trent City Council. The Friends also made good use of publicity opportunities offered by the three-day Birmingham International City Tattoo, and the by now familiar goalkeeper logo was much in evidence.

Useful in its own right as a solid piece of publicity in a widely read and respected magazine, the *Staffordshire Life* article described on page 115 also provided a peg for further publicity. Copies were sent to every MP and to each Branch Secretary and Area Chairman of the Friends. The article also provided the basis of a special feature in the *Birmingham Evening Mail.*

Mogridge also responded at short notice to a request for copy from Brigadier Sir Louis Hargroves, who had persuaded his friend Sir Doug Ellis, chairman of Aston Villa FC, to make space available in a match programme. The advertisement, which neatly linked Club and Regiment, was seen by a crowd of 22,000:

> British Infantry without the Regiment is like the Premier League without the Villa. Both these seasoned professionals know that success comes from team work and years of experience. Quality means mastery of basic skills, the set piece, defence into attack, success on the break.

The most-time consuming, yet most productive, aspect of Mogridge's work was with local authorities. Many Council Chairmen were keen to give assistance by means of Motions of Support, but lacked the detailed knowledge necessary to persuade fellow-councillors. Mogridge met the Chairmen of Sandwell Metropolitan Borough Council (see page 103), and of South Staffordshire District Council and East Staffordshire Borough Council, as well as Barbara Rothwell, Town Clerk of Uttoxeter. She in turn briefed local journalists from Cheadle, Leek and Uttoxeter with very positive results — all three papers carried a report the following weekend. The motions passed by East Staffordshire and Uttoxeter councils also helped to remind Sir Ivan Lawrence, the local MP, of the strength of local feeling. During late October and November no less than seven councils wrote to the Secretary of State to express concern at the proposed amalgamation.

The county was never allowed to forget how the campaign was progressing. A second *Staffordshire Life* article in November entitled 'The fighting breed of Staffordshire' neatly interwove the Regiment's desire to remain independent and the struggle to maintain the purity of the Staffordshire Bull Terrier breed. It was written by Colonel David Hancock MBE, an authority on terrier dog breeds, a Kennel Club judge, and National Trust Director at Shugborough. As a former member of The Somerset Light Infantry he was strongly sympathetic to the Staffords and happily waived his normal writing fee. The splendid photograph of Watchman III and Sergeant Malcolm Bowers was also donated by The Animal Photography Partnership of Cheltenham.

Only very occasionally did the campaign attract negative publicity. One such story appeared in the *Birmingham Post* of 8 July 1992, which screamed 'Hopes dashed for saving Staffordshire Regiment'. Levey and Nayyar swung rapidly into action to quash this inaccurate speculation, quickly faxing a letter to the editor setting the record straight before any lasting damage could be done to the campaign's credibility.

At Campaign Committee meetings in August and November Levey and Mogridge reviewed the regional position: 'the county was quietly simmering away with considerable support available when required' said Levey. Both now agreed that the campaign should focus on the Infantry at Westminster. According to Freer, the county was saturated with publicity which was beginning to cost too much — in February 1993 the *Walsall Express and Star* estimated that £50,000 had been spent; in reality, the figure was rather higher. At this point there was no need to boost the campaign; the established bedrock of support was available as necessary; the branches of the various regimental organisations could continue to use the free publicity made available by the regional media; and one-off events, such as the forthcoming Central Television documentary about the Staffords, gave the Regiment and the campaign sporadic high-profile publicity.

A television broadside

On the evening of 3 December 1992 Central Television transmitted a special 25-minute edition of its *Central Lobby* programme on The Staffordshire Regiment. It began with a short opening announcement over a blank screen:

> In 1990 Defence Secretary Tom King announced *Options for Change* — the Government's response to the changing world order and the expected peace dividend.
>
> For The Staffordshire Regiment it means the loss of three hundred jobs as it merges with the Cheshires. Since the announcement the Staffords have fought in the Gulf War and been on emergency tour in Northern Ireland.
>
> This is their story as their three hundred year history comes to an end.

The programme started with a collage of images of Staffords in combat uniform on the streets of Northern Ireland. Accompanying this was a recording of Tom King announcing to the Commons that the Staffords and Cheshires were to be amalgamated.

Nigel Alderman, Commanding Officer of the 1st Battalion, and John Levey described the immense burdens on family life that short tour gaps created. Levey, by now as effective at the ten-second soundbite as most professional politicians, remarked that cutting fifty-five battalions to just thirty-eight was 'a cut too far'. But the real potency of the documentary derived from the fact that most of the observations about the pressures of service life came from the soldiers and their families. A serving soldier told of his sadness at the impending amalgamation, his pride in being a Stafford and all that it stood for; and he noted, poignantly, that a pair of twins and several fathers and sons served side by side in the Regiment. He told of the pressures of serving in Northern Ireland — on a six-month emergency tour it was not unusual to have only eight days R & R (rest and relaxation), and the only time out was on patrol, which of course had its own pressures. All this came immediately after a six-month tour in the Gulf in which the Staffords were in the thick of the action. A group of wives was featured. One made the point that a service wife married not only her husband, but the Regiment also — wives felt loyalty, experienced the pressures of separation, and understood the significance of the ending of a regiment's existence.

The documentary lingered reflectively at a meeting of the Staffords'

Regimental Association; repaired, wistfully, to the King's Head pub; featured an interview with Mac McLean, the Regimental Secretary; and included shots of Watchman III. In the closing moments of the programme, Archie Hamilton declared: 'I have enormous sympathy for the Staffords', although, with perfect consistency, he repeated his belief that ultimately all would be well once the regimental amalgamations had been seen through. With a distinctly untelegenic grimace, he concluded:

> We don't have any intention of going back [on the amalgamation decision]. And, as I've said, we will look again at numbers if there are extra long commitments. But the commitments we now have we can deal with, with the numbers that we are looking at, post-Options.

The programme ended with a dramatic sequence, filmed from above, of the Regiment marching, to the strains of Ravel's *Bolero*. As the final chords sounded, the last of the troops marched off screen: a well synchronised portrayal of the finality of the Regiment's proposed fate.

Levey and Nayyar immediately recognised the publicity potential of this skilfully crafted documentary. (The author would like wholeheartedly to thank Judy Laybourn, the producer, Nigel Warrack, the director, the crew of *Central Lobby* and Central Television for this extremely helpful programme.) Having elicited the permission of Central Television, SOS sent each of its constituency MPs a video of the programme with a letter encouraging them to watch it over Christmas.

During January 1993, John Levey wrote to local authority chief executives, Presidents of the Regimental Associations, and Friends of the Regiment thanking them for eighteen months of campaigning against 'the stupidity of amalgamating the fully recruited Staffordshire Regiment' and urging them to make a final plea — 'it could swing our case at the eleventh hour.' Such encouragement provides an insight into Levey's seemingly endless commitment to the campaign and his remarkably robust optimism.

The Select Committee's assault

The Defence Select Committee continued to dig away at defence policy away from the glare of publicity. Under its new Chairman, Sir Nicholas Bonsor (elected specifically because he would prioritise the Infantry issue), the Committee returned to its task of keeping the

MoD on the back foot. The inquiry that produced the report *Britain's Army for the 90s: Commitments and Resources* was largely built on the previous Committee's inquiry into *Options for Change: Army*.

The Committee rejected the Government's benign assessment of *Options for Change*, and agreed instead with the wide body of informed opinion that held that *Options*, far from giving the Army greater flexibility under changing conditions, was causing greater overstretch and putting commitments in grave doubt. Work on the new inquiry got under way after the summer recess, although the Committee staff worked throughout the summer to prepare the ground.

During a special Committee sitting in September on the UK peace-keeping deployment to Bosnia, Archie Hamilton conceded an important point about the emergency tour gap. This was a key to proving the disastrous effect of *Options for Change* on Army morale and effectiveness. John Levey paraphrased Hamilton's testimony in a letter to the author. Because of a two-battalion reinforcement for Northern Ireland and the deployment of British troops (including Cheshires) to Bosnia, the 'much trumpeted twenty-four-month gap between unaccompanied tours was now unsustainable and the gap between tours would be reduced to fifteen months.' (Even this concession by Hamilton failed to point out that in some cases units were experiencing gaps of only seven or eight months between tours of duty.) 'The lengthened tour gap was originally cited as one of the central tenets of *Options for Change*, which would ease overstretch for the Infantry. This assumption has proved disastrously inaccurate.'

Sir John MacMillan provided a concise analysis of the impending tour gap crisis in a letter to the Committee in November 1992. He stated that the MoD, in submitting information to the Committee, had made 'economies with the truth', and that the significance of tour interval information was that:

> ... even an average tour interval which seems reasonable for the Army as a whole actually results in those units which can be made available often having a very much higher rate of operational deployment, not just in one or two years, but over a prolonged period. This will get infinitely worse as the number of units in the Army is reduced. ... Morale will be hit ..., because the necessity to do the chores [peacetime security, ceremonial and other tasks performed in the UK] will take priority over the training that is essential if soldiers are to feel confidence in their ability to meet the pressures of the war for which they are equipped.

The issue of undermanning and overstretch provides plenty of evidence of the MoD's *hauteur* in the face of the Defence Committee's probing into Army *Options*. The transcripts of hearings show that Committee members were exasperated throughout the inquiry by the dogmatic approach and sheer evasiveness of MoD witnesses and evidence. An exchange involving Brian Hawtin (Assistant Under Secretary of State for Programmes at the MoD), the author and Sir Nicholas Bonsor illustrates the difficulties regularly encountered:

Mr George

760. On a number of occasions the General and Mr. Hawtin have not even subliminally but blatantly said to us, or implied to us, that one of the reasons for the amalgamations was to overcome the problems of undermanning. It seems to me undermanning was as much deliberate Government policy as an accident of recruiting or demography. There was a deliberate attempt to hold down recruiting. It seems a rather harsh reaction to undermanning deliberately induced by the Government to merge regiments which, if given encouragement, would have been able to recruit up to the level which they required. ...
(*Mr Hawtin*) I think we have tried to explain to the Committee that full manning is a very important objective and has long been an important objective. The reasons for the amalgamations and the general principle that lay behind that again have been exposed to the Committee and debated on a number of occasions.

Chairman

761. Very unsatisfactorily, Mr Hawtin, I am afraid. On the question of individual units, no attempt has ever been made either in this Committee or on the floor of the House to explain why fully manned battalions have been scrapped in absolute opposition to the Government's own guidelines on the subject. I do not want to get drawn into that. I know you cannot answer the point. If we may, we will stick to the question of current manning levels and the way in which you think that might help the interim position between now and 1995.
(*Mr Hawtin*) I think it will help very considerably, Mr Chairman, in the kind of way that we have tried to describe, and in particular in the operational sense that General Wheeler [Assistant Chief of General Staff] has described. I think he explained to the Committee that a fully manned unit is far better

than and preferred to one that is undermanned.
Chairman: I am sure that is right. It does not answer the point.

The Committee and the campaigns shared a mutual unhappiness with the MoD's attitude to releasing information about areas of concern as important as the effects of wider defence policy on the Army's operational effectiveness. It was difficult for the Committee properly to scrutinise defence policy when it was continually being given misleading information and evasive answers. This was one of the most important facets of the relationship between the Defence Committee and the campaigners. The campaigners helped the Committee members to identify swiftly and easily those areas which the MoD was most keen to avoid discussing, and to ensure that the Committee asked the right questions.

While the Defence Select Committee plugged away at the MoD with the constant support of Levey, MacMillan and Nayyar, the Campaign Committee was becoming increasingly concerned by the absence of any indication — other than Hamilton's admission of reduced tour intervals — that the Government's position was shifting. When the Campaign Committee met in November 1992, it discussed the evidence given by the MoD to the Select Committee. It was depressing, Levey noted, that whenever the issue of addback was discussed by MoD officials it was always in the context of addback of soldiers, not units.

After many months of attempting to pry information out of the Ministry, the Select Committee finalised its Report, concluding that the mildly expressed fears and coded criticisms in the previous Committee's report had not been without good reason. The Bonsor Report dispensed with most of the niceties of the previous Committee, preferring a combination of the hammer, hatchet and rapier. Whereas the previous Report had talked of the Committee's 'concern' about Army *Options*, the new Report said, in plain English, that Army *Options* was disastrous. Additional commitments in Northern Ireland had, for instance, 'made nonsense of the figures used in 1991 to justify the Army strengths proposed'. The price of refusing to reconsider the July 1991 proposals would include 'the inability to respond to requests from the United Nations for military assistance on a scale commensurate with the United Kingdom's position as a Permanent Member of the Security Council.' The forceful criticisms throughout the Report were summarised in these words:

The ultimate determinant of the meeting of tasks, however, is

> the total number of units available. If flexibility is understood to mean that the Army can cope with more peacetime commitments within a certain manpower ceiling, it can only be achieved at the expense of a shorter interval between emergency tours for individual units and greater turbulence and family separation for individual soldiers. This will reduce the Army's ability to respond flexibly to demands which may be put upon it to fulfil its primary wartime roles. Furthermore, it is nonsense to talk as if the flexibility was inherent in the structure of the Army: it is not. It is exclusively dependent on the long-suffering individuals in the Army.

Whereas the previous Committee had largely been prepared to give the Government the benefit of the doubt, the new Committee under Sir Nicholas said that it was now convinced that Army *Options* would undermine the Army's operational effectiveness and would adversely affect Britain's defence and foreign policy:

> We consider it inappropriate and ill-advised to carry through the proposals for the restructuring of the Army in their entirety, and recommend that the Government cancel all amalgamations or disbandments of UK Infantry battalions currently planned.

Chapter 14

Darkness before Dawn

January 1993 to February 1993

A feeling of inevitability

Attitudes within the uppermost echelon of the Ministry of Defence may have altered slightly, but nevertheless, after more than a year of political street-fighting, an undeniable sense of fatalism was creeping into the Staffords' campaign. The comments made by Nicholas Benson in the introduction to his excellent book *Rats' Tales* typified this feeling of inevitability. Referring to the Staffords' action in the Gulf as their 'swan song', he wrote:

> When I started work on this project, *Options for Change*, the Government's defence review, had been suspended because of the Gulf War. When it was resurrected in the summer of 1991 few people imagined that the Staffords would suffer the cruel fate of being selected for amalgamation. When this was in fact announced, a massive campaign got underway in an attempt to try to save the Regiment. Unfortunately this appears to have failed, so Operation GRANBY will probably be the last large-scale operation in which The Staffordshire Regiment will have served.

People were beginning to steel themselves to accept that the threatened amalgamation would take place. This was not a signal to capitulate; the campaigners had come too far, had too much faith in their cause, to give up now. But it was necessary to realise that, even after their Herculean labours, they might have to bow in the face of the Government's intransigence. John Levey told the Campaign Committee in November that he saw 'no sign of reconsideration by the Government' and that time was 'getting short'. The Committee agreed to hold its next meeting on 9 February 1993; in fact, it took place on the 11th. Its realistic assessment of the situation in November bore no relation to the very different mood at that next meeting.

Preparation for amalgamation

Without the Defence Select Committee's continuing sessions on the Army manpower question, it would undoubtedly have been very difficult to sustain an active campaign. Nor would it have been unreasonable for some people's optimism to wane, especially those who sat on the Amalgamation Committee which was responsible for the technical details of the amalgamation. The Amalgamation Committee, which had been formed in December 1991, consisted of six members of each Regiment, and was chaired jointly by Ian Freer, for the Staffords, and James Percival, for the Cheshires; meetings alternated between Whittington Barracks and the Dale Barracks, Chester. Mac McLean, who was simultaneously a member of the SOS Campaign Committee and the Amalgamation Committee, recalls that the latter's meetings were 'democratic' and conducted in good spirit.

The Committee had many tasks, from agreeing the location of Regimental Headquarters to the design of tracksuits. Some were carried out with little difficulty. The new regimental name (The Cheshire and Staffordshire Regiment) reflected the priority of the Cheshires in the Order of Precedence of Regiments and Corps of the Regular Army. The uniform design, including the chevron backing colour, the design of the cap badge (by the Royal College of Arms), collar badge, parade belt buckle and shoulder title, was easily agreed. Other items proved far more contentious. The location of the Regimental HQ — neither Regiment would settle for the other's current location — proved particularly difficult. An emotive aspect of the amalgamation was the selection of Queen's Colour Battle Honours; the Queen's Colour would hold forty-two First and Second World War Battle Honours, the Regimental Colours thirty-nine from all other campaigns. Together the two Regiments possess over three hundred battle honours, and the conundrum centred on which to select for the new Colours. Who, also, dared to guess what the new Regimental March would sound like? The requirement was put out to competition 'to all bandmasters in the Army', but was never heard. There was also the sensitive and difficult issue of the Colonel-in-Chief; the choice lay between HRH The Prince of Wales, The Colonel in Chief, The Cheshire Regiment, and HRH The Duke of York, The Colonel in Chief, The Staffordshire Regiment.

To those people, such as Mac McLean, with dual responsibilities, preparations for the amalgamation did not seem at odds with campaigning to save the Staffords. Those chosen to sit on the Amalgamation Committee had to proceed with its work. Mac McLean testifies to the personal difficulty that he felt in 'having to work on both sides'; he felt like a 'double agent', and it was a mental strain. Yet his, and others', experience of the amalgamation of the South and North Staffords in 1959 assisted the Staffords-Cheshires amalgamation plans, and also helped them personally to meet the challenge. 'I knew the problems inside and out', McLean says, 'and was not going to be beaten.'

Ian Freer knew that the signs were not good; as Colonel of the Regiment he had to continue to prepare for the worst no matter his personal feelings. Hence, towards the end of 1992, he wrote to the Regiment:

> Regimentally, we must recognise that we are approaching a cross-roads. Many stalwart supporters understandably want to fight on. However, the reality is that the two 1st Battalions who have to carry out the amalgamation are at the stage where they need to be positive. I would therefore be grateful if they could be given our enthusiastic support from the New Year onwards.

This message was not well received by the campaigners, not so much for its content as for the fact that it appeared in the *Stafford Knot*. They felt that it represented something of a public smack in the face. The advantage of coded messages, however, is that they can be ignored, and the campaigners continued undeterred.

Work on the amalgamation, and the dilemma concerning the priority to be placed on amalgamation and opposition to it, was not confined to members of the Amalgamation Committee. The Warrant Officers and Sergeants Past and Present also had to consider their future status. At their Annual General Meeting on 5 November 1992 they discussed the vexing question of whether to remain separate from, or to merge with, the Cheshires' Mess. By all accounts, the debate was heated. Few were able to take the more relaxed approach adopted, presumably, by Sid Chaplin, who had served in the Cheshires, the South Staffords and the Staffords.

Thus, by early 1993, with only eight months left before amalgamation became reality, there was a widespread feeling of inevitability. There would be bitterness, but the people of Staffordshire and the West Midlands could proudly claim that they had done all they could. Indeed, it is difficult to imagine what more could have been done, short of mounting barricades around Lichfield.

Hints and denials

During the Christmas parliamentary Recess, Bill Walker, the Conservative MP for Tayside North and Chairman of the Scottish Conservative MPs, was quoted in a Scottish newspaper as saying that he had been given to understand that early in the New Year the Ministry of Defence was likely to have some good news for Scotland. Walker interpreted this to mean possible Infantry addbacks. Just before the New Year, Simon Nayyar spoke to Walker, who now claimed that he had been misquoted.

As the Christmas recess ended, there was an atmosphere of pregnant anticipation. SOS was unclear whether or not to believe a reprieve was really on the cards. It so happened that on 12 January, days after Parliament resumed, Defence Question Time provided an opportunity to find out. Inevitably, Army manpower featured prominently. The second Question, from Alex Salmond, the leader of the Scottish National Party, was on the future of the Scottish regiments. In his supplementary Question, Salmond asked the Defence Secretary whether he would:

> Acknowledge that it is becoming abundantly apparent ... that the regiments and the Infantry are becoming overstretched on current commitments? Given that, will the Secretary of State further acknowledge that a reassessment of the Government's position on regimental mergers in Scotland would be welcome? The Secretary of State will have seen the comments of the hon Member for Tayside North [Bill Walker] that he has already been engaged in such a private reassessment. Is that the case and, if so, will he take this opportunity to share that information with the rest of the House?

Rifkind replied enigmatically that Salmond's supplementary Question referred to 'Army manpower as a whole' — despite the fact that Salmond had been asking about the Infantry and the Scottish regiments. Rifkind went on:

> I am satisfied that at present we can meet all our obligations without undue overstretch. If I ever came to a different conclusion, it would be appropriate to review the assumptions of *Options for Change*.

Extraordinarily, Rifkind passed by the opportunity to slate Salmond and the press for engaging in unhelpful and misguided speculation. Nor, as the House would have expected, did he seek to deny the remarks that had been publicly attributed to Bill Walker.

The sense of anticipation on Government and Opposition benches was almost palpable. At this point, Bill Walker, the focus of so much unwanted attention, intervened to set the record straight:

> Will my right hon and learned Friend [the Defence Secretary] confirm that he has always made it clear that Army manpower and the pressures on the Army are subject to constant review in the light of events? That is what I have been saying. Will he also confirm that the Scottish regiments are part of the fabric that makes the United Kingdom united ... and that the political implications must also be taken into consideration?

Rifkind replied:

> I can certainly confirm that the Scottish regiments have made a fine and honourable contribution to the requirements of the United Kingdom armed forces over many years and I am sure that that will continue.

Again, neither Rifkind nor Walker made any attempt to scotch the rumours of a possible reappraisal of *Options*. Equally, Walker did not seek to deny the substance of the stories that the press had attributed to him.

The tenth Question to Defence Ministers that afternoon was from David Trimble, Ulster Unionist MP for Upper Bann. Trimble asked Archie Hamilton about the average interval between unaccompanied tours in the Province. Hamilton grudgingly conceded that there had been a significant deterioration in the tour gap interval, but emphasised that the target twenty-four-month gap would be achieved when restructuring was complete. Trimble asked when this might be and, meanwhile, what impact the Ministry of Defence reckoned this had on the families of servicemen. Hamilton replied lamely that, 'so long as there are no new commitments in the next two years, we estimate that we shall be able to return to twenty-four months.' He acknowledged the adverse impact that restructuring was having on servicemen's families.

At this point, Michael Fabricant, a staunch supporter of the Regiment at previous Defence Question Times, weighed in:

> A number of reports in the *Scotsman* and other newspapers have said that there may be a reprieve possibly for some Scottish regiments. Can my right hon. Friend reassure me and my constituents that any review of Scottish regiments will go hand in glove with the review of The Staffordshire and Cheshire Regiments?

Hamilton, manifestly dismayed at yet another Question about the future of the Staffords, replied:

> I do not think that we are talking about a review of the proposals for the amalgamation of regiments under Options for Change. We still feel that we have the right number of regiments. We do not think that long-term commitments have changed sufficiently to want to change that.

Taken at face value, this appeared to be another nail in the Staffords' coffin. Yet it did not entirely accord with what Malcolm Rifkind and Bill Walker had earlier said — or, to be more accurate, had not said.

Political storm in Scotland

On 15 January, just three days after these Question Time exchanges, the *Scotsman*, Scotland's premier newspaper published a deeply shocking interview with Malcolm Rifkind by journalist Severin Carrell. The front page, bearing a strident 'Exclusive' tag, shouted 'Regiments' hopes dashed'. On the leader page was an in-depth interview with Rifkind and an editorial.

Entitled 'Rifkind relaxes into his new role', and the product of an hour-long interview with Rifkind, the article ranged widely over Iraq, Bosnia, the European Fighter Aircraft (later known as Eurofighter 2000) and the future of the Rosyth dockyard (another major Scottish defence issue in the early 1990s). At its core was a carefully targeted and defiant message to Save Our Staffords and Keep Our Scottish Battalions:

> The other problem [besides Rosyth] in Scotland is the continuing campaign to prevent the merger of the regiments. There have been persistent rumours over the past year (gaining more impetus over the past month or so) that Rifkind will give them a reprieve. He made a clear denial that that was the case. 'The crucial point to take on board with regard to that issue is that the only legitimate debate is about whether there is going to be enough Infantry to meet the army's requirements over the next few years. If the answer is "yes", then that is the end of the discussion.'
>
> If the argument was 'no' and it was persuasive, then the problem would have to be rectified. 'It does not automatically follow that even if you thought there was a problem and wanted to rectify it that the answer would be changing the decision on individual regiments and battalions.
>
> 'You might want, for example, to bring up to strength battalions that are under strength. Our current assessment is that we are well able to meet our existing obligations.'

This last point was bad enough. The concept of bringing under-strength battalions up to strength was at the heart of the campaigners' concerns that the Ministry of Defence had allowed itself to be seduced into believing that merging two weak battalions would produce one strong one. It seemed that Rifkind was setting on the record his own belief in this particular nostrum. As for his contention that resources matched existing commitments, this appeared to confirm everything that Archie Hamilton had said in the Central TV documentary just before Christmas 1992.

Worse was to follow. The article placed on the record Rifkind's view that troublespots such as Bosnia did not change the equation, despite the insistence of the campaigners and most independent Westminster observers. With obvious irony, this claim also overlooked the fact that, just the day before, Rifkind had announced to the House the dispatch to the Adriatic of the aircraft carrier HMS *Ark Royal*; three helicopters; Sea Harriers; Royal Artillery 105 mm howitzers; two frigates; and three support ships to demonstrate the UK's willingness militarily to face down any threats to its UNPROFOR forces.

The article concluded:

> 'I think there is a natural sadness whether it be in Scotland, or in Stafford or Cheshire, or wherever if an old regiment is being amalgamated.' There had been amalgamations before; regiments were 'not sentimental creations', nothing remained static.

The detonation of this high-explosive warhead was sensational, and was clearly designed to be. For it was extraordinary that a busy Secretary of State for Defence should find the time to lavish suspect sympathy on campaigners who were seeking to overturn just three of the proposed eighteen Infantry amalgamations. It was curious, too, that despite his marginal seat, Rifkind should use his local newspaper — for many of his Edinburgh constituents were inevitably also *Scotsman* readers — to pass on the news that he had no intention of saving The Royal Scots, despite the intense pressure on him to review the decision.

But, from Save Our Staffords' point of view, most devastating of all was Rifkind's evident desire to snuff out any rumours of a reprieve for The Staffordshire Regiment. It was also startling that Rifkind had elected to use a Scottish newspaper to convey the news to Staffordshire that the campaigners there should call it a day. In fact, this was a backhanded compliment; it showed that the Ministry of Defence was

convinced that, because of the close co-operation between Save Our Staffords and Keep Our Scottish Battalions, the *Scotsman* was a suitable vehicle for this unwelcome news. The compliment brought the Staffords little consolation, however, who regarded it instead as an indication of the MoD's determination to brazen it out.
The *Scotsman*'s accompanying editorial noted sagely:

> If it can be shown that military supply has come to outreach demand, then the glory of old names should not impede reform. But eighteen months after the cutbacks were first proposed, there remain doubts as to whether that imbalance can yet be demonstrated. ... As yesterday's decision to reinforce the British presence in Bosnia illustrates, the humble squaddie is still a necessary commodity. There is no sign that a changing geopolitical picture has diminished the requirement for that sort of role. Indeed, there are some grounds for believing the reverse ... the interview today still suggests that all the hints of a change of heart have come to nothing. If Mr. Rifkind is indeed intent on pushing through the cuts, he will have to show convincingly that his reasoning extends beyond mere dogmatism — that he has done his own sums and can prove them to be correct.

Save Our Staffords was now in a quandary. Conflicting messages were coming from Ministers. National newspapers — the *Scotsman* interview notwithstanding — and gossip on the Westminster circuit still pointed to a satisfactory outcome, and soon. Throughout the second half of January 1993, there was increasing speculation, fuelled by journalists working on Scottish newspapers, that Rifkind's *Scotsman* interview had not meant what it said. Gradually, some of the national broadsheets picked up on the issue. Even the *Scotsman* now began to suggest that something was afoot. Were some regiments to be reprieved? There was plenty of hearsay to add fuel to the fire. For instance, the Staffords learned on the grapevine that Lord Sanderson, Chairman of the Scottish Conservative Party, had told one of the Scottish campaigners in confidence that the Ministry of Defence was about to announce the reprieve of some, including Scottish, Infantry regiments. Was this true? And, if so, which regiments?

With less than eight months to go before the Last Post was sounded, Save Our Staffords began to consider other parliamentary activity they might encourage their MPs to initiate. This was not a time to be downhearted. Initial ideas included a second Adjournment Debate, an early day motion (an expression of opinion useful for gathering support for a cause but never debated in the House), and a further bombardment of Parliamentary Questions. In addition, much hope was invested in the long-awaited report of the Defence Select Committee which, it was confidently anticipated, would vindicate everything the regimental campaigners had said, and provide a useful hook on which to hang much-needed, sympathetic national publicity.

Chapter 15

Victory at Dawn

3 February 1993

Reprieve

The Defence Select Committee met to agree the final draft of its report on 14 January 1993, and decided to launch it at a press conference. This radical departure, intended to maximise the impact of the report's many criticisms and heighten the Government's discomfort, reflected the strength of feeling about the need for Infantry addbacks and the commitment of many Committee members to individual regiments. The Committee was moving beyond its accepted role as analyst of defence policy towards becoming a campaigning Committee, eager to expose MoD complacency and to ensure that the report would not be pigeonholed, the fate of so many Select Committee endeavours. Publication and the press launch were scheduled for 9 February. With a breather, as it seemed, before publication, John Levey and Simon Nayyar agreed a further letter to the Staffords' constituency MPs. Then Levey set off on a short skiing holiday in Switzerland, intending to return in early February.

Levey's letter reminded MPs that the amalgamation was imminent, left no doubt about the increasing urgency, and contained too, for the first time, a hint of desperation in the face of Ministers' apparent unwillingness to listen to the blindingly obvious. Above all, the campaigners' quietly courageous determination to battle on shone through. Levey remained undaunted, unbowed, and adamant that Parliamentary support continued in these, the final days of The Staffordshire Regiment, to be of crucial importance:

> You will be aware of the tremendous support that we continue to receive from all the local authorities within our recruiting area. Equally, you will be aware of the increasing national press comment calling on Ministers to look again at overall Infantry numbers; the forecasts which Ministers appear to be using are worryingly wrong. As you know, on 9 February the Defence Select Committee will publish its long-awaited report, which we are confident will fully vindicate us in the case which we have, through so many months, been patiently attempting to explain.
>
> For us, however, time is fast running out. As one of the best recruited regiments in the Infantry, we make the point that, particularly in these unsettled times, it is curious for Ministers to

> be claiming that it is sensible to put highly trained and motivated officers and soldiers of The Staffordshire and The Cheshire Regiments on the dole. We would, therefore, very much welcome your help in optimising the value of the publicity that the Committee report will doubtless generate by using the occasion to set on the record your concerns about overstretch in the Infantry.

By an ironic twist of fate, Levey and Nayyar agreed that the letters should be dated, and delivered, on 3 February.

There was nothing particularly unusual about Wednesday 3 February 1993. Levey was on the piste in Switzerland with his wife Jackie, who had always been equally strong in her support for the Regiment. Simon Nayyar was in his office about 100 yards from the Palace of Westminster preparing for a meeting later that day with a City client; unbelievably, he did manage to devote time to other clients. Mac McLean was busy with his usual wide-ranging duties at RHQ. Major General Ian Freer, by this time Commander Land Forces, Northern Ireland, was in his office in Lisburn. Finally, the author was attending a meeting of the Defence Select Committee, during which he noticed on the 'annunciator' system — television screens throughout the Palace of Westminster that announce the day's Parliamentary business and, when a debate is in progress, show which MP or Peer is speaking — that there was to be a Statement on Army Manpower at 3.30 pm. After all the speculation of the previous months, this was an intriguing development.

The author rushed out of his meeting to telephone Nayyar at 10.30 am, telling him to be in the Strangers' Gallery that afternoon because something very important was to be announced. Nayyar began frantically telephoning Save Our Staffords' many contacts at Westminster trying to discover what was about to break. From Phil Johnston, a lobby correspondent of the *Daily Telegraph*, he learned that, at that morning's briefing by Number 10, parliamentary Lobby journalists had been told that Malcolm Rifkind would be making a Statement on Army Manpower to the House.

Nayyar felt increasing unease mixed with anticipation. After all, Rifkind could, conceivably, have been about to announce further manpower cuts. However, given the Government's admission the previous September of the reduction in the emergency tour gap, this surely stretched credibility. The Statement must therefore concern an upward revision of manpower levels, most likely in the Infantry. Even this possibility left many questions: Rifkind could announce a new global Army manpower figure and leave it to the Army to decide internally how to reapportion the extra (or the non-obsolete) manpower; he could yet announce, despite the debate over manning levels, that an addback in numbers would achieve the Government's goal of fully-manned battalions; or he could specifically identify for retention regiments earmarked for amalgamation. If these questions made Nayyar uncertain, he felt even more unsure about how to approach the SOS campaigners — if he were too optimistic he might unnecessarily raise their expectations only to have them dashed by Rifkind. He therefore decided to get as much evidence as he could before telephoning RHQ and the Campaign Committee.

Nayyar had often looked forward to the day when he would make one particular telephone call. He had always assumed that it would be to John Levey; but at 11.45 am, with Levey cutting tracks in the Alps, Nayyar decided to ring Ian Freer in Lisburn. Captain Simon Banton, Freer's ADC, answered immediately, and Nayyar asked to speak to Freer urgently. Moments later, clearly surprised to receive this call from Westminster and wholly unsuspecting, Freer came on the line to hear Nayyar recount the morning's events. Nayyar urged Freer to treat the rumours with great caution, but he could sense the controlled excitement and anticipation in Freer's voice. Nayyar then rang RHQ, where, in contrast, he says the reaction was one of fairly undisguised celebration.

From then on, the telephones, civilian and military, were abuzz with excited speculation across Staffordshire, the West Midlands and Cheshire and around Westminster. BBC Television News carried a lunchtime report suggesting that Malcolm Rifkind's Statement would include a reprieve for The Staffordshire Regiment. Some MPs telephoned Simon Nayyar to get his opinion of the rumours, which was, of course, one of guarded optimism, nothing more. Members of the Defence Select Committee attempted to elicit 'hot' inside information, only to meet the usual silence. Meanwhile, John Levey, the key player throughout this long and arduous campaign, remained blissfully unaware of the pandemonium that had broken out in Westminster.

On 3 February, at 3.31 pm — 561 days (to the very minute) since Tom King had announced that the Staffords were to be sacrificed on the altar of peace — Malcolm Rifkind rose to stand before the Despatch Box. The House was hushed and expectant. Rifkind launched into his Statement, keeping up the suspense:

> The requirement to allow sufficient leeway to deal with the unexpected was one of the major considerations underpinning the original work on *Options for Change*. My predecessor and I have also made clear that we shall keep the position under review and that, should we judge it necessary to look again at planned force levels and the balance between capabilities, we shall do so.

This seemed to be a pretty clear hint of what was about to come. Listeners might have been excused for being momentarily thrown when Rifkind stated that the 'judgments made in *Options for Change* remain valid'. But he returned to his theme, which minute by minute sounded more realistic than anything MoD had said for a very long time:

> Since 1991, however, there have been a number of developments which have added significantly to the commitments that the Army is required to meet at the same time as it is in the process of reorganising. Additional battalions have been deployed to Northern Ireland, and our overall contribution to United Nations peacekeeping tasks — in Cyprus, Cambodia, the former republic of Yugoslavia and elsewhere — has almost trebled. The effect of these additional commitments, combined with the disruption caused by the restructuring and drawdown, is placing increasing pressure on individual soldiers and their families.

The author was as nervous as when awaiting the results of his parliamentary elections. Rifkind now disclosed what many had long suspected: 'I have been considering for a number of months, with my military advisers, the need to adjust the force levels set out by my Right Hon. Friend [Tom King].' Inevitably, this raised quite a few eyebrows, for it begged the question why he had publicly declared, just a fortnight previously, that there would be no reprieves. However, this was not the time to examine motives, but to listen to the unfolding news. Rifkind now continued:

> I have concluded that there is a case for an adjustment in the planned strength of the Army. ... First, I am announcing that the planned strength of the Army in the mid-1990s should be increased by 3,000 to 119,000. In determining how to use that additional manpower, I have been influenced by two considerations. The first is that it is desirable to bring up to strength a number of units which would otherwise have to be reinforced in order to undertake their peacetime operational

> commitments. ... The second consideration is that the Government attach importance to increasing the emergency tour interval towards the target of twenty-four months, to which we remain committed. That can best be achieved by revising the number of battalions that will be available in future. I have decided therefore to permit the retention of two further Infantry battalions. There will therefore now be a total of forty battalions ... in 1998, compared with the thirty-eight previously planned. That will have the effect of increasing the average interval between emergency tours from fifteen to seventeen months this year and providing an additional margin above twenty-four months once restructuring is complete, which would make it easier to accommodate any further commitments.

This had the House on tenterhooks. Which regiments was he about to name?

> I have consulted the Chief of General Staff and my other colleagues on the Army Board of the Defence Council. ... After considering all the reductions currently under way or planned, it is our unanimous view that the amalgamations of The Cheshire Regiment and The Staffordshire Regiment and of The Royal Scots and The King's Own Scottish Borderers should not now proceed.

Hansard does not record for posterity the tremendous roar of jubilation that greeted this last sentence. Members on all sides of the House cheered wildly, some waved their Order Papers, and the Secretary of State paused, momentarily unable to continue with his Statement. To his left, on the plush green leather front bench, sat his MoD colleagues, including Archie Hamilton, whose face revealed not a trace of emotion. Interestingly, on his immediate right sat Ian Lang, the Scottish Secretary (not customarily present for defence business), whose face broke into a momentary smile as Rifkind announced the reprieve of the two Scottish regiments. And, to his credit, on the back benches sat Tom King, who had the good form and grace to sit through the partial undoing of his own out-of-date policy.

As the Secretary of State sat down, many MPs on all sides of the House immediately rose in an attempt to catch Madam Speaker's eye, and offer their own thoughts about the reprieves. Madam Speaker, noting the immense interest in the Statement, warned:

> I cannot possibly call all the hon. Members who are rising. ... I

> appeal to hon. Members to ask the Secretary of State a single direct question, with no accompanying statement or preamble.

The author managed to make an early contribution:

> Your warning [about limiting speeches], Madam Speaker, and my elation at the saving of The Staffordshire and Cheshire Regiments inhibits me from gloating or saying 'I told you so' but I very much welcome the belated decision and thank the Secretary of State and his predecessor for being here to make it. However, does it not reflect badly on how decisions are made? First, there was the stupidity of making the decision in the first place, but the strength of our system is that stupidity can at least be rectified by the House, by a Select Committee and by public opinion. Will the Secretary of State try very hard to ensure that there is a little more far-sightedness in future, because the rationale that he gave for changing the decision was obvious to everyone eighteen months ago, even before the decision was made?

Nicholas Winterton noted that the Secretary of State's announcement would be 'warmly welcomed by the Services, not least The Staffordshire and Cheshire Regiments'. Sir Nicholas Bonsor, Chairman of the Defence Select Committee, rose to make the point that the Statement offered significantly less than his Committee would be seeking in its forthcoming report. But, with customary unfailing good grace, he added that 'nonetheless, I wholeheartedly welcome [the Secretary of State's] Statement and thank him for showing the flexibility of being prepared to move towards the level of manpower that our armed forces need.'

Bill Cash, an unflagging SOS supporter said:

> ... there will be great rejoicing in Staffordshire at the reprieve of The Staffordshire Regiment. Will [the Secretary of State] bear in mind that The Staffordshire Regiment fought a tremendous battle in the Gulf and that the Cheshires are fighting such a battle in Bosnia?

Reasons for the Victory

While neither Tom King nor Malcolm Rifkind — nor, for that matter, any of their MoD or Cabinet colleagues — seems to have borne in mind the fact that the Staffords had fought with great valour in the Gulf, it cannot be doubted that the Cheshires' Bosnia deployment had much to do with the Staffords' reprieve. There are several reasons why the SOS campaign was vindicated, justifying every ounce of effort that had been expended. First, while the Scottish battalions had presented the best emotional case and political rationale for a reprieve, the Staffords' supremely directed and logically coherent campaign meant that they were best positioned when the reprieve for the Scottish battalions had to be balanced by a reprieve for two English battalions; it was widely known that politics would demand matching reprieves in the two nations. Second, the deterioration of the emergency tour interval (brought about by the reduction in Infantry battalions and the potential increase in Infantry commitments) and changes in the actual security environment (including the requirement to addback two battalions owing to the situation in Northern Ireland and Bosnia) came together to legitimise and justify the campaign's often-repeated strategic arguments. Finally, Ian Freer's shrewd move in securing a one-year delay in the amalgamation timetable brought sufficient time to ensure that the reprieve short-list included the Staffords.

It was either a remarkable coincidence, or shrewdness on the Government's part, that the addback was announced immediately before the release of the Defence Committee's Report *Britain's Army for the 90s*. The Report was released on 9 February with a press conference — for the first time in the Committee's thirteen-year history. The Grand Committee Room of the House of Commons was packed. The two Johns — Levey and MacMillan — were present to thank the Committee for its work and to express empathy with those regiments still to be amalgamated.

The Report's arguments were watertight and its recommendations were uncompromising. Its explosive potential made its release one of the most important events of the campaign, and signified that, from the Government's perspective, the campaign had maintained, and could still increase, its momentum. It is patently obvious that by acceding only in part to the Report's extremely painful demands the Government hoped to avoid the furore that they knew publication would create.

It would be very interesting to complement this account of the campaign with testimony from a Government insider about the decision-making process from the time of the amalgamation decisions to the moment when the partial reprieves were agreed. However, the secrecy shrouding this aspect of the affair makes it difficult to do anything but speculate about the whys, wherefores and whens of very important decisions. We do not know when the change in the Government's position occurred, who knew what about the change, or what caused the rethink. Likewise we can only assert our belief that *Options for Change* was a frantic exercise to tailor defence policy to economic parameters; the Government simply contradicts that view without furnishing any evidence whatsoever.

It is of little help to look at the public utterances of Ministers. They denied any possibility of a rethink right until the end of January 1993 — yet other indications are that the option of reprieves had been studied for some time before the announcement. All the Ministers involved wrote letters throughout the campaign stating that there was no reason to re-examine the amalgamations and that the Army should be left to get on with restructuring (and also insinuating that any adverse effects on Army morale were caused by the critics of amalgamation, not by overstretch). As late as 22 December 1992, Archie Hamilton wrote to David Knox (Conservative MP for Staffordshire, Moorlands) that:

> I remain satisfied that the restructuring will deliver a balanced force that is well-matched to our future needs and able to meet the challenges of the mid-1990s and beyond. Should circumstances change, and we are faced with new long-term commitments, as I have already indicated, we will have to look again at Army manpower levels. Nothing in recent events, however, convinces me that this is yet necessary.

The reprieves forced Hamilton into an abrupt about-turn. Only fifty-two days later he wrote to Mark Fisher (Labour MP for Stoke-on-Trent Central) as follows:

> Tom King, Malcolm Rifkind and I have always made it clear that if we judged it necessary to look again at planned force levels and the balance between capabilities we would do so. As Malcolm said in the House on 3 February there have been a number of developments since 1991 which have added significantly to the commitments the Army is required to meet at the same time that it is being disrupted by the restructuring and need to reduce in size. Additional battalions have been sent to Northern Ireland and we are now providing a major contribution to the UN peace-keeping operation in the former Republic of Yugoslavia. This has had the effect of placing increasing pressure of [sic] individual soldiers and their families.

Malcolm Rifkind's *volte face* was rather more dramatic. An editorial in the *Scotsman* on 15 January 1993, only nineteen days before his statement to the House, quoted Rifkind as saying that no reversal of any amalgamations was planned.

Could it be that the Government only recognised the flaws in its defence policy after 15 January? It would not appear so. In his 3 February statement, Rifkind also mentioned that a working group (consisting of himself and his military advisors) had been studying the amalgamations for months, so at the very least we can be certain that some doubt about the Army cuts had existed for some time before the announcement. Indeed, as early as 28 August 1992 John Levey had written to Patrick Cormack suggesting a possible reason for the strange state of the Government's policy:

> I cannot believe those advising Ministers have the slightest idea of the strain on the Infantry. ... If they do, and some rumours suggest they do, they are, then, proving unwilling to present Ministers with unpalatable (military and political) home truths.

That may be so, but at some late point Ministers did become aware of these home truths, since Archie Hamilton cited increased commitments as the reason for the reversal of two amalgamations. In fact, ever since the announcement of *Options for Change*, the Government had been warned that the strategic environment was almost certain to throw up unforeseen commitments. The Government was given the information, but chose not to use it.

Instead of accepting that overstretch would inevitably be exacerbated by Army reductions, the MoD boxed itself in by suggesting that full manning of fewer units would relieve overstretch and that there was sufficient 'leeway' within its proposals to allow for unforeseen commitments. This claim was shown to be false, but this was never acknowledged until 1993. By stating that the proposals would remain open to reconsideration if unforeseen circumstances warranted it, but at the same time saying that no such circumstances were likely, the Government could claim to be operating a flexible policy.

The simple truth of the matter is that the initial *Options for Change* proposals were Treasury-led, and contained not an ounce of strategic justification. Once the Government's announcement of specific proposals in June and July 1991 made possible a thorough critique of *Options*, the MoD was increasingly forced to defend the indefensible. It ignored the criticisms of the Treasury's role, stonewalled over (and sometimes refused) requests to submit information for detailed scrutiny, and blindly adhered to its course, claiming that overly intrusive examination would undermine the Army's ability to perform its tasks. By accepting a partial reversal of its policy on 3 February it was able to deflect the massive damage that the Defence Select Committee's Report, released six days later, would have inflicted in its unassailable conclusion that the Army's ability to perform its tasks was being undermined.

Chapter 16

Celebration

February to July 1993

The Regiment receives the news

There are probably thousands of people who will always remember where they were and what they were doing at 3.30 pm on 3 February 1993. For those people, that moment vindicated one and a half years' work, during which the possibility of victory, constantly denied by the Government, had always been uppermost in their minds. Many people, while refusing to give up, were preparing for the worst. Hence, when the announcement did come, it came like a bolt from the blue.

Even Lieutenant Colonel Nigel Alderman, the Commanding Officer of the 1st Battalion, did not know for sure until immediately before the announcement. It was not until midday on 3 February that Simon Nayyar rang to offer his 'cautiously confident congratulations'. Alderman then received a 'phone call from Ian Freer, telling him to be home at 2.30 pm, at which time he was, finally, officially informed of the Regiment's reprieve; even then he was instructed not to tell anyone whatsoever. The closest he could come was to inform the commander of a company out on the road to tune in to the radio, but he could not be any more specific. He then summoned company commanders into his office, and divulged his secret minutes before the Secretary of State's announcement. As soon as Rifkind had finished, the champagne was cracked open.

Alderman then told the Regimental Sergeant Major to assemble the battalion immediately in the Quartermaster's Compound. The atmosphere, he remembers, was tense, and the battalion knew that something big was about to break — it isn't every day that the battalion is summoned to be addressed by the CO at such short notice. Alderman reports that he spoke slowly and at length. He said that the Secretary of State had announced the Staffords' reprieve from amalgamation 'with another regiment' — he could not bring himself to say 'The Cheshire Regiment'. A great roar of relief went up; many men had feared altogether different news. Alderman continued, telling them not to celebrate in town, because of the bad publicity this might generate, but to stay in camp, and 'to have sympathy for all those other great regiments whose amalgamations are going ahead. Treat this wonderful victory with humility and maturity.' There were three cheers and, with this, the battalion dispersed to begin the inevitable celebrations. After completing the day's business, Alderman returned to the Officers' Mess to find celebrations already underway. The atmosphere, he says, was 'euphoric, indescribable, one of sheer joy'.

A soldier in the 1st Battalion, who has since left the Regiment (but who was no less pleased about the reprieve for all that), confirmed to the author the tension at the briefing and the surprise the men felt. He was working in oil-smeared overalls when his Section Corporal told him to get ready for a briefing. He was filled with foreboding — unscheduled briefings were rare, and he swears he saw officers walking around with long faces; many others attended in the same frame of mind. He had half an hour to get ready, so he quickly shined his boots, pressed his trousers and made his way to the Quartermaster's Compound. The men stood at ease, while officers flanked the CO as he prepared to read his briefing. There was a depressed atmosphere, and the occasional oath — 'I'm getting out' — could be heard. Alderman's speech, of which this soldier remembers little, was 'good, but too long'; he recalls only Alderman's final admonitions. After a short pause to digest the unexpected message of salvation, a great cheer rose up. Everyone was ecstatic, and everyone proceeded to ignore Alderman's advice by heading straight to their respective Messes to consume large quantities of beer.

There were extraordinary scenes in the NAAFI: long queues at the telephones and at the bar, men hugging and kissing each other. Even men in the Glasshouse received some liquid refreshment (Alderman later said he regretted not having released those on detention for the celebrations, as had the Scots). Most people stayed in the barracks to celebrate, although not everyone managed to find their way back from the NAAFI!

Rumours abound about the huge increase in alcohol sales that night. The *Daily Telegraph*'s 'Peterborough' column the next day caught wind of the celebrations. *Rats' Tales* author Nicholas Benson was reported as saying: 'I am sure the messes will be serving Stafford Knot, the lethal regimental cocktail.' The prediction was correct. The day after that 'Peterborough' recorded this offering from:

> a groggy voice ... on the line from The Staffordshire Regiment's Officers Mess: 'Noticed your reference to the Stafford Knot, our cocktail,' it said, quietly. 'I must say, we got through twenty-nine bottles of champagne last night. Feeling a bit jaded.'

According to *The Times*'s 'Diary' of 5 February, Watchman was

> recovering, along with many of his officers, from the impromptu

> celebrations marking the reprieve that saved the Regiment from the planned amalgamation with the Cheshires. After all, who's ever heard of a Cheshire bull terrier?'

To honour Watchman's part in the victory, he was promoted from Lance Corporal to full Corporal at Burton Town Hall on 19 May 1993 'for the excellent effort that he and his handler, Sergeant Malcolm Bowers, made to promote the Regiment in Staffordshire, the West Midlands, London and Edinburgh in recent months'. Since then, Watchman has been promoted to Sergeant.

The SOS response

The reprieve caught the normally well prepared John Levey unaware. His daughter Henrietta (who is married to Nigel Alderman) telephoned him at his hotel in Switzerland but, unable to reach him, faxed the hotel to send a bottle of champagne to his room together with the news. At about 6.00 pm Nayyar caught up with Levey, who was by now enjoying his celebratory champagne, and over the telephone they agreed the campaign's final press release. Nayyar raced across to the House and placed copies of this in the Parliamentary Press Gallery, for the use of Lobby correspondents:

> The Save Our Staffords campaign committee warmly welcomes the Statement to the House by Malcolm Rifkind this afternoon, announcing that The Staffordshire Regiment will not now amalgamate with The Cheshire Regiment.
>
> The decision reflects the serious and substantive concerns which we have set out to Ministers since Tom King made his announcement to the House, in July 1991, that the Regiment, founded in 1705, should not be amalgamated. The Staffordshire Regiment is well-recruited, it has an outstanding record of service to the county and to the country, and it met all the criteria laid out by the Army Board that should have militated against its amalgamation.
>
> We are delighted that Ministers have recognised that overstretch in the Infantry is gravely serious, that there are presently too few soldiers to meet current commitments at home and abroad, and that they have now sought to address this issue while there are still regiments in hand.
>
> The Regiment is particularly grateful for the warm support which it has at all times received from the county, the local authorities within its recruiting area, and from all its Members of Parliament.

The county rejoices

As soon as the final words of Malcolm Rifkind's Statement were out of his mouth — even before that, according to some accounts — hordes of the Regiment's supporters telephoned each other to spread the news. There were more than a few warm telephones that day. Writing in the 1993 *Stafford Knot*, Mac McLean, the Regimental Secretary, gave a vivid account of the afternoon's events at RHQ:

> In RHQ it had been a normal working day. At approximately 1400 hours we were advised that there was going to be a statement on the Armed Forces in Parliament at 1530 hours; the subject was not clear but it might have something to do with the amalgamations.
>
> At 1530hrs after a certain amount of finger trouble with the radio RHQ managed to listen in to Radio 4 to hear the news and it was good. There was a very pregnant pause when you could have heard the lightest of feathers crashing to the ground, then all hell was let loose. Every telephone (3) in RHQ erupted and kept erupting until well into the evening, with literally hundreds of messages of goodwill from all over the Regiment, the county and the country and even BAOR. The traffic swamped the military telephone exchange at Shrewsbury by 1730 hours and they gave up.

Ann Johnson first caught wind of the imminent announcement on the lunchtime news. She rang RHQ, went to a meeting and left the video running. When she returned her daughter presented her with a long list of callers, and it was 11pm before she managed to watch the tape of the news.

Wendy Gordon (office manager of the Campaign Control Centre) telephoned Mike Mogridge at home in Sidmouth with the news that Rifkind was to make a Statement. He turned on the television, greeting the announcement with great elation — he felt no disbelief and says that, for him, the result had never been in doubt. At this moment the telephone started to ring, and rang almost continuously for some time.

The award for hearing the reprieve in the most unfortunate location must surely go to Councillor John Mellor, Chairman of Sandwell Friends, who was flat on his back in the Intensive Care Cardiac Unit after failing angio-plasty. 'It was', he (under)states, 'the only good news I'd heard that day.' Following close behind was Patrick Cormack MP, who could not be in Parliament to hear the announcement because he had a particularly infectious case of mumps. He did receive some consolation: Malcolm Rifkind's private office telephoned him earlier in the day to tell him that the Secretary of State would be making a Statement that afternoon in which he might be interested. After he informed the caller of his condition, a courier arrived to deliver a copy of the statement at precisely 3.30. Cormack was rather touched by the gesture.

A historic victory

John Levey returned to the UK like a conquering Roman general returning to Rome. Hundreds of supporters of the campaign and, by no means least, the Regiment itself hastened to weigh him down with richly deserved plaudits and praise. Levey, with characteristic modesty and diffidence, shrugged it all aside.

On 9 February Levey wrote to Malcolm Rifkind for the last time:

> I am writing to express our warmest appreciation at your willingness to take account of our concerns inherent in your decision to relieve the pressure on the Infantry and, in particular, to set aside the proposed amalgamation of The Staffordshire Regiment. With a recruiting area represented by twenty-six Members of Parliament, our sustainability is, as you know, beyond question.
>
> You will, of course, have been aware of the intense anxiety within the County and the West Midlands about the way the decision to amalgamate the Regiment was reached. The relief and pleasure felt by all sections of the community — to say nothing of the Regiment itself — is almost tangible.
>
> It is, therefore, no exaggeration to say that your Statement to the House on 3 February represents, for those of us living in the heart of England, a truly historic occasion. It provides, too, a source of deep satisfaction to Members on all sides of the House who have helped to articulate our concerns about the Infantry, and about the future of The Staffordshire Regiment, through so many months.
>
> I appreciate the very severe financial pressures you are under but the reprieve of the two battalions really only scratches the surface of the problem faced by the Infantry as a whole.

The last point was succinctly made and heartfelt. The Staffords had been reprieved, but the lot of the ordinary infantryman had not been significantly improved, despite Malcolm Rifkind's overflowing optimism.

Levey's letter was presented to the Secretary of State the moment it arrived at the Ministry of Defence. Astonishingly — given that on average Ministers take about a month to reply to a letter — Malcolm Rifkind answered within just twenty-four hours:

> Thank you very much for your letter of 9 February. I am pleased that what I said last week was so well received. I set out in my statement the way in which our plans for the future of the Army could be adjusted to meet the challenges posed by a changing world. The Staffordshire Regiment will have a part to play in this, in the future as in the past.

Rifkind's reply betrayed nothing of the complex, lengthy and secret discussions that had led to the unravelling of the original amalgamation decision. Nor did it address Levey's closing comment about the continued existence of overstretch. Finally, it ignored the effectiveness of the campaign that had ensured the retention of the Staffords rather than another regiment. The reason is, of course, that Government policy changes are never publicly discussed, less still justified, especially by a department as secretive as the MoD. The campaigners will probably have to wait for the Thirty-Year Rule to allow the release of the relevant documents.

The final meeting of the Campaign Committee on 11 February 1993 was an unexpected celebration. None had realised, at the previous meeting less than three months before, that victory was so close. Yet, as old soldiers steeped in military history, they would have known that some of the finest victories, including many belonging to The Staffordshire Regiment and its predecessors, were won when least expected; the fortunes of war change at the least likely moments. Unlike the reprieved Scottish battalions, the Committee and its supporters now set about planning an extended round of celebrations.

The first of these was the annual dinner of Warrant Officers Past and Present held in the 1st Battalion at Chester on 2 April 1993, and presided over by Jim Ellison. The dinner enabled insiders to relax and express their feelings in what was very much a family setting. John Levey took to the podium to disclaim that he had simply acquiesced in Freer's request that he head a campaign to save his son-in-law's job! It was time for the tensions of the campaign to be forgotten and for the lighter side of things to come to the fore, even though there were still a few administrative loose ends to clear up. The author treasures the memory of Ian Freer presenting him with a framed print of 1st Battalion Staffords fighting in the Gulf; John Levey and Mike Mogridge were also honoured thus. But, lurking in the back of many people's minds, was the question of whether the Regiment could ever afford to be caught off-guard a second time. The unquestionable right to celebrate was already being tempered by the realisation — the shock — of just how close the Regiment had come to the abyss.

There followed in May a luncheon in the Officers Mess of the 1st Battalion when Patrick Cormack, John Levey and the author were the principal guests, In his speech Patrick Cormack highlighted the cross-party support throughout the campaign, as demonstrated by the author sitting opposite him at lunch.

Champagne receptions were held in Stafford and Walsall to commemorate the contributions of all the campaigning organisations and individuals in those areas. The celebrations continued after the formal part of the proceedings was complete — the author bumped into a very merry group of Staffords officers and wives in an Indian restaurant on the night of the Walsall reception.

Later came another series of Freedom Marches. These were very well attended, even though security dictated that advance publicity be muted. Ostensibly these were not organised to celebrate the reprieve, although everyone knew otherwise. After Operation Granby the Regiment had said thank you to the people of the Midlands for their support in a military victory; after the reprieve from *Options for Change*, it said thank you to the same people for their support in a political victory. In Walsall, the march went through the town centre, past the Town Hall, where the Mayor took the salute, and then on to the cenotaph. From there the men marched back again past a slightly surprised and dispersed crowd, which thought that the spectacle had finished — not for nothing is The Duke of York the Staffords' Colonel in Chief.

The Freedom March in Lichfield followed a Service of Thanksgiving in the Cathedral on Friday 2 July 1993. It was an especially emotional occasion, for Lichfield is the Regiment's home town, and the extent of the city's support for the Regiment cannot be exaggerated. A thick file of messages of congratulation in RHQ from those who campaigned hard (and from some who wished they had campaigned hard) bears testimony to the Regiment's standing in the community.

The Service of Thanksgiving echoed with gratitude for the preservation of the Regiment and with celebration of the united struggle that had achieved that goal. The Dean's opening address set the tone: 'Today we especially give thanks for the preservation of our Regiment and for the continuation of its honoured name.' The psalms and hymns caught the atmosphere, one imploring:

> High King of heaven, thou heaven's bright Sun
> O grant me its joys after vict'ry is won.

So too did one prayer in particular:

> We rejoice that our Regiment with its honoured name will continue to play its part in the furtherance of peace and justice wherever it may be called upon to serve, and we pray that its members may be bound together in loyalty and comradeship for the benefit of the common good.

Epilogue

Does it go without saying that all the effort expended by the Save Our Staffords campaign has seen The Staffordshire Regiment safely on its way into a rosy future? Not necessarily. Several factors, domestic and international, could have a serious bearing on the Regiment's future and should encourage it to maintain the political links established during the SOS campaign. Nevertheless, the instability of the international security environment and the relentlessness of reductions in the defence budget throughout the post-war period — which have reduced British out-of-area capabilities to a minimum — should restrain future governments from any further opportunistic savings and should bode well for the Regiment.

The economy has an enormous influence on defence policy, and pressures on public spending have played a pivotal role in the contraction of the defence budget since the beginning of the 1990s. There is no reason to believe that, without a change of outlook, the gradual steady decline in the defence budget will be arrested before it reaches a dangerously low level — low enough, one has to add, to bring into question current commitments and resources to the extent that no Infantry regiment could consider itself safe from future mergers or disbandments.

A change of orientation in Government policy-making, away from the incessant Treasury-driven mindset of the 1980s and 1990s, would be likely to arrest the decline, if not reverse it. The Labour Party's repeated criticisms of the Conservative Government for its failure to conduct a strategic defence review have forced it to take its own position seriously. Politically it would be extremely expensive for an incoming Labour Government not to undertake a 'thorough-going strategic defence review' after demanding one for the better part of a decade. However, this book is not a party political tract. While we have criticised the Conservative Government of the 1990s, that is merely because it was this Government that took the knife to defence policy. Had a Labour Government done the same, it would have faced the same opposition to its plans and would have been documented similarly. Likewise there is no hard and fast rule that a Labour Government would honour assurances any more than its opposite number, so The Staffordshire Regiment would be well advised to look sceptically at any promises or hints of security in the future.

A defence review would not, of necessity, hold defence spending at an irreducible level — it could reduce commitments to match reduced resources. Yet reducing commitments is itself politically risky given the UK's globalist leanings. Labour's approach is that a defence review will have the effect of 'ring fencing' the defence budget. By approaching defence policy from the direction of strategic need, rather than of public expenditure, the Ministry of Defence will be on firmer ground in budgetary negotiations with the Treasury and other spending departments than it has been previously.

Public spending is not the only economic consideration. The relative growth of the economy must also be taken into account, and the position of the UK within the global economy has some bearing on this question. A stagnant or slowly growing economy will limit growth in the defence budget. The development of the economy, and the relative abilities of future governments to control it, will be important factors in the future for the Army, the Infantry and, therefore, The Staffordshire Regiment.

There will be other, more transient, factors to cope with as well. Northern Ireland has proved itself to be as unpredictable as ever. We have already seen that an important factor in the decision to reprieve the Staffords was the need in 1992 to reinforce Northern Ireland with two additional battalions. After a period in which many people began to assume the permanence of the paramilitary ceasefire first announced by the IRA on 31 August 1994, a new mainland bombing campaign in 1996 led observers seriously to doubt the Sinn Fein/ IRA commitment to the peace process. The ceasefire brought about a substantial reduction in the Army's profile in the province, and the troops were happy to remove their helmets and don regimental headgear. After the resumption of bombing the Army returned to patrolling and checkpoint duties and put its helmets back on — a significant psychological change for the troops and, presumably, for the terrorists. Few would now be willing to predict security requirements in Northern Ireland. The gradual withdrawal of troops during 1995 could as easily become a gradual build-up.

The economy and instability in Northern Ireland thus play potentially competing roles in the formulation of defence policy. Globally also, while some commitments continue to diminish, others threaten to take up the slack. The torrent of decolonisation during the 1960s and 1970s has dried up, except for the handing-back of Hong Kong to China on 30 June 1997 (an event which bears on the Staffords, discussed below). While that event will marginally reduce Infantry commitments, unfolding conflicts around the world raise the possibility of new United Nations peace-keeping operations and additional requests for British Infantry contributions, especially in the light of the tough reputation British forces have carved out for themselves in Bosnia. Equally, having changed dramatically since the days of the Cold War's armour-intensive planning scenarios, the core commitment to NATO could place new demands on British Infantry if operations such as the NATO Implementation Force (IFOR) in Bosnia become the norm.

In addition to the unfolding or settlement of conflicts, the regimes which manage security — alliances or looser conferences of states such as NATO and OSCE (Organisation for Security and Co-operation in Europe) — are by no means flux-free. Both main parties in Britain oppose a European Army, and will work to prevent the replacement of a US SACEUR (Supreme Allied Commander Europe) with a German, French or British equivalent. They therefore oppose any strengthening of the Western European Union as an instrument of common European defence policy. Whether other EU members see things in the same way is an important question for the future. External influences also add to the uncertainty of European security institutions. For instance, Russia continues to remain unpredictable in both its domestic politics and its policy towards Western security organisations. Of equal, or even greater, importance is the United States' future role in Europe and NATO, which is by no means certain. The way these countries evolve over the coming years will have an enormous bearing on the defence and security policies of the Western European states.

At present most of the conflicts around the world are intrastate (i.e. internal) rather than interstate, so the most likely assumptions about UK military planning therefore involve either UN peace-keeping operations, as in Bosnia (UNPROFOR), or NATO deployments such as IFOR. However, UK defence planners must also anticipate needs for power projection capabilities other than in peace-keeping or peace implementation operations. Peace enforcement operations such as the US-led Gulf coalition against Iraq (which one would usually expect to be conducted under UN auspices, although there could be exceptions) and out-of-area deployments in support of national interests (such as the Falklands task force) are examples of such deployments.

All these planning assumptions entail flexibility and mobility and, most critical of all, a high degree of Infantry participation. It is difficult to plan for such deployments without knowing whether they will mushroom in the future or decrease, or what the balance might be between the different types of deployment. In addition, the nature of the battlefield could have untold repercussions for the Infantry. Growing technological sophistication and an enormous increase in the lethality of weaponry would seem to have enormous consequences for the infantryman; yet the range of military tasks in all types of deployment will continue to demand a substantial Infantry presence until well into the next century.

However the European security environment develops, there is likely to remain a role for the UK's Infantry well into the future. As Russell F. Weigley deliberately understates in his 1991 book *The Age of Battles*, 'humankind is unlikely to forgo wars in the foreseeable future.' We can also safely assume that, although the UK is unlikely to become involved in a European war in the foreseeable future, there is every possibility that at some (probably unexpected) time the UK will be called upon in one or more ways: through its commitments to the UN, NATO and the Western European Union; through commitments such as the Five Power Defence Arrangement and defence 'consultation' with Brunei and Belize in the event of a threat to their integrity; or through a direct threat to a dependent territory.

It is extremely difficult to attempt to forecast how countless existing conflicts or latent tensions might affect the UK in the next five years, let alone the next twenty-five. Many analysts would urge governments to err on the side of caution in planning for such a range of scenarios, and would argue that the Infantry component of the Order of Battle (ORBAT) should be sufficient to undertake the huge number of tasks that the volatile security environment might demand. It is worthwhile commenting on the bizarre situation whereby the Infantry, already overstretched following substantial cuts, is short of men and must go on a recruiting drive to bring itself up to its reduced establishment. (The Staffords, it should be noted, have one of the best recruitment and retention records in the Prince of Wales's Division.)

What does this signify for the Staffords? For one, the unfolding global security climate and the continued aim of British governments to maintain a position of influence within NATO and the UN mean that minimum capabilities must be maintained in order to meet the UK's obligations. The British Infantry (and other Arms undertaking Infantry roles) have been stretched in meeting only one overseas deployment in Bosnia. In addition, the result of the cadreisation of peace-time forces and the heightened emphasis on Reserve forces to bring Regular units up to operational readiness is that there simply are no surplus Infantry regiments. This should ensure the safety of the Staffords from the MoD's paring knife. Furthermore, the importance of the 3rd Staffords to national defence and the flagship NATO ACE Rapid Reaction Corps, and their survival in the recent Reserve restructuring with the loss of only the 81mm mortar platoon and MILAN platoon (both as part of a concentration of the fire support function), mean that both Regular and Reserve battalions are indispensable to the Army. Second, as long as the Treasury continues to hold undue power over defence policy by restricting, or demanding reductions in, the defence budget year upon year, there can be no guarantee that any regiment remains immune from amalgamation or disbandment. However, a change of government might reduce the Treasury's influence, and a defence review should establish some sort of baseline into the 21st century below which UK defence capabilities will not be permitted to drop. Furthermore, since the end of the Cold War there has been a marked return to a political consensus around defence which will be less tolerant of cost-cutting exercises that lack strategic justification.

As things stand in mid-1996, 1st Staffords are firmly ensconced in Tern Hill, Shropshire, where they were posted upon completion of their two-year tour in Ballykinler, Northern Ireland. The lead elements began to arrive in February 1996, and the entire battalion was in place by the end of March. There they will remain for a short time on a slightly more relaxed basis undertaking mainly training duties. In the second half of September 1996 they will again be on the move, this time on an unaccompanied tour to Hong Kong until February 1997, when they will hand over the reins to the Black Watch, who will remain until the final handing-over on 30 June 1997. (The Staffords were disappointed at missing the honour of being last out, since the 98th were the first regiment to garrison the colony in 1841.) In Hong Kong the Staffords will adopt a modest profile, as befits their role in presiding over an event of such significance as the return of a colonial possession (especially one of great economic importance) to its 'owners'. The emphasis of the posting will be on training rather than on ceremonial or operational tasks (although, as in any posting, the battalion will be required to undertake whatever tasks arise). After leaving Hong Kong the Battalion will return to Tern Hill to prepare for the next instalment in its diverse history.

The Staffordshire Regiment has every reason to feel proud and to feel confident. Since *Options for Change* was announced in 1990, the 1st Battalion has acquitted itself well militarily in the Gulf, the 3rd

Battalion has come out of the Reserve restructuring relatively unscathed, and the Regiment has fought a successful battle for its own survival. There is plenty to be proud of in those achievements. The Regiment now publishes a regular newsletter for MPs to maintain the links that were forged during the anti-amalgamation campaign. This is just one part of a forward-looking strategy for an uncertain 21st century. The expertise and spirit that were built up during the Save Our Staffords campaign should be kept alive. If this happens the Staffords should be able to look forward confidently to new battle honours worthy of a distinguished county regiment.

Index